Personal and Organizational Transformations

Valentines Day
1997

For Bob
It's a life long
pleasure!)
Bill

D1361302

Titles available in the McGraw-Hill Developing Organization Series

THE ORGANIZATIONAL LEARNING CYCLE
How We Can Learn Collectively
Nancy Dixon
ISBN 0-07707937-X

THE WISDOM OF STRATEGIC LEARNING
The Self-managed Learning Solution
Ian Cunningham
ISBN 0-07707894-2

DEVELOPING STRATEGIC THOUGHT
Rediscovering the Art of Direction-giving
Edited by Bob Garratt
ISBN 0-07707986-8

PERSONAL AND ORGANIZATIONAL TRANSFORMATIONS
The True Challenge of Continual Quality Improvement
Dalmar Fisher and William Torbert
ISBN 0-077078349

LEARNING AT THE TOP
Alan Mumford
ISBN 0-077090667

LEARNING ORGANIZATIONS IN PRACTICE
Michael Pearn, Chris Mulrooney and Keri Roderick
ISBN 0-07707744X

CONSULTANT'S JOURNEY
Roger Harrison
ISBN 0-077090896

THE COLLECTED PAPERS OF ROGER HARRISON
Roger Harrison
ISBN 0-07709090X

For further information on these titles and other forthcoming books please contact:

The Product Manager, Professional Books, McGraw-Hill Publishing Company, Shoppenhangers Road, Maidenhead, Berkshire, SL6 2QL, United Kingdom

Personal and Organizational Transformations

The true challenge of continual quality improvement

DALMAR FISHER AND
WILLIAM R. TORBERT

The McGraw-Hill Companies

London · New York · St Louis · San Francisco · Auckland
Bogotá · Caracas · Lisbon · Madrid · Mexico
Milan · Montreal · New Delhi · Panama · Paris · San Juan
São Paulo · Singapore · Sydney · Tokyo · Toronto

Published by
McGRAW-HILL Publishing Company
Shoppenhangers Road, Maidenhead, Berkshire, SL6 2QL, England
Telephone 01628 23432
Fax 01628 770224

British Library Cataloguing in Publication Data
Torbert, William R.
   Personal and Organizational Transformations: True Challenge of
   Continual Quality Improvement. – (McGraw-Hill Developing
   Organizations Series)
   I. Title II. Fisher, Dalmar III.Series 658.562

   ISBN 0–07–707834–9

Library of Congress Cataloging-in-Publication Data
Torbert, William R.,
   Personal and organizational transformations: the true challenge of
   continual quality improvement / William R. Torbert and Dalmer Fisher
   p.   cm. – (The McGraw-Hill developing organizations series)
   Includes Index.
   ISBN 0–07–707834–9 :
   1. Total quality management. 2. Organizational change.
I. Fisher, Dalmar. II. Title. III. Series.
HD62.15.T67   1995
658.5'62–dc20   94–39570
                                                                      CIP

McGraw-Hill

A Division of The *McGraw·Hill* Companies

2345 CUP 9876

Typeset by Computape (Pickering) Ltd., North Yorkshire
and printed and bound in Great Britain at the University Press, Cambridge

Printed on permanent paper in compliance with ISO Standard 9706

Contents

Series preface

The McGraw-Hill *Developing Organizations* series is for people in the business of changing, developing and transforming their organizations. The books in the series bring together ideas and practice in the emerging field of organizational learning and development. Bridging theory and action, they contain new ideas, methods and models of how to get things done.

Organizational learning and development is the child of the organization development (OD) movement of the 1960s and 1970s. Then people like Schein, Beckhard, Bennis, Walton, Blake and Mouton *et al.* defined a *change technology* which was exciting and revolutionary. Now the world has moved on.

The word 'technology' goes with the organization-as-machine metaphor. OD emphasized the *outside-in* application of 'behavioural science' which seems naive in the context of the power-broking, influence and leverage of today's language. Our dominant metaphor of organizations as organisms or collective living beings requires a balancing *inside-out* focus of development and transformation of what is already there.

Learning is the key to our current dilemmas. We are not just talking about change. Learning starts with me and you, with the person—and spreads to others—if we can organize in ways which encourage it.

Learning is at a premium because we are not so much masters of change as beset by it. There is no single formula or image for the excellent company. Even the idea of 'progress' is problematic as companies stick to the knitting and go to the wall. Multiple possible futures, the need for discontinuity almost for the sake of it, means that we must be able to think imaginatively, to be able to develop ourselves and, in generative relationships with others, to organize and reorganize ourselves continuously.

Organizations are unique, with distinctive biographies, strengths, opportunities. Each creates its own future and finds its own development paths. The purpose of these books is not to offer ready-made tools, but to help you create your own tools from the best new ideas and practices around.

The authors in the series have been picked because they have something to say. You will find in all of the books the personal voice of the writer, and this reflects the voice which each of us needs in our own organizations to do the best we can.

Bill Torbert got my attention twenty years ago with his dash and daring in various learning community experiments. Here was a man prepared to live out his ideas and values not only in student programmes but in summer camps and in the public 'Theatre of Inquiry' performances in Boston. From him I picked up some ideas which have stayed with me; the notion that shared purpose, quality work and self-direction all require one another; the riddle of 'liberating structure'. Since then he has developed his idea of personal and organizational transformation in a number of books. His 'The Power of Balance' (Sage 1991) is autobiography, odyssey and an attempt to build a new theory of organizational development. It is described in the foreword by Donald Schön as 'a document of shocking grandiosity'.

In recent years, Torbert has found a committed co-author, Dal Fisher, a writer with an abiding interest in managerial effectiveness and communications ('Communication in Organizations' West 1993). Together Torbert and Fisher have developed their ideas to present a challenging and engaging vision of organizational learning as CQI—continual quality improvement. As you might have guessed, this is no safe, ordered programme; it demands nothing less of those who would transform their organizations than they must also transform themselves. By the time you get to the last case study it will not surprise you to find Captain Kirk's successor and the crew of the Starship Enterprise on stage. Here are authors who really do 'boldly go' . . . and who also take you with them. Hold tight!

Mike Pedler

Acknowledgements

We would like to thank all of the evening MBA students at Boston College, USA, who also work full time each day and who have so enthusiastically tested out the ideas in this book in their everyday work lives. As the reader will discover, many of their accounts of their experiments have been included, with their permission, in the following pages as illustrations and as encouragements for you, our reader, to continue this process of personal testing.

We would also like to thank the various companies and their senior managements whose transformational stories appear in the pages to follow. They, too, have been willing to take many a real-time risk in applying the ideas presented here to their own executive development and to restructuring their whole company. In particular, we want to bring Jackie Keeley, David Rooke and their consulting company, The Harthill Group, to the attention of any of our readers who wish to pursue the executive development and organizational development implications of this book. Generously seeking our guidance, David, Jackie and the rest of their team have fully explored their personal and organizational dynamics using this theory and have adapted it for consulting purposes. We urge that you address any inquiries concerning applications of this work in a business environment to them.*

Among our scholarly colleagues, we are particularly grateful for the ongoing support and conversation we enjoy with Marcy Crary, Judi Marshall, Richard Nielsen, Joseph Raelin, Peter Reason, Diana Smith and Sandra Waddock about issues of learning, development and consulting.

As their names on the title pages of Chapters 9 and 10 attest, we were pleased to have Barbara Davidson and Melissa McDaniels join in our research at Sun Health Care,

* The Harthill Group, Gloucestershire, tel. 01594 530223.

and very much appreciate their collaboration in the writing of those chapters. Several other research assistants over the past dozen years helped us with studies that contributed to this book. We are grateful to Kathleen Beale, Keith Merron, Larry Pike, Paul Skilton and Rosemary Tin.

Our editors, Mike Pedler and Julia Riddlesdell, have been especially supportive and responsive in helping us craft a book that is intended to be accessible, useful and enjoyable for a wide reading public. We now invite your judgement about how successful we have been.

We are both deeply grateful for the nurture we receive from our families.

Introduction

Quality improvement is the challenge in management today. Continual quality improvement (CQI) or total quality management (TQM) is the 'rage' not just in manufacturing but also in service, public sector and not-for-profit organizations. Legions of managers are responding to the quality challenge. Probably most managers world wide, if not deeply involved in a quality effort, are learning and thinking about it.

But the true challenge of quality is understood by very few managers, even those deeply involved in CQI. We argue in this book that CQI/TQM will become just another former management fad if the manager does not begin to understand and practise it in a new way: with the central focus placed on changing (not just once, but repeatedly) his or her own way of learning, understanding and acting. Put most simply, this book is addressed directly to what you, the reader, can do to improve the quality of your own work and your own work environment—no matter what your hierarchical role in the organization and no matter whether your organization is 'officially' engaged in quality improvement.

We are not saying that the CQI concept is wrong, but that it is incomplete. What is missing is a close-up focus on the thought and behaviour of the manager: the person who leads and energizes CQI. Here, for example, is as good a definition of CQI as can be found today, given by Marshall Sashkin and Kenneth J. Kiser in their book *Putting Total Quality Management to Work*.[1] Sashkin and Kiser say there are three foundations of CQI:

> The first concerns tools and techniques that people are trained to use to identify and solve quality problems. The second factor centers on the customer as the focus of [CQI]. The third factor is the organization's culture. A [CQI] culture is based on certain values and leadership vision.

There is certainly nothing wrong with defining CQI in terms of its tools and techniques, its focus on the customer, and its dependence on a supporting organizational culture, informed by leadership vision. But, important as these elements are to CQI, they appear in this definition more as end results than in terms of the actions necessary to reach them. There is no mention in the definition of the moment-to-moment management action through which training, customer focus and vision-based culture are brought about. Nor is inquiry mentioned, though it is an element that must be crucial to learning how to manage in a fashion that both exhibits and encourages continual quality improvement.

To stimulate improvement in the global competitiveness of American industry, the US government presents annually the Malcom Baldridge National Quality Award to honour organizations that attain 'world class' quality in their products, services and operations. The judges base the awards on the degree to which companies fulfil eight characteristics, which shed further light on how CQI is viewed today[2]:

- A plan to keep improving all operations continuously.
- A system for measuring these improvements accurately.
- A strategic plan based on benchmarks that compare the company's performance with the world's best.
- A close partnership with suppliers and customers that feeds improvements back into the operation.
- A deep understanding of the customers so that their wants can be translated into products.
- A long-lasting relationship with customers, going beyond the delivery of the product to include sales, service and ease of maintenance.
- A focus on preventing mistakes rather than merely correcting them.
- A commitment to improving quality that runs from the top of the organization to the bottom.

Like Sashkin's and Kiser's definition, the Baldridge Award criteria are an impressive and admirable list of end states, but the list tells us little about what is required to bring them about. In this book, we shall refer to the managerial skills that both enact and encourage continual quality improvement as *action inquiry*. One quite imposing fact about achieving CQI is that it requires a decade or more. This has been the experience of Motorola, Ford, Xerox and the few other companies that are deeply committed to the process. Why is

CQI such a challenge, and why does it take so long? For the answer we must again look to the element missed by the existing definitions and criteria: the individual manager. Any manager who assumes the lead in CQI—either just in one's own work, or in encouraging CQI throughout one's own work group(s), or in influencing a whole organization—must travel a lengthy and up-ending journey, in order to succeed in meeting the true challenge of CQI. We offer three propositions to explain why this lengthy action inquiry journey is necessary[3]:

Proposition 1. CQI requires combining productivity with inquiry. This seems obvious, because inquiry and learning are clearly necessary to improve quality. But the modern world separates the 'real world' of action from the 'ivory tower' of reflective inquiry. Why? So as not to paralyse action and not to bias inquiry. But CQI calls for flexibility and correction of errors at the very moment of seeking to make a sale, or in the midst of a management meeting. This requires a heightened awareness that inquires and corrects itself in the midst of action. Modern science and professional education do not cultivate this kind of heightened awareness. To do so requires that we transform our basic assumptions about the relation of action and inquiry. We must learn to speak in such a way as to combine action and inquiry at the same time. This way of speaking will be clearly defined and illustrated in Chapter 3 and is part of what we call action inquiry.

Proposition 2. CQI requires the exercise of an unfamiliar type of power—transforming power. Transforming people's basic assumptions cannot be accomplished by force, diplomacy or other traditional forms of power commonly used to influence external behaviour. These types of power are likely to generate conformity, dependency or resistance, not transformation. Transforming power is a rare, little understood type of power that invites mutuality, seeks contradiction and requires heightened awareness of the present. The exercise of transforming power makes everyone present (including the person exercising the power) vulnerable to transformation.

Continual quality improvement can be sustained only if it begins to transform the way you as a manager (or parent or team member) use power. If the current power possessors—the chief executive officer (CEO), the board of directors, and top management—say that they favour quality improvement, but they use power in unilateral or otherwise manipulative ways, they will in fact generate resistance to CQI. If you, whatever your position, say you favour quality improvement but use power in manipulative ways, you will generate resistance to CQI. Only if executives engage in awareness-heightening inquiry in the midst of action, and use power differently, generating CQI in their own immediate activities and relations, will CQI become a credible and effectual activity within their organization. CQI can only sputter and fail if it is introduced first at the shop-floor level.

Proposition 3. If an individual manager is to transform his or her assumptions about power and organizational working relationships to the point of truly and continually engaging in quality improvement, then that *manager will very likely need to work through several personal developmental transformations.* According to developmental measures of managers, which we shall describe later, the typical manager is three transformations away from the stage where transforming power is fully understood and practised. Moreover, each personal transformation requires a minimum of two years, and three to five years are usually spent consolidating one's competences at the next stage before one begins to appreciate its limits and wish to grow beyond them[4].

Each of these three propositions alone, and certainly all three taken together, suggest why establishing CQI within any given organization will, realistically, require at least a decade. This may seem daunting or discouraging. The reader may well ask, 'Are transformation and CQI really worth the effort?' We think the examples in this book of individuals who have begun to reap the rewards of personal and organizational transformation will help to answer this question. Furthermore, developmental progress, and its accompanying payoffs, can begin in small ways immediately, as the following example shows.

Amy, a systems analyst in the claims division of a motor insurance company, wanted to increase her personal effectiveness and her visibility to her managers with an aim to moving up to a managerial position. Although she approached the challenge of personal change very tentatively, she nonetheless approached it.

> My experiments were by no means a threat to my job, but were my way of beginning to dabble in the 'art' of action inquiry.

Amy served as a member of a committee developing new software and claims-processing procedures for her division,

Claims Processing. The committee's members included George, the vice-president of the division, her own manager, John, and other senior managers in the Claims and MIS divisions. She saw her position on the committee as an obvious opportunity to work on her developmental goal and set as a specific objective,

> To participate more fully in committee meetings by asking questions to clarify directives and my specific responsibilities, instead of waiting and assuming someone would let me know what tasks I should be doing.

She went on to describe this effort

> The full committee has met only once in recent months. In that meeting, Property Division personnel felt we were ready to begin use of the new software with actual incoming claims. Some members of the MIS Division expressed concern that we had not tested the software and procedures enough. During this meeting, I attempted to ask questions and clarify the concerns of the MIS people. Being ingrained in the software development and the claims handling processes, it was difficult for me to understand their hesitation.
>
> In another meeting with George, John, and the two other Property Division managers, we discussed claims handling procedures. The procedure manual had been written and reviewed, but George was not yet fully comfortable with it. Training for the first unit member using the system and procedures was scheduled for the next week. In the meeting, many ideas about how to process newly assigned claims were laid on the table. I realized the ideas were all good ones and we needed to have the best possible procedures in place. But I was feeling very stressed during this discussion because training was due to start and we needed to make a decision about what procedure to follow. The procedure manual had to be ready for the training. I spoke up in the meeting stating that at some point this manual had to be finished, but that training and the start of handling live claims would help us find the areas which needed to be examined and redesigned.
>
> The significance of these two examples is not obvious, but had these two meetings taken place three or more months ago, I would have acted differently. I would have kept quiet during the meetings and let my frustration increase. Later, I would have complained to someone else about how nothing ever gets done in meetings. Now I am willing to be more open and speak up. In doing this I am, hopefully, improving communications between myself and the people with whom I have to work. I may also be increasing my own job effectiveness by making sure I have resolved conflicts I feel exist.

This book will help the reader to understand and perhaps even to begin the developmental journey as Amy began it. We shall illustrate the inquiry-in-action process with many more examples. Further, through exercises and guided journal writing, we shall invite readers who are interested to enter into the inquiry-in-action process. We shall begin with the focus on the individual manager, then expand it outward to teams, then to organizations, and, finally, to society and human living in general.

In Part One we view the individual manager in action as the 'gene' of CQI. We offer, in Chapter 1, further evidence that organizational learning requires individual learning and mutual learning, and that the essence of CQI must be seen as the individual manager in action with others. Chapters 2 and 3 describe very concretely a way of acting with others—action inquiry—which generates learning and is at the heart of the personal development and CQI processes. Chapters 3 and 4 both contain exercises which offer you an opportunity to begin building your own action inquiry skills. More exercises are given in Appendix A.

Part Two puts the spotlight on leadership towards CQI in relation to one's immediate associates. Chapter 5 explains, through examples and exercises, how adult personal development occurs in stages, or 'frames', each including a new orientation towards leadership, as the developing individual moves towards transformational leadership—that is, towards being a catalyst for the development of others. The exercises are designed to help you recognize your own frame and learn to recognize others' frames—the starting point for setting a developmental course for yourself as well as for those with whom you work. In Chapter 6 we focus on one of the later developmental frames, one we call the 'Strategist' frame. We illustrate how 'Strategists' exercise transformational leadership that generates CQI.

In Part Three we widen the scope, viewing CQI at the level of groups and total organizations. In Chapter 7 we offer a plan and a process for convening a group that is committed to improving its members' practice. Our focus is on how you may be an entrepreneur and lead such a group. In Chapter 8 we show how personal development relates to corresponding stages of group and organization development. We discuss how business meetings may be managed with a sensitivity to developmental process and describe two organizations that are making developmental transitions. Chapters 9 and 10 continue with a more penetrating look at one of these organizations as it makes a breakthrough to an advanced stage of development we refer to as 'Collaborative Inquiry'.

In Part Four we look beyond the experience of most persons and organizations, suggesting 'reach' objectives for both. These levels of CQI have rarely been reached, but we offer evidence that they can be. At the personal level of experience, Chapter 11 describes a personal frame beyond that of the 'Strategist', and offers glimpses of the kinds of action awareness and the potentials for transformational leadership that become possible at this level of development. Chapter 12 describes an advanced stage of organization development we call 'Foundational Community'.

Such an organization would integrate personal and social transformation as well as spiritual, political and economic transformation. We picture such an organization, and also speculate about it, through a look at several real organizations that may be attaining that stage and then at a fictional organization that appears to touch it briefly following transformations through all the earlier stages. In Appendix B we offer a glimpse of a still later, ultimate stage of organization development we call 'Liberating Disciplines'. Chapter 13 continues and broadens our 'reach' towards higher quality experience. We suggest components of 'the good life' implied by the understanding of CQI and of personal and organizational transformation presented throughout the book.

Most of this book deals with making managers and organizations more effective. However, it should be clear from our introduction to Part Four that we believe action inquiry and CQI apply not just to a manager's work—not even primarily to work—but to the total life experience of the person. And they apply not just to improving an organization's quality in terms of its competitive position as an enterprise, but in terms of its cooperative enhancement of the common good. Understood this way, the aims of CQI are broad, deep and, as we have said, involve a lengthy journey. The starting point, however, is closer to home and quite manageable. It is the individual's own thought and action here and now in the current moment. We invite the reader to begin examining with us this moment of action and in so doing to commence the journey.

Notes

1. M. Sashkin and K. J. Kiser (1993) *Putting Total Quality Management to Work*, San Francisco, CA: Berrett-Koehler Publishers.
2. The Baldridge Award criteria are taken from S. K. Yoder, G. Fuchsberg and B. A. Stertz (1990) 'All that's lacking is Bert

Parks singing 'Cadillac, Cadillac', *Wall Street Journal*, 13 December, A-1, A-4.

3. The three propositions were originally stated and discussed in William R. Torbert (1992) 'The true challenge of generating continual quality improvement,' *Journal of Management Inquiry*, **1** (4), 331. Adapted by permission of the publisher.

4. Just after the final version of this book was submitted to the publisher, the very useful special issue of *The Academy of Management Review* (Vol. 9, No. 3, July 1994) on 'Total Quality' appeared. We hope that the following very brief comments on the articles in this special issue will further highlight the powerful and timely contribution that the developmental, action inquiry approach presented in this book can make to the theory and practice of quality improvement.

In her article, Spencer points out that much of the TQM literature and practical rhetoric is 'functionalist' in nature, suggesting that 'following certain procedures or establishing particular structures will lead to desired ends' (pp. 461–2). By contrast, Spencer suggests that an 'interpretivist' approach to TQM would highlight stakeholders' different desired ends, would encourage discussion among them, and would foster both human development among the members and the development of the organization as a whole. The developmental theory presented in this book is precisely such an 'interpretivist' approach to quality improvement. Indeed, we believe that developmental theory represents the most sophisticated interpretivist theory available today because it specifies a number of common frames of interpretation (including 'objectivism' and 'relativism'), shows how they relate to one another, and shows how they transform.

In a distinction that closely parallels Spencer's, Sitkin, Sutcliffe, and Schroeder contrast 'the singular emphasis on control' that has characterized TQM to the 'Learning-oriented requirements associated with higher levels of uncertainty' (p. 537) that are in fact characteristic of today's rapidly self-reframing persons, companies, and industries. Again, you will see that the developmental model presented in this book directly addresses the dilemmas of helping managers and organizations transform from a unilateral-control orientation to a mutual-learning-and-transforming orientation.

Several of the articles (e.g., Dean and Bowen, Reger, *et al.*) in the *AMR* special issue on TQM comment on the irony that it is most difficult to engage in quality improvement of those processes with which one is most closely identified. Thus 'statistics profs who teach statistical process control for manufacturing systems [may] be unable to apply TQM concepts to their own classroom' (p. 570); and 'strategic management researchers . . . have devoted little attention to the improvement of strategic processes' (p. 405). Chapters 9 and 10 of this book are quite specifically about improving the strategic process within a particular company; and the emphasis throughout the entire book is on improving those processes with which one is most closely identified, starting with one's own actions and one's own immediate work group. Once again, the developmental theory used here highlights that applying a concept to oneself and correcting disharmonies between theory and practice is a major developmental challenge that some managers are not yet prepared to meet, and that requires years of dedicated practice from anyone who does accept the challenge. Finally, Reger, *et al.* present a cognitive theory that explains why managers often seem to resist beneficial change. We agree with these authors about the importance of understanding this phenomeon and see their article as a step in the right direction. At the same time, however, we believe that the developmental theory presented in this book is far more powerful and apt as a guide to understanding and transforming action than the theory they present. Whereas they limit their focus to 'cognitive sources of resistance to beneficial change' and state that 'other sources of resistance to change, such as those that stem from political concerns or guileful self-interest, are beyond our immediate scope' (p. 567), developmental theory encompasses all these sources of resistance to change and shows at what stage of development each is likely to be most heavily emphasized (e.g., referring to Chapter 5, you can see that 'guileful self-interest' is typical of the Opportunistic developmental frame and 'political concerns' tend to preoccupy persons who inhabit the Diplomatic developmental frame).

Moreover, whereas Reger, *et al.*, construct their cognitive theory of resistance to beneficial change as though it is a theory of general validity, developmental theory suggests something strikingly different: that the mental structuring they describe is characteristic of all the early and middle stages of development (where 90 per cent of all managers are measured), but not of later stages where flexible, self-referential, analogical thinking becomes characteristic. Thus, developmental theory not only describes the social realities that are constructed from the currently most common modes of interpretation that people apply to their worlds, but also points toward a normative direction for personal, organizational, and social development that it invites each of us to consider and to explore. The later chapters of this book open out towards this empirically uncommon frontier.

PART ONE

THE 'GENE' OF CONTINUAL QUALITY IMPROVEMENT (CQI): ACTION INQUIRY BY INDIVIDUAL MANAGERS

1 CQI and the manager in action

In this book, and in our consulting work, we use the phrase 'continual quality improvement' rather than 'continuous quality improvement' or 'total quality management'.

Why? What difference does it make which bit of jargon we use?

Let us pause, here at the beginning, to look at what these three phrases actually mean. If we do *not* do this, we are asking you, the reader, to begin by adopting a somewhat meaningless slogan that *we*, the authors, have chosen.

- The process we are describing would then become *ours* rather than yours.
- Your task would be to conform to an activity *we* are prescribing.
- We would be back in the traditional world of organizing, where someone above tells someone below what to do.

In other words, we would be contradicting our mission of empowering you. So let us first point out what is most obvious about the three phrases—namely, their similarity, in that they all include the word 'quality'.[1] They are also concerned with improving quality. A product, or service, or managerial action or work of art that has more quality is more useful, more effective, and more valuable. While economics relates to the monetary cost of things—i.e. their *extrinsic* value when exchanged in a market—quality improvement is concerned with increasing their *intrinsic* value. We know that these two kinds of value are only distantly related. One family can work constantly on their home for ten years, vastly improving its plumbing and its appearance, only to find themselves needing to sell in a 'down' market and barely recouping the money they originally paid. Another family can do nothing to improve the quality of their home for ten years, but sell in an 'up' market and make twice as much money as they originally paid.

Since quality improvement is only distantly related to the price that a product, or service, or managerial skill can command, why are so many organizations engaging in quality improvement? Part of the reason may be that no one in the organization has done the little thinking exercise that we have just done here. Other organizations are adopting the latest fad, so top management is simply joining the bandwagon. As soon as it becomes clear that this newest top-down quick-fix costs time and money and may not yield immediate economic returns, the initiative fades.

Another reason why organizations adopt some kind of quality improvement programme is that they, and perhaps other companies in their industry, have already tried a variety of purely economic strategies to improve profit-ability—strategies such as using lower cost, lower quality parts, personnel layoffs, mergers and acquisitions, or redu-cing the amount they spend on research and development and putting that money directly into current advertising to increase sales. Desperately, they latch onto quality improve-ment as one more method of improving profitability, not fully realizing that quality improvement is fundamentally different from a purely economic strategy and is only contingently related to increased profitability. If they adopt quality improvement as though it is a programme for reducing costs and increasing profit at the point of exchange, rather than a way of increasing the intrinsic value of the service they provide, the programme is again likely to fade very quickly.

Having just explored a little of the common territory that pertains to all three of the most-used quality slogans—'total quality management,' 'continuous quality improvement', and 'continual quality improvement.'—let us now examine the differences between the phrase 'total quality management' and the two other 'quality improvement' phrases that sound very similar. The most obvious difference here is that 'total quality management' implies an observant god, like Zeus, who surveys the entire organizational scene and manages its totality by effective, illuminating, discombobulating lightning thrusts and thunderous sounds. We know many executives who act in discombobulating ways, but very few who qualify as simultaneously effective and illuminating in ways that lead everyone to enter into the quality improvement contra-dance. Instead, the phrase 'total quality management' seems to us to encourage managers to imagine that they have latched onto a sure thing—indeed, that they have encountered in TQM 'the final fix'.

By contrast, the two phrases about 'continu(ing) quality improvement' speak from our actual positions, at our very *best* moments as managers and as human beings. Our actual position at our very best moments is to recognize ourselves as being *inside* a process of learning, producing, or loving—or *inside* a process of weaving past interpretations, present actions, and future ends into a pilgrimage of learning. Executives do not merely run such a process from the outside, like Zeus or Athena. On the contrary, top executives have the hardest job of all in a quality improvement process, for they need to learn not only new knowledge, skills, and strategies that others already know, but, even more importantly, they need to learn how to sculpt the company or agency into a 'learning organization', which no one has yet managed to do. (We will have a lot more to say about learning organizations in Chapters 8–12.)

Everyone who encounters a quality improvement process, from whatever angle, has the same initial dilemma: how to get inside the process so that the learning and quality improvement start to come from within rather than being put on like a new set of clothes. These are the reasons why we favour a phrase that focuses on continuing quality improvement to describe what we are advocating and illustrating in this book.

In our continuing exploration of the meaning of these three phrases, let us now compare 'continual quality improvement' and 'continuous quality improvement.' What is the main difference between 'continual' and 'continuous'? Those of you who have taken calculus, or even heard about it as a distant rumour, may know that the word 'continuous' refers to equal increments of change over equal time periods, or to equal increments of acceleration over equal time periods. By contrast, the word 'continual' refers to intermittent and unequal, but still frequent and unceasing, changes over time.

Why quibble about this difference?

Because it isn't a quibble. No one can show you *continuous* change in any known organizational variable. Continuous change can only occur in a mechanical or automated process (such as the flight of a cannonball), where no human action intervenes once the mechanical process is set in motion. To speak of 'continuous quality improvement' is to speak of engineering improvements, or of an automated process of feedback, whereby, for example, people who have bought nothing from a mail order catalogue in the past seven or ten mailings are automatically deleted from the mailing list, while people who buy regularly are sent extra notices of 'favoured customer specials'. If your entire image of quality improvement is ruled by this sense of mechanistic, continuous change, you will inevitably focus away from your own and your colleagues' learning (which comes in discontinuous, unequal lumps at best) toward things that are easily countable and automatable. These, in turn, are just the things that competitors can easily copy and that are, in general, the least difficult things for an organization to learn. Thus, in our opinion, the frequent references to 'continu*ous* quality improvement' show that the organizational change agents and managers who use the term are not thinking very clearly about their biggest quality dilemmas. The most significant quality dilemmas are concerned with widening, deepening, and transforming (a) your vision (b) the vision of other members of the organization and (c) the capacity for vision, learning, and improved performance by the organization as a whole.

We hope to capture all of this in the phrase 'continu*al* quality improvement', and we'll bet you didn't infer all of that from the phrase when you first read it! So now, let us think together about this discontinuous, lumpy process of learning.

Quality improvement and learning

Continual quality improvement (CQI) has at its heart a central process. That process is *learning*. We know from our own experience that learning is not continuous—sometimes we learn, but often we do anything but—and our learning is never total. Yet it does continue. As humans, we are designed for learning. Children have a built-in urge to learn. They do not have to be 'taught' to talk or to walk.

Society, however, has put large barriers in the way of the process of learning. Not the least of these is the traditionally accepted way in which organizations are managed. W. Edwards Deming, a leader in the quality movement, criticizes in particular the prevailing practice of merit rating:

> The idea of a merit rating is alluring. The sound of the words captivates the imagination: pay for what you get; get what you pay for; motivate people to do their best, for their own good.
>
> The effect is exactly the opposite of what the words promise. Everyone propels himself forward, or tries to, for his own good, on his own life preserver. The organization is the loser. . . .

Merit rating rewards people that do well in the system. It does not reward attempts to improve the system. Don't rock the boat.

If anyone in top management asks a plant manager what he hopes to accomplish next year, the answer will be an echo of the policy (numerical goal) of the company.[2]

Deming is saying that most of society's institutions train their members to perform to the standards of others rather than develop their own innate capacity to learn. Indeed, it is clear that even some institutions fail to learn. A study by Shell Oil Company showed that 'a full one-third of the Fortune "500" industrials listed in 1970 had vanished by 1983'. However, according to former Shell planning director Arie de Geus, the study also revealed a small number of companies that had survived for 75 years or longer. The secret to their survival appeared to be their ability to 'experiment' by continually examining new business and organizational opportunities that made growth possible.[3]

This experimentation is the act of creating what we shall describe more fully later in this book as 'liberating structures'. The idea of a liberating structure can be approached through a situation in which there is *no* liberating structure to support learning for organizational members.

In response to market demand, one of the largest US consulting firms has recently organized a group explicitly mandated to help large firms with general organizational change. However, while the members of the group have impressive technical business skills to solve specific problems, virtually none of them has the political skills to support a general organizational transformation that increasingly empowers the client organization members to solve their own problems. Instead, they tend to retreat back to offering piecemeal technical advice. Moreover, the rest of the consulting firm tends to be allergic to this new group, rather than trying to learn from its experience.

A liberating structure would turn the tensions, dilemmas, and gaps evident in this illustration into occasions for learning and improved competence. A liberating structure is a type of organizing that is productive and at the same time educates its members towards self-correcting awareness. Engaging in a process of mutual self-correction requires ongoing effort among participants to recognize and correct errors and incongruities in the midst of action, an effort we find to be the primary requirement for continual quality improvement.

Managers typically lead in a different way than this: they

attempt to impose their vision and their learnings on others. The result is that others do not share ownership in the vision and learnings. Because they have not been invited to share in the vision and learnings, they see them as faddish and abstract—not really connected to the realities they encounter and deal with in their work. This situation is illustrated in the comments a young market research staff member, Jennifer, makes about her company:

The company has established very strict rules and systems for getting the job done, getting the product out on the market and measuring its success in the market. I would even go so far as to say there are unwritten rules about how one should act in the company. I think the company has been in this by-the-book mode for decades. But there is some evidence that efforts are being made to change this.

For approximately two years, the company as a whole has been involved in a 'quality movement'—looking for better ways to do things. It is my belief that senior management has realized our company cannot keep doing business the same old way in today's competitive environment. Most people in the company have been involved in some quality training. My opinion is that this movement on the whole and within my sector has not been very effective to date. The culture of the company is such that the large majority of employees are very comfortable with what they do and how they do it. They are not encouraged or motivated to think of ways to improve processes. Change is avoided and rejected at all costs. In order for this quality movement to be successful, it is necessary that quality is embraced from the lower levels and move upwards, rather than the traditional 'top-down' method. This is something that is extremely unfamiliar in my company. People are still waiting for management to tell them what to do with these quality initiatives.

A majority of the people in my sector have been through some sort of quality training. In order to enforce this quality training and for quality to become part of our everyday work, our senior management came up with a 'We Create Quality' programme. The format of the programme was as follows: all employees were to form themselves into 'quality teams'. (Teams could be departments, subsets of departments, cross departments, what-ever.) These quality teams were supposed to identify the services they provided and to whom they provided them (i.e. identify their 'customers'). Once that was determined, the team was supposed to pick a process that could be improved upon. One major problem with this 'We Create Quality' programme was that these were the *only* guidelines. People were very confused about what they were supposed to do. To be more specific, the guidelines weren't the problem, it was just that people in my company are so used to being told what to do and how to do it, they could not understand why management wasn't telling them what to do.

Jennifer's description is typical of the all-too-common situation where people do not feel personally connected to CQI, where someone up there is doing it *to* them. As Jennifer says, the problem is not that top management is the starting point for CQI and is providing the guidelines; in those cases where CQI really takes hold, its starting point is at the top. But the crucial question is: *What is it* that starts at the top? The top is only a good starting point for CQI if the top actually *does* CQI—i.e. practises the learning process instead of merely giving the abstract 'guidelines' that came from the management of Jennifer's company.

Jennifer also believes that CQI has to be 'embraced from the lower levels and move upwards.' Taken as a whole, her argument is that CQI has to move in both directions— downwards and upwards—in the organization, and we agree. CQI has to be set in motion from the inside out. Initiative has to come from personnel at all levels. As Peter Senge puts it: 'Organizations learn only through individuals who learn.'

At the heart of CQI: individual involvement

The importance to CQI of grassroots involvement by employees throughout the organization is strongly supported by a survey of 313 Fortune 1000 firms conducted in 1990 by Edward Lawler, Susan Mohrman and Gerald Ledford.[4] Their research revealed that while 75 per cent of these organizations use specific quality management practices (such as direct exposure to customers, self-inspection, work simplification, cost-of-quality monitoring, collaboration with suppliers in quality efforts, just-in-time deliveries, or work cells) to at least some extent, these practices affect less than 40 per cent of employees in the typical organization. The study further revealed that various forms of employee involvement in management existed in 86 per cent of the firms surveyed. These included such practices as quality circles, quality of work life committees, parallel organization structures, and survey feedback to work groups.

The researchers found that both total quality practices and employee involvement practices were related to organizational effectiveness on a variety of measures, but they saw important differences between the contributions each made. Employee involvement focuses on the individual by assigning responsible, motivating jobs and by basing rewards on performance. This emphasis on arousing the commitment and creativity of the individual differs from the more 'top-down' nature of many total quality programmes that we mentioned earlier. On the other hand, a key contribution of the total quality movement has been its emphasis on processes that cut across the entire sweep of the organization, exposing some employees directly to customers and involving others in collaborating with suppliers' quality efforts. Because total quality and employee involvement contribute to organizational performance importantly, but in different ways, Lawler, Mohrman and Ledford wondered how the two efforts are related in organizations that have used them. They found that of the Fortune 1000 companies that had used both employee involvement and quality management, about one-third conducted them as separate programmes, one-third coordinated them, while one-third ran them as one integrated effort. The choice was a crucial one:

> Running the programs separately reduces the impact on the transition to a high-involvement culture. Companies that run them separately are less likely to achieve a participatory management style, move decisions lower, and achieve broad skill development and information flow. They are also less likely to remove layers of management, which was found earlier to be associated with fuller implementation of both quality and employee involvement. Finally, they report less improvement in their technology and in organizational processes and procedures.
>
> In short, it appears that having two separate organizational initiatives, quality and employee involvement, strongly reduces their impact. Companies that take this approach do not attain as complete an implementation of either one and are not as likely to obtain their desired outcomes. This is a very important finding in view of the number of companies that have two different initiatives and two different support staffs vying for attention. It is quite possible that such separation precludes recognition within the organization of the fundamental conceptual and action overlap and leaves organizational members confused and/or cynical about the change strategy. In fact, the two initiatives may be implemented incompatibly.

By emphasizing how important it is that quality management be integrated with employee involvement, the Lawler, Mohrman, and Ledford study confirms the competitive advantage of understanding CQI as an action process at the level of the individual person in the organization, not merely as an abstract programme. Transforming the organization means transforming it person by person. Contributors to a

1993 *Harvard Business Review* forum confirm the point. Asked whether CQI can survive economic adversity, including company downsizing, these experts, all extensively experienced in quality management, explained how CQI can become so well established in some organizations that it is able to withstand difficult periods. One participant, James L. Broadhead, chairman and CEO of Florida Power and Light Company, noted that where CQI really takes hold in an organization, it moves from a 'developmental' stage, where format and structured procedures are emphasized, to a 'mature' stage, where employees are

> allowed to apply more freely the problem-solving methods they had learned from the program without being criticized for not following specific procedures or formats. Following changes in our approach to allow greater freedom and creativity, our employees have introduced countless improvements and helped us achieve ever higher levels of productivity and customer satisfaction.[5]

This statement again spotlights the importance of CQI at the level of the individual. The need for CQI to go deeper than the level of an abstract programme is echoed by Bernardo de Sousa, corporate quality officer of Ciba-Geigy Ltd. He notes that where CQI is seen 'as a programme and not as a continuous (*sic*) process, the company has been practising a quality system but not total quality management. . . . managers are only partly committed to TQM.'

Our earlier point that CQI has to be real rather than programmatic for top managers, not just for their subordinates, is also confirmed by the *Harvard Business Review* commentators. Jeff Haley and Peter Cross, systems engineers at an East Coast, US engineering consulting firm whose quality effort was derailed by a business downturn, reported that

> Our firm lost its direction implementing TQM. The owners viewed TQM as a marketing tool, enabling them to tout our company as being part of the fashionable total quality movement. But an empty TQM effort is worse than none at all. . . . The owners chose not to participate in the 'open' discussion sessions conducted in the TQM culture. . . . They just wanted us to 'do TQM' as if it meant flipping a switch, while they went about business as usual. . . . Our company owners have yet to recognize that the TQM process is not now, and probably never will be, in place. But when asked if we are a total quality company, the answer is always a resounding yes.

In the remainder of Part One of this book, we define and illustrate the specifics of the kind of action individuals can take to assume personal ownership of CQI and make it real for themselves and their organizations. We call this behaviour *action inquiry*. Action inquiry is the gene of continual quality improvement. It is behaviour through which persons build the process of learning, which can make possible transformation for themselves and their organization. Our argument is that you can continually improve in your own work only to the degree that you practise action inquiry and that you can influence others to engage in continual quality improvement only to the degree that you practise action inquiry. So . . . what is this magical elixir?

Notes

1. For those eager to pursue, or even mildly interested in pursuing, a longer path of adventurous inquiry into the world of intrinsically valuable 'quality' than this short book provides, our first recommended alternative text is Robert M. Pirsig (1974) *Zen and the Art of Motorcycle Maintenance*, New York: Morrow. Pirsig refuses to define 'quality', but at one point tells us that 'quality is not a thing; it's an event'—an act we take, a social theatre in which we participate—a point to which we shall return explicitly in our final chapter, but which we are coming back to implicitly throughout the book whenever we focus again, with you, on **your actions** *in the management setting*.
2. W. Edwards Deming (1986) *Out of The Crisis*, Cambridge, MA, Massachusetts Institute of Technology, Center for Advanced Engineering Study, p. 103.
3. The Shell Oil Company study is reported by Arie P. de Geus (1988) 'Planning as learning', *Harvard Business Review* (March–April), 70–4.
4. Edward E. Lawler III, Susan Albers Mohrman and Gerald E. Ledford Jr. (1992) *Employee Involvement and Total Quality Management: Practices and Results in Fortune 1000 Companies*, San Francisco, CA: Jossey-Bass. The quotation is reproduced by permission of the publisher.
5. Reprinted by permission of the *Harvard Business Review*. Excerpt from Daniel Niven (1993) 'When times get tough, what happens to TQM?', *Harvard Business Review* (May–June 1993) Copyright © 1993 by the President and Fellows of Harvard College. All rights reserved.

2 Action inquiry: the gene of CQI

By *action inquiry* we mean a kind of behaviour that is simultaneously inquiring and productive. It is behaviour that simultaneously learns about the developing situation, accomplishes whatever task appears to have priority, and invites a redefining of the task if necessary.

When truly practised, action inquiry enhances the actor's as well as the organization's *efficiency*, *effectiveness* and *legitimacy*.

- By weaving together action and inquiry rather than separating them, as does most managerial action, action inquiry can save you time and thus increase efficiency.
- By making explicit and testing the appropriateness of your purposes, strategies, inferences and outcomes, action inquiry results in the correction of errors, increasing the immediate effectiveness of outcomes.
- By testing and potentially redefining your own strategy, or the strategy of a group or an organization, action inquiry generates long-term term effectiveness.
- By making explicit and testing your own and others' purposes and visions, action inquiry develops increasingly shared corporate purposes and visions.
- By redefining when current strategies are shown to contradict the vision, action inquiry increases the legitimacy and integrity of the enterprise to its members and clients. In this way, you also guard against being seduced into illegitimate enterprises, since a good test of legitimacy is whether you can make your vision or purpose explicit to other participants without damaging the chance to achieve it.

This kind of behaviour is not merely a set of technical tools, though we shall treat it that way in the next chapter when we provide guidelines to enable you to experiment on your own. Instead, when used effectively, this approach generates a reframing of your entire foundation for, and aim when, working with others. The aims of work become *not* attaining preconceived objectives through unilateral manipulation, but rather:

(a) increasing your own and others' awareness of a shared mission;
(b) increasing mutuality and internal commitment among the players;
(c) increasing communication about lack of alignment of individual, group and corporate objectives and actions and about lack of validity of assumptions;
(d) increasing action towards alignment between personal aims and actions and organizational mission and operations.

Thus, action inquiry heightens your awareness of your purposes and assumptions, of the quality of your conversation moment by moment with other individuals or at meetings, and of how your action in the moment relates to group and corporate quality. The power of action inquiry is in its potential for linking both *personal* quality improvement and quality improvement in the immediate conversation with quality improvement longer term in the work group and the wider organization.

We feel the best way to begin to gain an appreciation of the potential of action inquiry is to see it in operation. In this chapter we shall present two examples, the first two among many appearing throughout this book. Both represent 'first tries' at action inquiry by evening MBA students taking a course requiring a six-month action inquiry project. In the first, Jennifer, whom we met earlier, takes action that breathes life into the quality improvement programme within her own small department—the programme that had fallen dormant because people 'could not understand why management wasn't telling them what to do'. In the second, Anthony, a staff member in a consulting firm, employs action inquiry in a way that sparks change across the entire top management of his organization.

Jennifer's experiment

Jennifer's department consisted of four women. Jennifer, Louise and Margaret reported to the department manager, Donna. All four comprised the department's quality team, with Jennifer having been appointed by Donna as its 'team leader'. Jennifer gave her view of the quality project, dubbed the 'We Create Quality' project by her company:

> I will admit that I initially felt some resentment since I had no desire to be responsible for this project. Anyway, as team leader I had done a miserable job if you judged my performance by what actually got done, which was nothing. There are many reasons (excuses?) why nothing was accomplished: (1) Louise was out on short-term disability, (2) our department is very busy, (3) it is very hard for us all to get together (Donna is out at least one day a week), (4) our department does not work well together at all (there are personality conflicts), (5) it is difficult to think of a process to improve which affects all of us in the department, and (6) I have no managerial responsibility. But it became extremely important to me to do something with this failure. Before I began to study action inquiry, I had just given up, because I didn't know how to handle the conflicts which arose whenever I tried to make progress on the 'We Create Quality' project. It was easier to do nothing. I was accustomed to doing individual projects I could have complete control over. But this project would force me to work on a 'team' and to take others' points of view into account.

Jennifer shows a willingness to jump in and try action inquiry in a difficult situation. She also shows an explicit desire not only to restart the quality programme, but to break out of her shell and develop her own teamwork capabilities. Thus she links her personal developmental effort to her departmental group's quality improvement effort, which is in turn a part of the total company's effort. She then gave her views of some further features of the situation that she saw as important, as well as her goals for her effort at action inquiry:

> Although my company has always been managed from the top down, and change has been minimal, things could be starting to change. The fact that the company is trying to formulate alternatives to the current health insurance situation, given the [US] government's attention to national healthcare, shows the company is trying to *work with* instead of *react to* the government in this major reform. . . .
>
> I joined the department less than a year ago. Donna, who was also new, told me she had decided to change the way the department operated. She wanted to shift responsibilities around so that the other two members of the department could learn new things. The previous manager had never done this. Thus, not only was there a new member—myself—but everyone in the department ended up with new responsibilities. These facts led me to believe the department is assuming an experimental bent— starting to search for new ways of doing things. . . .

Donna treats each of us very individualistically. There is no real 'team' atmosphere in our department. Although none of our projects requires that we work with other people in the department, I believe we would produce higher quality work if we knew what everyone was doing. I usually have no idea what anyone else is working on. I have also felt that Donna 'withholds' or does not share information with the rest of us. My hopes have been that with time this tendency would fade if she were shown an alternative method of managing the department. . . .

I knew this was the situation I wanted to deal with for my action inquiry project. It is a situation which encompasses the organization, the department, all of my associates, and myself, individually. It was a project that would help me with some of my current professional goals:

1. Increased 'visibility' to my supervisor, which includes taking initiative to go above and beyond the responsibilities of my job.
2. A better working relationship with both Louise and Margaret.
3. Somehow get Donna to share information she has about our sector of the company with the rest of the department.

We can see that Jennifer began her action inquiry attempt with several foundation pieces in place. First, she viewed her situation as having several nested layers: the organization's incipient struggle to become less bureaucratic, her department's need for teamwork, her manager's start at trying to build the department's flexibility and versatility juxtaposed with the manager's own tendency to withhold information, and Jennifer's own professional objectives of visibility, upward influence, effectiveness as a team member and her desire to rescue the quality improvement programme along with her record as its leader. Secondly, she made explicit, written statements of several of her objectives. Finally, she implicitly assumes that it is worth while to try changing patterns of behaviour even though they may be ones that are well established (her manager's and colleagues' reluctance to share information, her own reclusiveness, etc.). Building on these foundation elements, Jennifer began her action inquiry experiment by having a discussion with her manager, Donna.

I went into her office and began by saying, 'Remember that "We Create Quality" project?' She kind of laughed and said she did. I went on to explain why I thought it had failed at first, but how I thought it would be a good idea for our department if we got together to meet about it. It would bring us together and get us working on something in a 'team' manner instead of how we usually did our work, which is in a very 'individualistic' manner. I said I thought we could learn from each other working in this manner. I was taking a risk at this point because I didn't want to come across as criticizing her management style. I just wanted to offer an additional way for our department to work. She didn't really show any reaction at this point.

I went on to say I knew Louise would be very resistant to the idea. (She has a serious personality conflict with Margaret, which Donna is aware of.) I asked for her support in this project and to help me out if I came across serious conflict between Louise and Margaret. She assured me she would. I told Donna I planned to go to Louise and Margaret separately and remind them about this project and say I would really like to start it up again. I asked for her advice at this point—did she think it was a good idea? She thought it was. I went on and said I would ask them to think about it for a few days to see if they could come up with any ideas for a 'quality initiative', my thoughts being that if ideas came from them they would be more willing to work on them. I then asked her to do the same thing, except I prefaced this with the fact that I knew she was very busy on some task forces and if she knew of anything our department could help her with, this would be a great opportunity to do so. I felt it was important to frame this part of the conversation in this way. Working on her own is something Donna was and is very used to doing. She thought for a moment and said, 'That's a good idea, I'll think about it.' I left her office feeling as though I had accomplished some small feats—I got her support, encouragement, and also got her thinking about the possibility of sharing with the rest of the department what she is working on.

In this conversation, Jennifer made conscious use of four specific elements of action inquiry. She *framed* the conversation at the start by referring to the 'We Create Quality' project and her current view of it, making her agenda clear to Donna. She *advocated* by saying what her recommendations were. She *illustrated* by telling how she planned to proceed (e.g. go to Louise and Margaret separately). Finally, she *inquired* by asking Donna for her advice. In the next chapter, we shall explain framing, advocating, illustrating and inquiring in more detail. Suffice it to say at this point that Jennifer's artful use of the technical tools of action inquiry in her conversation with Donna got her effort off to a running start.

She next went to Louise, and then to Margaret. She encountered the resistance she had expected from Louise, who didn't want anything to do with Margaret. Jennifer persisted, however, reminding Louise of their friendship, admitting she had failed so far with the quality improvement programme and saying how much she wanted it to be different this time. She continued that this would be a good way to get Donna to share information about what is happening. She found that 'this comeback worked, because she is very interested (as we all are) in what is happening in the company outside our department?' In response to a request by Jennifer that she think of projects the group could work on, Louise agreed to do so. Then, over the next two days, Jennifer returned to remind Louise to think of things they could suggest at a meeting of the team. Louise came up with the possibility of conducting a survey of field personnel—an idea Jennifer strongly confirmed, and suggested that she bring up at the meeting.

Jennifer's meeting with Margaret went smoothly. Jennifer began the conversation with a few friendly pleasantries, then moved rather quickly to the business at hand, an approach she knew from past experience that Margaret found comfortable. Margaret responded with enthusiasm to the idea of reviving the 'We Create Quality' team and agreed to be of help.

When Jennifer convened the first meeting of the team she had momentary feelings of panic. She was vulnerable. She recalled how she had never really taken charge in previous meetings and they had not gone well. Things 'just happened'.

The day of the meeting finally came. This time I took a leadership role and reiterated the fact that I really wanted to do something on this project this time. I stated I was committed to this since senior management endorses the quality movement. I asked if anyone had ideas they wanted to share.

Donna said she had been thinking about a variety of projects, but there was one in particular we would all be able to work on. She said we needed to look at our survey process. We all agreed this was certainly a good project to begin with. I then suggested we could split it up: Louise and I could look at the in-house process costs since Louise had dealt primarily with internal people, while Margaret and I could look at the outside vendor costs, since we were the ones who usually dealt with vendors. I made this suggestion because I knew Louise was not going to work with Margaret on anything. The reasons I suggested I work on both parts were because I was team leader and because this would be a good way to work on my goals of creating more effective working relationships with Louise and Margaret.

I asked if anyone had other ideas. Louise made the suggestion she and I had discussed about conducting a survey of our field people. Both Donna and Margaret agreed this was a good idea. Donna suggested Louise and I make a draft of the survey, since we had never done a questionnaire ourselves, and then she and

Margaret would look at it and make comments, presenting an opportunity for us to get trained in survey design.

After this was decided, Donna said one of the task forces she was working on would need a monthly newsletter about managed care and other issues dealing with the healthcare question in Washington. She said she would talk to Louise later about her ideas. Margaret asked about the task force, noting that she does a monthly newsletter for the field personnel and wondered how it might be affected. After I followed with some questions of my own about the task force, I think Donna realized we were all interested in these outside-the-department task forces she works on. To end the meeting, I suggested that we meet again when we had made definite progress on our separate projects so we could share with each other. I thanked them all for coming and for their commitment to the project.

I felt great about what had just taken place. By preparing everyone individually a few days before, I think people spent time thinking about what could be done. What I felt most optimistic about was Donna's sharing of information with us. This was really something new.

In the days that followed, Jennifer began working collaboratively with both Louise and Margaret. Good progress was made in both cases, although she found working with Louise stressful at times:

> One of the most difficult things to deal with is her unpredictable nature. I can never tell whether she will be willing to do something or not or what sets her off. I have noticed that she tends to have outbursts when she is unsure of herself. This realization has helped me. I take a few seconds to think about how I will reply to an outburst. At another time, I might have yelled back, or just cut her out of a project and finished it myself. But now, it has also become clear to me that I cannot always be prepared in dealing with her and have to perfect my actions on a moment-by-moment basis.

The project continued to enable Jennifer to fulfil her goals of having more contact with Donna and increasing the overall information sharing within the department:

> Just keeping her up to date on our progress on each project gave me more opportunities, and I was more candid than I had been before in telling her about problems I and my associates were running into. I told her how I appreciated working with each of them because I was finding out what they were working on and learning new things. Donna said she was glad about this. I also told her I was glad she was telling us more about the things she was working on. Again she said that was good.

As an aside, although Louise's and Margaret's interaction had not increased, they were both aware of what the other was working on because I had shared that information with them.

Jennifer commented in her written report on her action inquiry project that she saw her efforts as having 'only just begun'. In writing this she shows an understanding of something that is as basic to action inquiry as it is to quality management, namely that both are continual. They are processes, not monuments that, once completed, always sit there. In this and other ways her description shows she is not just practising action inquiry as an external behaviour, but is also experiencing it implicitly and internally. She marshalled the inner courage to act on a previous failure. She thought hard about her colleagues' internal, individual points of view, realizing the importance of making her thinking clear to them and strengthening her personal relationships with them as a foundation on which to conduct the team meeting. She paid close attention to what she knew about their idiosyncrasies and adapted her approaches accordingly. She had her specific personal goals in mind while in action, as when she set up the task assignments in a way that confirmed her role as team leader while simultaneously developing her relationships with Louise and Margaret. She also began to realize the importance of practising 'moment-by-moment' action improvement—awareness of her own actions and results as they occur—as she did in connection with her successful responses to Louise's 'outbursts'. Here she was beginning to experience one of the ultimate destinations of action inquiry, moment-to-moment awareness and experimental actions in the midst of ongoing situations. In addition, Jennifer helped others to realize internally the significance of incidents by summarizing and explaining events to them, as when, at the end of the meeting, she thanked her team members for their commitment to the project, and when she ended her conversation with Donna by saying she was glad Donna was 'telling us more about the things she was working on'. Thus, in several ways, Jennifer illustrates what we mean when we say that quality improvement requires a special kind of on-line awareness by the individual. Quality improvement has to happen from the inside out.

Jennifer re-invigorated a CQI programme within her department. Our second experimenter in action inquiry, Anthony, had an impact across the top management of his organization.

Anthony's experiment

Anthony saw his action inquiry project as an opportunity to try breaking out of a cocoon. As a benefits consultant in a local office of an international human resources consulting firm, he had for the past two years immersed himself in the narrowly specialized world of a very complex method for comparing company benefit programmes for large corporate clients. He became one of the firm's few experts in this method, which fulfilled his personal ambition to

> do something unique to differentiate myself. There were very few people who worked with this system, so I was on my own much of the time. I enjoyed knowing that every new barrier I was crossing was separating me further and further from other young associates. However, at times my perfectionist nature would cause me physical and mental stress. I would find myself obsessing about minutia in an effort to rationalize every last variation in my results.

The opportunity to break out presented itself in two ways. First, the organization of the office was non-hierarchial, with the office divided into 12 teams, each headed by a coordinator, who reported to the office manager. This allowed Anthony ready access to the office manager and the team coordinators, who were the office's strategic management team. Secondly, Anthony saw a quality improvement opportunity. The team coordinators were plagued by a problem he felt he could help them address:

> As an employee, I encounter shortcomings in a myriad of administrative functions such as billing, training, hiring and new employee initiation, career pathing, work allocation, and performance review. Our team coordinators are supposed to oversee all this while simultaneously bringing in new clients and working with ongoing clients. The coordinators are constantly forced to juggle priorities amid tight time constraints. Clients, employees, and the coordinators themselves suffer severe consequences. I developed a plan to help ameliorate some of the team coordinators' problems.

In much the same way that Jennifer strategized and planned before talking with anyone about her project, Anthony developed a detailed set of steps he proposed to take with the team coordinators. First, he would meet with the office manager to discuss the project, then meet briefly with each team coordinator to explain his proposed approach. Next, he would prepare questions for interviews and for a survey instrument and would administer both. After analysing the data, he would present feedback to the team coordinators at one of their monthly meetings. A collaboratively determined action plan would then be developed and implemented.

With this plan in mind, Anthony met with Don, the office manager. Scheduled for half an hour, this meeting, as Anthony put it, 'blossomed into two hours of discussion about our team coordinator problems and how this project could help address them'. An important clarification occurred in this meeting. Don suggested that Anthony should make recommendations to the team coordinators after collecting his data, but Anthony responded that he did not intend to recommend solutions, 'but rather to facilitate a collaborative effort involving all of the team coordinators'. A framework and timetable were established for the project and Anthony was pleasantly surprised with the success of this meeting.

> Even with this initial meeting, I began to achieve several of my objectives. After overcoming my initial nervousness, I settled into a productive give-and-take discussion with the highest ranking person in our office. Comments and observations from each of us were given equal weighting. Several times I provided insights that enlightened Don about the perspectives of lower-level staff members. Throughout the course of this meeting, I realized that several of my objectives were beginning to take shape:
>
> 1. To differentiate myself from the average staff member.
> 2. To increase my exposure to senior management.
> 3. To purposely place myself in a high-risk situation.
> 4. To force myself out of my own consulting specialty and into other service lines within our company.
> 5. To improve my presentation and public speaking skills.

Anthony proceeded with the survey and interviews. After several further discussions with Don, he decided to survey the team coordinators explicitly on their responsibilities—which should they retain, which should be delegated to their team members, and which should be handled through a centralized office administration. Anthony was also stimulated by these meetings both in terms of the work accomplished and in terms of progress he was able to make in developing his action inquiry skills.

> My follow-up discussions with the team coordinators were fantastic opportunities to experiment with my behaviour on a one-to-one basis. They were very willing to open up and discuss

sensitive subjects and were also appreciative of my efforts to make their lives easier.

Each coordinator directs a given consulting specialty. I had to constantly be aware of how to frame questions, which areas to hone in on, which to tactfully sidestep. For instance, on several occasions, I drew a chart with 'market growth' and 'market penetration' on the two axes (the old star/dog/cash cow diagram). While talking with the coordinator of a health care team, I marked his team in the star category, and a defined benefit team in the dog category. Should the leaders of these two teams have the same set of responsibilities? Perhaps the health care coordinator should let expenses rise to permit getting more revenue, while the defined benefit coordinator should work on cutting costs to increase profit.

In any event, the chart proved to be a perfect arena for using my framing/advocating/illustrating/inquiring skills. You can't just *tell* a senior manager and expert who's been in the business 25 years that he should change his behaviour. But the components of action inquiry verbal behaviour came right out of me. 'Let's talk about revenues and expenses for the next few minutes (framing). I don't think that two separate team coordinators should necessarily share the same focus regarding profit generation (advocating). Look here on this chart. See how the pension team is at the opposite end of the spectrum from the health care team (illustrating)? Would you have them focus on the same issues (inquiring)?' It was an opportunity to increase the team coordinators' awareness.

After completing this round of interviews and tabulating the survey results, it was time for Anthony to give his presentation to the monthly meeting. When the day arrived, he suffered an attack of stage fright.

I was to wait at my desk and they would call me when it was time for my presentation. The minutes ticked by, I paced a while, read memos in my in-box, listened to my phone messages, and paced a little more. Finally, they called me in.

I broke the ice a bit by saying I felt like a bachelor who had been waiting backstage on the Dating Game. I then began the meeting by framing what I intended to accomplish (following the standard public speaking guidelines, 'Tell them what you're going to tell them, tell them, then tell them what you told them'). We then entered a lengthy and somewhat spirited discussion of a chart showing results of the team coordinator and team member surveys. I sensed that several coordinators interpreted the chart as saying that they weren't doing their jobs well. I quickly thought how I could rephrase my lead-in and then announced, 'The shaded responsibilities are areas which stand to gain the most through refocused attention and delegation to other team members'. They were more comfortable with this way of looking at it.

The meeting lasted for over an hour and produced encouraging results. In terms of practising and enhancing my action inquiry skills, I could not have asked for a better forum. I was surrounded by every member of our senior management; they all had a vested interest in the subject matter; there was a constant interchange of ideas and opinions; and I was leading the meeting. Add to that that each team coordinator represented a different service line and years of ingrained behaviour. We ultimately decided to pilot test a delegation of certain coordinator responsibilities to three teams. I am continuing to work with the office manager and the various teams as we move forward with this initiative.

Anthony's case shows that CQI at the senior management level shares certain features with CQI within a lower level work group like Jennifer's. Anthony's effort, though not labelled as part of a formal quality improvement programme, was one in which he saw malfunctions in the work setting and developed specific plans for bringing them to light. Then he set the stage, testing and revising his plans with the key people involved, building their support and at the same time developing personal rapport with them, much the same as Jennifer did with her department manager and the two associates.

Summary

Both Anthony and Jennifer began a process of organizational transformation that depended not just on programmatic planning, but on putting into action a venture in personal development. Both decided to 'break out' of roles where they acted more as individuals than as team members, and to 'break into' roles which required more of themselves and also influenced better performance by others. Both were willing to take risks, cope with initial nervousness, and move into unfamiliar territory. Conversations embodying inquiry, mutual influence, and learning were at the heart of both of these successful efforts.

From their initial conception on through to their outcomes, Jennifer's and Anthony's cases are personal as well as organizational. In the preceding chapter, we said that CQI must be understood at the level of the individual's on-the-spot action. We said quality improvement is continu-*al*, not continu-*ous*, and is never 'total'. It is not programmable, like a machine, where all the parameters are known. It occurs through the fits and starts of individual learning. We quoted researchers and executives who testified to the importance of 'involvement' as crucial to quality management—the necessity that CQI permeate into and transform the on-line thought and action of the individuals in an organization.

Jennifer's and Anthony's cases show in practice the link between CQI as organizational transformation and as individual transformation. Through inquiry in action, both established a reciprocity between themselves and their organization. Jennifer's actions—to help her associates to gain more information about what was going on, and help her boss to have a reduced workload—required a developmental 'break-out' by Jennifer herself, and laid the foundation to make her department a place that would keep her functioning at a higher level of personal effectiveness in the future. The same is probably true for Anthony, whose personal developmental surge shows others that he is a person who can move the organization.

You may have noticed an additional aspect of how both Jennifer and Anthony acted. Neither of them had formal organizational authority to do what they did and neither of them tried to force their proposals or opinions on others. Instead, they *gained* authority through their way of working in the actual situation; and their way of working was to exercise the power of vulnerability—the power of actively seeking through inquiry with others what is best for the larger situation. We will talk more about this power of vulnerability that characterizes action inquiry as we continue.

We hope you, like Jennifer and Anthony, are beginning to think about the possibility of 'breaking out'. Or you may be looking for more evidence that it is worth the risk, or perhaps more specifics on how to begin the process. In the next chapter we shall address these concerns by describing in a more complete, step-by-step manner the action process Jennifer and Anthony adopted that helped them increase their effectiveness. In short, we shall provide you more fully with the tools of action inquiry. While doing so, we shall also add more evidence that if you take the challenge of starting CQI at the personal level, you will find the effort to be worth while.

3 Fundamentals of action inquiry

As shown in Chapters 1 and 2, continual quality improvement (CQI) involves organizational learning, and organizational learning requires learning by individuals. In highly effective organizations, those who are at the top as well as those who are at lower levels engage in the process of learning. In fact, in the *most* effective organizations, those at the top engage in the most risky and most transformative learning, for they must lead the organization precisely in this domain—they must teach their subordinates more about learning.

This does not mean, as most books on quality improvement inveigh from beginning to end, that quality improvement must be practised by *everyone* in the organization before it can work. Heavy pressure for everyone in the organization to participate in a new quality programme is a recipe for generating blind faith at the outset among some; next, it is likely to generate temporary conformity to a new 'unquestionable' official jargon; then, finally, it is likely in the long term to generate increased cynicism about the organization. A quality programme begins to die from the inside the moment it becomes unquestionable religion, orthodoxy, jargon—i.e. as soon as it ceases to be a vehicle for true adventures in learning, in invention, in corporate strategy, in service and in daily actions.

We saw examples in Chapters 1 and 2 of people who undertook CQI not in abstract, symbolic terms, but in real-time action. Our students, Jennifer and Anthony, made clear headway towards increasing their own effectiveness and that of their organizations by taking the risk of experimenting with what, for them, was a new way of engaging with other people in the course of their work: action inquiry.

We hope these examples help to encourage you to begin your own continual quality programme in tentative, testing fashion. The examples suggest that even if only one or a few persons in an organization practise quality improvement with regard to *their own actions* and their immediate group, a process leading to organizational improvement may begin. Widespread commitment to, and participation in, CQI may be the eventual outcome, but it is not the starting point.

If your organization is *not yet* involved in a quality programme, you can be at the forefront when it begins one. If your organization is *already* involved in a quality programme, you can use the ideas and exercises in this book to establish your own position, to see through the shortcomings of a brand-name programme, and to discover how to contribute constructively to, and improve, your organization's programme.

If you are a senior executive in an organization that is now championing a quality improvement programme, you might encourage your key colleagues to question and improve the process you are currently engaged in, and to commit themselves more deeply to improving their own managerial effectiveness. Chapter 7 is dedicated in particular to examples, exercises and procedures that can help senior management teams with their individual and team development. Chapters 9 and 10 show one particular senior management team radically improving the quality of its meetings as part of an organization-wide quality programme.

If you are a member of the board of directors, you might ask the CEO what the organization is doing about quality. Ask him or her to present something on quality to the board—and you could offer a copy of this book! (In the US, with outside boards and legal precedents regarding board members' fiduciary responsibilities, this suggestion may seem entirely appropriate. By contrast, in the UK, with inside boards and the CEO as chairman, this suggestion may seem entirely *inappropriate*. The point, of course, is to imagine the most effectual quality-improving initiative for your circumstances. The discussion in this chapter can help you think about how to shape what you might say.)

Our point is that encouraging *individuals* to engage in constructive inquiry, awareness stretching and self-initiated behaviour changes in the midst of ongoing work ultimately provides the key to continual quality improvement. It is, however, a difficult process to begin and even more difficult to sustain, and one that can only be convincing if it begins, again and again, with one's own actions.

Why is action inquiry so difficult to start up in oneself and to prompt in others? It is difficult to start up because the vast majority of people who are under the stress of having to perform in managerial or professional positions in organizations simplify their lives by encasing their awareness and thought within assumptions they do not test. Even senior executives are not immune to this encasement.

In 1981, Kathleen Kenefick, a young lender for Continental Illinois Bank, wrote a memo to her superiors saying, 'The status of the Oklahoma accounts (particularly Penn Square) is a cause for concern, and corrective action should be instigated quickly.' In fact, corrective action was never instigated. Kenefick's message was explained away in upper echelons as a personality conflict with her boss, and Kenefick left the company. A year later, Penn Square was closed by regulators, and Continental was left holding $1 billion in bad loans. Continental itself underwent a federally supported reorganization in 1984.

Continental's higher management assumed that since Kenefick had a personality problem, her report was invalid. (Whether her conflict with her boss was fact or assumption, we don't know.) Higher management likely also assumed that a young staff member could not be correct in saying that such important loans, overseen by much more senior and experienced officers of the bank, were in danger when no one else was saying so. Though her warning was factually true, it did not penetrate these assumptions.[1]

Kenefick's communication to her superiors was by memo, but simplistic assumptions can prove to be just as impenetrable in face-to-face communication. In their book *Managing for Excellence*, David Bradford and Alan Cohen offer the following prototypical conversation between a manager and a subordinate. The manager is a good example of someone who is sealed within assumptions[2]:

Subordinate: We're having trouble delivering disposable widgets to Techcorp.

Manager: But they're our most important customer. Have you talked with Dan in Production?

Subordinate: Yes, but he says that yields are off because of poor material.

Manager: He always uses that as an excuse. Have you checked the materials report?

Subordinate: Yes, I've got it right here. I thought we ought to check . . .

Manager: [interrupting] Look at that. The material quality is within 1.5% of our usual standard. That can't be the problem. Anyway, yields can be increased by reprocessing material on overtime shifts.

Subordinate: That's right. We could use overtime.

Manager: OK, here's what to do: Get Alice to go over and tell Dan to increase the percentage of alloy by 7% and decrease the time in the second-batch processing. In fact, never mind—I'll call Dan myself and explain that, along with how he can shift extra materials over to widget making. Then he won't have any excuse.

Of course, it could be that material within 1.5 per cent of standard is not satisfactory in this particular case, or that technical factors of the kinds addressed by the manager are not really the problem. Indeed, if the manager routinely deals with Dan, as proposed here, by leaving him without 'any excuse', then the working relationship between the manager and Dan could be the main problem. Preventing the manager from exploring these possibilities are the assumptions (a) that technical factors are the only ones worth considering, (b) that the manager's own experience and current state of knowledge should be sufficient to solve any problem, (c) that people's options should be circumscribed so that they cannot give 'excuses', and (d) that this subordinate's options in particular, right now, should be circumscribed totally by the manager. On the basis of these assumptions, the manager takes over the problem from the subordinate, diagnoses it personally and acts on it personally. The manager's assumptions are not tested in order to learn whether they are right or wrong; nor does the manager create an opportunity for the subordinate to learn.

The manager allows no opening through which new information might come into his awareness to modify these assumptions. The situation is taken to be fully known and factual. The manager does not say, 'I think Dan may not know what is really delaying the widgets job, or may not want to tell if he does'. Nor does the manager *propose* the action to be taken (by saying, for example, 'What I think we should do is this . . .'). Nor does the manager say why increasing the alloy percentage and shifting extra materials over to widget making are the best choices of action to take. Such statements would have allowed the subordinate to view the manager's thinking and thereby to contribute relevant information or suggestions. Further, the manager could have invited the subordinate's input by asking, 'What do you think?' after proposing the suggested action. The way the manager spoke reinforced an attention that was narrowed within a single interpretation of the situation and prevented the assumptions on which that interpretation was based from being tested and modified.

Widening our attention

The example of Kathleen Kenefick's superiors at Continental Bank may seem a bit extreme, but we expect that many readers may not immediately have noticed what was 'wrong' with the responses of the manager in the case of the widget delivery problem. This manager's responses seem quite normal or typical. Most of us don't realize how many assumptions we make and how much learning we inhibit by our typical responses.

But, even if you, our reader, are willing to admit in a hypothetical way that you *may* be making assumptions of which you are unaware, you can argue that there is no way and no time for *anyone* to become aware of *all* their assumptions. 'Things must be done,' you say. 'The market will not wait for us to become wise. Thus we cannot help but act on our assumptions at times.'

You are right, of course. In fact, one way we learn about our false assumptions is to act on them without being aware that they are only assumptions *until* they prove themselves through our failure. The later in life you wait to learn about your false assumptions, the more painful are the consequences of these ultimate failures likely to be. They can result in lost jobs, injured organizations, divorce or alienated children, to name just a few of life's tragedies when we learn too late.

It is true that we cannot become aware of all our assumptions and that we cannot help but act on assumptions at times. But it is also true that it is profoundly important to learn how to test assumptions in the midst of everyday actions. By doing so, we create a climate in which (a) others in the organization become more aware that they, too, are making assumptions, (b) others become more willing to help us test our own assumptions (sometimes even before we are aware we are making assumptions), and (c) others gradually become more willing to test their assumptions as well.

Not all assumptions will be tested, and not all those that are tested will be tested well. But *many* assumptions *will* be tested and will generate learning, subsequent *success* and higher morale, rather than *failure* (and lower morale, without a subsequent chance to learn).

With sustained risk taking and ingenuity, an organization can generate a culture in which not only high-quality products and services are valued, but also high-quality awareness that tests assumptions early. This would be a true learning organization. No organization can test every assumption and thereby altogether avoid the risk of failing to test problematic assumptions, but an organization that cultivates courageous, intelligent, competent testing of assumptions will have an enormous competitive advantage over those in the same field that do not.

In the meantime, however, the more immediate question is how you, the reader, as an individual manager (and you do manage at least your own time and actions), can become more aware of, and less bound within, your implicit untested assumptions. The first step is to begin to recognize how limited our ordinary attention is and therefore how inadequate even our factual knowledge is of what is occurring at any moment in our lives—within us, around us and beyond us. There are four reasons why this is true.[3]

First, our attention simply does not register a great deal of what occurs. Reading this book, for example, you are likely to become oblivious for periods of time to sounds and other events in your environment; oblivious, too, to your own body position and breathing; oblivious even to the fact that this book is a physical object with size, weight and texture as distinct from the cognitive meaning of the words and sentences. Being reminded of these facts now may momentarily jolt you into a widened awareness, but you may simply shift your attention to the outside world territory from the cognitive territory, rather than widening it to include both—becoming transfixed, for example, with the view from the window.

A second limit to our attention on what is occurring at any moment is the very narrow cognitive-emotional interpretive net we apply to our perceptions. For example, most of us think in only one language and in one mood, without feeling how these patterns limit our awareness of what is occurring. (Those of you who speak a second or third language quite well can try to think about the same human issue—for example, a disagreement with a colleague or a member of your family—in each language. You will see that you think different thoughts and even discover different feelings as you talk to yourself about the issue in each different language.)

A third limit of our attention is that, although our own actions generate much of the knowledge we receive from others and from the environment, we are rarely aware how our actions skew what we know. Let us say, for example, that in a bright and cheerful manner you regularly pop into co-workers' offices briefly to find out things you need to know, always careful to make your visit as short as possible. You may not learn for years that they view you as a constant interruption, putting your agenda first, with the effect that they withhold significant information and oppose you much more than they otherwise might.

The simple fact is that we are rarely aware of our own behaviour and the reactions of others as we act. Seeing and hearing yourself on videotape for the first time (if you have done so) was probably a shock. You had no idea of the gestures you were making in public, of the facial expressions, the tones of voice, the run-on sentences, and so forth. But seeing oneself on videotape is not the same as direct awareness of oneself as one acts. First efforts towards this awareness typically generate paralysing self-consciousness. How to cultivate an ongoing awareness of how one is acting is key to continual quality improvement, both personally and organizationally, and is itself an inquiry and a practice for a lifetime.

A fourth limit on our attention to what is occurring at any given moment in our lives is that the data we have about the outside world is ordinarily about the past, not the present, is drastically unsystematic and incomplete, and is rarely tested for validity on the spot. Even the best of scientific studies can never prove that a proposition is *unequivocally* and *invariably* true (that is, true for all moments, and thus true for the present moment as well). At best, scientific methods can unequivocally *disconfirm* a proposition, but cannot unequivocally confirm it.

Again, because our knowledge at the moment is less than we need it to be, we rely on simplifying assumptions, as the executives at Continental Bank did, and as the manager in the widget case did. Once formed, these assumptions can blind us to the need to inquire in action, preventing the start-up of quality improvement.

The fact that our assumptions often veil us from what is going on means we must test them frequently whenever our best intuition in the midst of an ongoing business situation suggests the need. Doing this testing means you begin to behave in a way that reveals the unknown, enabling you to make your actions more consistent with your intentions, exemplifying a pattern that helps others to improve, and inviting others by example to join in such testing.

Even if you are deeply engaged in a personal quality improvement process, you may well fail to encourage others to engage in such a process. But you most certainly cannot successfully encourage quality improvement in anyone else unless you are deeply committed to it yourself.

Once you increase your credibility as a practitioner of CQI, you are more likely to be effective at inviting your immediate work associates to participate in a way that helps each of them to find his or her own motivation. And still later, with more practice, you can enter the rougher seas of inviting a wider sector of the organization to participate in CQI. This practice is what this chapter and the three that follow are about.

Let's start with an exercise. This exercise contains five steps and is intended to get you to pay much closer attention to how you act at work. So, let's go to work.

Improving the quality of your own action

Think of a recent incident, at work, in which you were involved that did *not* materialize in the way you had hoped, expected and sought. Choose an incident, if possible, that is ongoing or may recur, so that you can actually try out what you learn from this exercise if you wish. Make it a significant incident: one that matters enough to make it worth your while to discover how you can get a better outcome. Now, jot down in Step I the outline of what happened.

STEP I—*The incident. How it started, how it went, how it ended:*

. . . .

. . . .

. . . .

Quite possibly your recollection about the incident is that the unsatisfactory outcome was someone else's fault, or was the result of cumbersome or inappropriate organizational procedures, such as a meeting format that doesn't allow people to discuss the real issues. And you may be perfectly correct in the culprit you have chosen.

However, this way of telling the story gives you no direct control over improving the quality of the outcome. The only way you can directly improve the quality of outcomes in any situation is for *you* to act more effectively than you did in the incident you are remembering. This does not mean, of course, that you were solely, or even mainly responsible for the original unsatisfactory outcome. You may indeed have been the most constructive actor present. And, it may be that the way you can act even more effectively is to learn how to speak in a way that persuades 'the culprit' to change.

In other words, you can either wring your hands and blame the culprit in any negative situation, or you can ask yourself what *you* can do to improve it. (Of course, further inquiry may reveal that you were not quite the white knight in shining armour you imagined yourself to be.)

So, how do you find out how effective you actually were in the incident you are remembering, and how you might have become more effective? First, we suggest you make some brief notes, reconstructing in Step II the conversation(s) in which you participated at what you take to be the critical moment(s) of the incident you outlined in Step I. You probably won't be able to recall word for word what you and the other(s) said, but come as close as you can.

Step II

I said:	*He or she or they said:*
1.	1. . . . .
2.	2. . . . .
3.	3. . . . .
4.	4. . . . .

Now, let us suggest four simple categories into which all speech acts can be divided. You can apply these categories to what each person in the conversation said, but particularly to your own speech. Our claim is that your speech will be increasingly effective as you increasingly balance and integrate these four kinds of speech. In other words, if you find that your speaking is dominated by one or two of these types of speech, the recommendation is to try adding more of the other types. You can then test this claim by your own conversational experiments.

Types of speech

The four 'types of speech' are called *framing, advocating, illustrating* and *inquiring*.[4]

Framing

This refers to explicitly stating the purpose for the present occasion, the dilemma you are trying to resolve, and the assumptions you think are shared or not shared (but need to be tested out loud to be sure). This is the element of speaking most often missing from conversations and meetings. The leader or initiator assumes the others know and share the overall objective. Explicit framing (or reframing, if the conversation appears off-track) is useful precisely because the assumption of a shared frame is frequently untrue. When people have to guess at the frame, they frequently guess wrongly and they often impute negative, manipulative motives ('What's he getting at?').

For example, instead of starting with the first item of the meeting, the leader can provide and test an explicit frame:

> 'We're about halfway through to our final deadline and we've gathered a lot of information and shared different approaches, but we haven't yet made a single decision. To me, the most important thing we can do today is agree on something, make at least one decision we can feel good about. I think XYZ is our best chance, so I want to start with that. Do you agree with this assessment, or do you think something else is more important?'

Advocating

This refers to asserting an option, perception, feeling, or proposal for action explicitly in relatively abstract terms (e.g. 'We've got to get shipments out faster'). Some people speak almost entirely in terms of advocacy; others rarely advocate at all. Either extreme—only advocating or never advocating—is likely to be relatively ineffective. For example, 'Do you have an extra pen?' is not an explicit advocacy, but an inquiry. The person you are asking may truthfully say, 'No' and turn away. On the other hand, if you say 'I need a pen *(advocacy)*. Do you have an extra one *(inquiry)?*' the other is more likely to say something like, 'No, but there's a whole box in the secretary's office.'

The most difficult type of advocacy for most people to make effectively is an advocacy about how we feel—especially how we feel about what is occurring at this moment. This is difficult partly because we are often only partially aware of how we feel; also, we are reluctant to become vulnerable. For both these reasons, feelings usually enter conversations only when they have become so strong that they burst in, and then they are likely to be offered in a way that *harshly evaluates* others ('Damn it, will you loud-mouths shut up!'). This way of advocating feelings is usually very ineffective, however, because it invites defensiveness. By contrast, a *vulnerable description* is more likely to invite honest sharing by others ('I'm feeling frustrated and shut out by the machine-gun pace of this conversation and I don't see it getting us to agreement. Does anyone else feel this way?').

Illustrating

This involves telling a bit of a concrete story that puts meat on the bones of the advocacy and thereby orients and motivates others more clearly (e.g. 'We've got to get shipments out faster (*advocacy*). Jake Tarn, our biggest client, has got a rush order of his own, and he needs our parts before the end of the week' (*illustration*)). The illustration suggests an entirely different mission and strategy than might have been inferred from the advocacy alone. The advocacy alone may be taken as a criticism of the subordinate or another department and may unleash a year-long system-wide change, when the real target was intended to be much more specific and near-term.

You may be convinced that your advocacy contains one and only one implication for action, and that your subordinate or peer is at fault for misunderstanding. But in this case, it is *your* conviction that is a colossal metaphysical mistake. Implications are by their very nature *inexhaustible*. There is *never* one and only one implication. That is why it is so important to be explicit about each of the four types of speech and to interweave them sequentially.

Inquiring

This, obviously, involves questioning others in order to learn something from them. In principle, it is the simplest thing in the world; in practice, it is one of the most difficult things in the world to do effectively. Why? One reason is that we often inquire rhetorically, as we just did. We don't give the other the opportunity to respond; or we suggest by our tone that we don't really want an answer, at least, not a *true* answer. 'How are you?' we say dozens of times each day, not really wanting to know. 'You agree, don't you?' we say, making it clear what answer we want.

A second reason why it is difficult to inquire effectively is that an inquiry is much less likely to be effective if it is not preceded by framing, advocacy and illustration. Naked inquiry often causes the other to wonder what frame, advocacy, and illustration are implied and to respond carefully and defensively (e.g. 'How much inventory do we have on hand?'; 'Hmm, he's trying to build a case for reducing our manpower').

Back to your incident

Now, look back at your conversational actions in the unsatisfactory incident you have been describing and try to categorize which of the four types of speech you used and in what sequence (see Step III). How does your speech sound to you now? Are there one or two types of speech that you regularly omitted from your statements? Do each of your comments interweave two or more types of speech, or does a given comment usually only represent one type of speech? (As you work on identifying the types of speech you regularly use or omit, you may find useful the first section of Appendix A: 'Analysing, Framing, Advocating, Illustrating and Inquiring.'

STEP III—*Your notes about how you wove the types of speech together in the incident:*

. . . .

. . . .

. . . .

Are you beginning to see ways you might have acted differently and more effectively? Can you think of other ways of stating the central issues, in a gently assertive and inquiring way (Step IV) rather than in an accusatory, evaluative, self-righteous way? What about those things you would 'really like' to have said, but would never actually dare say? What about the last thing in the world you would ever say (stated in a revealing, descriptive way, rather than a blaming, evaluative way)?

STEP IV—*Notes about how you can experiment with new ways of weaving the types of speech together in an incident such as this:*

. . . .

. . . .

. . . .

Or does this entire exercise seem incredibly trivial to you?

Does the whole issue of how you sculpt comments seem like a super-psychoanalytical academic game that no one in management could possibly take time to attend to on a daily basis?

Developing our nuclear powers

Our claim, by contrast, is just the opposite. We claim that *speaking is the primary and most influential medium of action in the human universe*—in business, in school, between parents and children, and among lovers. Our claim is that speaking is the secret of conscious social life. The four types of speech just introduced represent, as it were, the very atoms of human action. If we can cultivate an awareness that penetrates our own actions, allowing us to arrange and rearrange the interweaving of these atoms as we speak, we will have harnessed, quite peacefully, the human equivalent of nuclear power.

People who speak of moving *from talk to action* are apparently blind to the fact that *talk is the essence of action* (and they probably talk relatively ineffectively). During this industrial age, we have become technically powerful, but have not cultivated our powers of action. Although we are in fact deeply influenced by how each of us talks (the very best managers often have an intuitive appreciation for much of what we are now saying and have semi-intentionally cultivated an art of speaking), we are rarely aware of how much we are influenced by the nuclear dynamics of conversational action. Instead of attending to the dynamic *process* of conversation, we focus all of our deliberate attention on the passive *content* of the conversation.

The four types of speech may seem trivial to you because they provide virtually *no* unilateral, technical power to get results. Indeed, using them to tell the truth and make ourselves vulnerable is deeply threatening to whatever momentum we have developed (or imagine we have developed) in manipulating situations unilaterally. A large part of each of us does not want our momentum interrupted, therefore we are hesitant to try a true framing, advocacy, illustration and inquiry because speaking like that may call forth true responses that interrupt our momentum and disconfirm our happy dreams.

But it is worth it. Earlier we listed four aims of action inquiry: (1) increasing our own and others' awareness of a shared mission; (2) increasing mutuality and internal commitment; (3) increasing communication about lack of alignment of individual, group and corporate objectives and actions and about lack of validity of assumptions, and (4) increasing action towards alignment between personal aims and actions and organizational missions and operations.

Together, the pursuit of these aims increases the likelihood of achieving effective outcomes. Do you see why and how this is the case? No? What are your objections (Step V)?

STEP V—*Your objections:*

. . . .

. . . .

. . . .

We shall not succeed in framing, advocating, illustrating, and inquiring effectively until we strongly and sincerely want to be aware of ourselves in action in the present—what our true frame/advocacy/illustration/inquiry is right now. Nor shall we succeed in framing, advocating, illustrating and inquiring effectively until we strongly and sincerely want to know the true response, *especially* when it disconfirms our current frame, advocacy and illustration. We have to feel in our bones that only actions based on truth are good for us, for others, and for our organizations. Developing that feeling is a lifetime journey in its own right.

Not only must we really wish to know the truth, but we need to act/inquire in a way that also convinces the other person(s) that we *wish* to be disconfirmed. Why? Because people generally are reluctant to disconfirm another person's frame, advocacy or illustration. To do so directly is often considered to be rude—as making the other 'lose face'. The more sensitive the question, the more important it should be to hear a disconfirming response, if that is in fact the *true* response, and you must convince the person with whom you are conversing that that is truly how you feel.

Transforming a conversation

To illustrate how the awareness/mutuality/alignment game can be played in a risky situation, we offer an example from an actual business situation.[5] The risk is very real to Jane—a new member of one of her bank's lending groups and the key player in the example—because she does not have unilateral power and fears her counter-player's intentions. Like Jennifer and Anthony in the previous chapter, Jane has been schooled in the concepts of action inquiry and is seeking opportunities to experiment with it.

Jane's experience

Having emerged from her bank's training programme, Jane is invited to join one of the bank's commercial lending groups. As is common, Jane is initially assigned to visit ten small companies where there is little business potential. In this way, the neophyte lender can practise her presentation skills and begin to learn what questions to ask, at virtually no risk to the bank's business. This procedure also permits the bank to test the new lender's ability to persevere through a string of frustratingly ambiguous and unrewarding experiences.

Jane aggressively calls on all ten potential accounts the first day. From the very first instant, she finds herself faced with a choice between giving up on a potential account, persevering unimaginatively, or inventing some ingenious way of gathering information about, and better access to, any given company.

Because self-study exercises have shown her that she gives up too easily on relationships when she hears the first hint of a no, and because she has also learned that simple doggedness frequently courts further rejection, Jane now makes use of a variety of resources (such as customers of the companies and other officers of the bank) to seek access to her potential clients.

Most bank training programmes advocate creative selling of this kind. However, the lesson is often forgotten because the training programme has not helped individual trainees to see what blocks them from creative selling (for example, their assumptions about the adequacy of their own current knowledge and their assumptions about the extent of commitments that must be made to obtain useful new knowledge).

Ultimately, Jane visits nine of the ten companies, and eight are 'dry wells', but to her surprise, the ninth is considering borrowing a million pounds for a major expansion. However, the company is already negotiating with another bank and expects to hear its terms within a week. Undaunted, Jane uses her bank's latest financial database (with the enthusiastic support of the MIS staff because she is the first lender to approach rather than avoid them after their offer to show lenders how to use it), and delivers her analysis, proposal and terms to the company on the same day as her competitor. When she calls the next day, she learns that both banks have offered exactly the same terms on the loan, leaving the company president in a quandary. He explains that he feels a prior commitment to the other bank but is impressed by her turn-around time and the implications that may have for the future quality of her service. On the other hand, he is not so naive that he cannot imagine a change in her motivation once the sale is made. Jane asks whether the president would like to meet to discuss these issues, but he says he must make up his own mind.

Two days later, Jane calls again to learn the president's final decision. He says he remains uncertain about the various legal implications of the loan. At this point she strongly urges him to meet with her at the bank, where she can call upon one of the bank's lawyers to assist them if necessary.

The meeting at the bank is a prolonged affair. The president anxiously asks for clarification of each legal term in the bank's standard agreement. After consulting with the lawyer for some time without achieving any sense of resolution, Jane begins to doubt whether the president will take either loan. The increasing frustration of circling and recircling through the morass of technicalities reminds her of similar situations in previous group projects when she learned that someone can sometimes break the vicious circle by disclosing one's perception of what is happening, in a non-accusatory, inquiring way.

At this point, action inquiry ceases to be an exercise done on paper or with a supportive mentor and becomes, suddenly, a risk she can choose to take now. Heart very much in mouth, Jane interrupts the flow of conversation to say,

> 'Can we stop and change tracks for just a minute? I'm feeling increasingly frustrated by our conversation because I sense it's not resolving your real concerns. Instead, we both seem to be growing increasingly anxious. This is the bank's standard agreement form. It's important for our ongoing relationships with our clients, as well as our general reputation in the community, that we write the agreement in a way that maximally protects both parties. It is in my interest to make sure that you are satisfied and not deceived, so that we feel that we are working together and can possibly develop an ongoing business relationship. But it seems to me that you don't believe any of that right now, or don't trust me. Is this true? Am I doing something that blocks your confidence in me? Or, if not, can you tell me what you are seeing as the real issue right now?'

With this, the president confesses that he has never before taken a major bank loan, and that the legal language high-lights his fear that he will lose the business he has founded and nurtured to forces that are beyond his capacity to control.

The two discuss the dangers, difficulties and opportunities that always attend the moment when an enterprise grows beyond the single-handed control of the founder. They also explicitly discuss their shared purpose for the first time—how doing the loan benefits both of them.

If you, the reader, are assessing Jane's performance in this meeting with an eye to the concepts we have been discussing in this chapter, you are very likely concluding that it exemplifies action inquiry, and we strongly agree. She uses all four of the 'types of speech', and frequently interweaves two or more of them. She very carefully and clearly expresses that she wants to reframe the conversation ('Can we stop and change tracks for a minute?'), and she continues to frame the situation by stating the dilemma: her view that the conversation is not satisfying the president's real concerns. She further frames while weaving in advocacy by adding that she wants to satisfy him and work together, but that the bank's standard agreement form nevertheless is important to discuss. She advocates (and illustrates) by expressing her increasing feeling of frustration. By referring to the bank's standard agreement form and by stating her 'interest' *as a representative of the bank* in developing an ongoing business relationship, she uses the bank's practices and her role as bank representative as illustrations to legitimize the line of effort she is pursuing in the conversation. Next, Jane advocates an inference she is making ('. . . it seems to me you don't believe any of that right now, or don't trust me . . .'), and immediately tests her inference with an inquiry, asking the president to say whether he trusts her and/or what he sees as the real issue. Because she makes herself vulnerable to whatever his answer may be, rather than guiding him towards an answer, her inquiry is likely to elicit a genuine response, not just a particular answer that she may want to hear.

Jane takes the risk of exposing an assumption in order to test it. It could have offended the president to be told that he appeared untrusting. Furthermore, she takes the risk of possibly heightening tensions when she interrupts the flow of the meeting. She also takes the risk of hearing something unpleasant about herself. However, her willingness to take these risks yields important learning as the president tells her about his fear of losing control of his business. Her willingness to test her assumption serves to invite the president into the learning process as well, and he responds by participating in a discussion that produces new information of value to both parties.

Or are these really risks ? From one perspective, they can all be written off as training in this case—a cost, to be sure, but a necessary one rather than an avoidable one. Furthermore, the risk Jane takes in interrupting may in fact be smaller than the risk of continuing the conversation without interruption. (Most managers who go very far in self-study find that they systematically *overestimate* the risks of acting differently in situations, computing all the possible costs but not the benefits. Conversely, they systematically *underestimate* the risks of acting habitually, computing all the possible benefits and blaming others for any costs.)

Another less visible cost in this case—but one that seems too high for many managers and prevents them from emulating Jane—is that she had to give up some basic assumptions she held in order to interrupt the legal conversation with the president. In a letter to her former instructor in the MBA course where she was trained in action inquiry, Jane describes her most basic assumption as having been that 'the deal hinges on reason alone'. From this assumption flow a series of corollaries, such as, 'trust is irrelevant', 'the legalese will be accepted as soon as it's explained', and 'negotiating an agreement is a deductive process of finding the correct path to a desired solution'. Jane found in retrospect that these underlying assumptions all appear to have been illusions.

Having thus discussed the costs, what were the benefits? The president decided to do business with Jane the next day. She thereby gained the visibility of having made a large commercial loan even before being appointed a company officer. Eighteen months later, one of the eight 'dry wells' took the initiative to contact her and shortly transformed itself into a 'gusher'. Another six months later she became the first member of the group of commercial lenders who had joined the bank at the same time as she to receive a major promotion. She also won the most desirable sales territory in her area of the bank.

Summary

In this case, we see a manager seeking to act *efficiently*, *effectively* and *legitimately* all at once, ultimately employing action inquiry to restructure a degenerating situation and achieve her aims. At the outset, her use of computer software along with plain hard work enables Jane to produce an analysis and loan proposal more *efficiently* (i.e. in less time) than her competitor. Her recognition that she is marketing a service to a client, not merely a logically correct financial analysis, results next in an *effective* series of initiatives towards the client after submission of the proposal.

Finally, we see in Jane's comments to the company president, in the midst of their meeting about the legal implications of the loan agreement, how deeply she is attuned to generating long-term success and *legitimacy*. First, she defines her own and the bank's entire interest in terms of establishing mutually beneficial, long-term, trusting relationships with clients. Second, she convincingly demonstrates that this is not mere rhetoric by interrupting her own attempt to persuade the president that the legal language is technically appropriate, in order to ask him whether in fact he has doubts about the ultimate legitimacy or wisdom of the loan. By engaging in a shared inquiry into the purpose and possible effects of the loan, Jane and the president create the sense of mutual learning, mutual trust and mutual benefit that was missing earlier. In general, a business negotiation becomes increasingly legitimate to all the parties involved as the negotiation itself is shown to be open to inspection, controllable and aimed at benefiting all the parties. We submit that quality management in any organization aims too low if it does not aim at increased legitimacy.

Obviously, not every business transaction requires such a fundamental and explicit exploration of legitimacy. The manager must sense when the issue of legitimacy is really at stake and must learn how to address it when it arises so that the very actions taken in addressing it themselves generate legitimacy. The problem is that too few managers appreciate the practical importance of the issue of legitimacy, and too few schools of management and organizations generate the kinds of rehearsals that teach aspiring managers and practising managers how to address the issue of legitimacy effectively in everyday business transactions.

Action inquiry, rehearsal, and personal development

In your own responses to the action inquiry exercise earlier in this chapter, you 'rehearsed' an incident after the fact. The case of Jane, the neophyte commercial lender, implicitly involved numerous rehearsals *before* the crucial meeting with the company president. Rehearsals in an atmosphere of inquiry, both before and after significant incidents at work, are essential to a lifelong professional commitment to action leading to quality improvement.

But the unique and essential feature of action inquiry is that 'rehearsal' and 'performance' blend into one another until they become simultaneous. The right kind of rehearsal does not replace questioning and uncertainty with answers and certainty. The ultimate performance at the conclusion of all one's rehearsals is not a polished answer but a more appropriate and penetrating inquiry.

Rehearsal and performance also blend into each other at the other end of the spectrum. Not even the earliest rehearsals can be entirely safe or entirely protected from real-life consequences. At each rehearsal that is in any way effectual, one's self-image is at stake and illusions of which one was not even aware may be exposed.

Thus, there is a performance aspect even to your own after-the-fact reflections as you wrote, or even thought about writing, the exercise earlier in this chapter. Your reflection can be viewed as a thought performance. You had to select an incident. You took the risk of learning something less than complimentary about yourself either from the writing or from the inevitable comparison you knew you would be making between what you wrote and what you would then find in the remainder of this chapter. You took the risk of deciding how you could experiment with new ways of speaking in the incident you chose. Perhaps you chose a relatively 'safe' incident—one in which you had already used all of the action inquiry 'types of speech'. Or perhaps you chose an incident in which your written experiment with action inquiry necessarily produced speech that strongly disconfirmed the speech you actually used in the original situation, realizing that if you chose a 'safe' incident your learning would almost certainly prove less effectual, less potent and less meaningful. Either way, you can learn something about the action of your thought, if you so choose.

Next, you may choose to take the risk of trying to interweave framing, advocacy, illustration and inquiry in new ways in an on-the-job conversation. You may choose to risk not just in thought, but in social action.

Ultimately, the sense of simultaneous rehearsal and performance in action inquiry introduces the manager to a new quality of awareness—to a continuous, silent, impartial observation of your own performance in thought and in action amidst others.

Notes

1. The Continental Illinois information and quotation are from *The Wall Street Journal*, 30 July 1984.
2. The manager–subordinate conversation about the widget delivery problem is from David L. Bradford and Alan R. Cohen (1984) *Managing for Excellence* , New York: Wiley, pp. 37–8.
3. The reasons why our knowledge in the moment is always inadequate come from William R. Torbert (1991) *The Power of Balance*, Newbury Park, CA: Sage Publishers, pp. 221–3. Adapted by permission of the publisher.
4. The four categories into which speech acts may be divided are based on prior theory and research found in Chris Argyris and Donald A. Schön (1974) *Theory in Practice: Increasing Professional Effectiveness*, San Francisco; CA: Jossey-Bass; C. Argyris (1981) *Reasoning, Learning and Action*, San Francisco, CA: Jossey-Bass; D. A. Schön (1983) *The Reflective Practitioner*, New York: Basic Books; W. R. Torbert (1987) *Managing The Corporate Dream*, Homewood, IL: Dow Jones-Irwin; W. R. Torbert, *The Power of Balance*, Newbury Park, CA: Sage Publishers.
5. The case of Jane, the new bank lender, is drawn from W. R. Torbert (1987) *Managing The Corporate Dream*, Homewood, IL: Dow Jones-Irwin, pp. 169–76.

4   Practising action inquiry at work

Reading about action inquiry is not *doing* action inquiry. You have read about action inquiry in the previous chapters. In this chapter, we invite you to begin *practising* action inquiry.

Let us be clear, first, that the exercise in the previous chapter was *not* a full action inquiry exercise. It was a *reflective* inquiry exercise about action inquiry. We invited you to reflect on how you and others speak and to categorize statements as one, or a combination, of 'framing', 'advocating', illustrating' and 'inquiring'. If, since reading Chapter 3, you (a) have *taken those ideas into action with you* at work (or at home, for that matter); (b) have *remembered them as you were speaking and listening* to others; and (c) after observing the conversation as it occurred, have *changed how you were speaking during the ongoing conversation*; then, having done all this, you have already begun to engage in action inquiry.

Indeed, if you have continued reading from Chapter 3, we recommend that you stop here. Turn off your bedside or office light for five minutes while you consider a situation in which you can try these ideas. Then go ahead and try them, before you continue reading this chapter.

Everything we say from here on will gain a much richer meaning for you if it enters a conversation not just with your mind as you read, but also with your mind, your feelings and your body as you act.

If you have already begun to practise action inquiry, you have almost certainly noticed one of its primary attributes—that it initially seems scary. One's heart has a disturbing tendency to jump into one's mouth as one approaches the moment of actually experimenting in a real-time situation with intentionally and awarely different action. For example, you may imagine all the worst possible consequences of speaking in this new way, or you may feel that your face is flushing and that others must be able to sense your self-consciousness and discomfort.

Once you have spoken differently in an experimental manner, you may become unusually self-critical: 'Oh no! That didn't sound right. Not what I meant to say—and my voice cracked.' Moreover, others may respond in a totally unexpected way, leaving you confused and depressed about what to say next. (It takes a lot of practice before one becomes adept at responding with action inquiry to *whatever* is said.)

Why does practising action inquiry generate fear and all these other negative feelings? Practising action inquiry brings us into contact with our fear because action inquiry is never entirely safe. *Action inquiry is inherently risky.* It is risky because it is played in real time with real relationships. It is risky because it is played in relation to one's own awareness and the unknown; and it therefore introduces us—sometimes gradually, sometimes suddenly—to alien experiences. (If we think about horror films such as *Alien* or about ethnic wars, we can become aware of just how much fear we project onto the unknown.)

Action inquiry is also risky because it usually sacrifices unilateral control over outcomes in favour of openness to the influence of others, and of decisions to which the parties are mutually and internally committed. Yet another reason why action inquiry is risky is that, in the interest of achieving a wider and better balance—between, for example, initiating influence and being receptive to influence—action inquiry takes us to the very frontier of our current method of balancing. It may even take us beyond our current method of balancing—out of *that* balance, perhaps temporarily altogether *off* balance—as our very method of balancing transforms.

Now: let us re-swallow our hearts and attempt some early action inquiry exercises—that will not, hopefully, send us totally out of balance. We can wait for such thrills until we are more familiar with, adept at, and committed to, action inquiry.

In the meantime, we can protect ourselves from our worst fears of what may occur in several different ways as we start. One way is literally to take one or more deep breaths, breathing new energy in through our fear when we feel it, and then exhaling the fear. Sometimes the fear will evaporate when so treated, or at least will cease to grip us in the same way, because we are brought back in touch with the reasons and feelings that urge us to act differently. A second way to make the moment of exercising action inquiry less fearful is to experiment in a situation of relatively high overall trust. Where trust is high, risks are lower than they otherwise would be, and honest failure costs less. A third way to reduce fear is to choose an issue around which your previous, more habitual, ways of acting have clearly failed; hence, you have nothing to lose by trying a new way and you probably have a much better chance of 'winning'. A fourth way to reduce risk and fear is to choose new ways of acting that appear so ordinary that no one else may even notice that you are 'acting differently'. When you sense that an action inquiry experiment is too risky, you may wish to return to these guidelines to invent a less risky alternative.

There is one last, but crucial, point before we offer you a series of action inquiry exercises that you are free to amend and embroider as you wish. The word 'exercise' no doubt makes some of you feel tired, just as the word 'experiment' may make some of you think of a cold, inhumane, manipulative science. However, the idea in action inquiry is to take risks that are fun, because they energize you and raise your awareness; risks that are rewarding because they increase the efficacy of your colleagues as well as yourself; and risks that highlight your own and others' capacity for initiative and mutuality. Consequently, when performing these exercises, ensure that you work at your own pleasurable pace.

Exercise I

OK. Ready?

Think of jogging around a long wooded path for daily, physical exercise (feeling tired yet?). But instead of imagining that you are dragging yourself out there for the run, pushing yourself fiercely then not going back out for a week or two because the prospect of repeating the performance is too daunting . . . and instead of imagining, in the other extreme, that this is something simple and habitual that you already do, imagine rather that this jog is an awareness-jogging adventure. Start, perhaps, at a walk. Then, perhaps, walk backwards slowly for ten paces, just to see how your balance/agility/alertness is and how you feel about others seeing you do this 'strange' thing. Perhaps you leave the path altogether, crouch in a small bower, and emit a few animal sounds. Next, you dash into a short uphill sprint, and so on . . . listening for impulses within yourself that you do not usually hear; sniffing the environment for clues of . . . you do not know what at the outset.

Are you willing to treat this as your first action inquiry exercise? Can you give yourself the time (we suggest allowing a whole hour), at least every other day for a couple of weeks, to take such an adventure? Can you enjoy the process of finding the right place (or places), if you don't already have a favourite trail? If you are balking at this whole idea, can you discover the feelings that are blocking you? (If you think 'facts' are blocking you [no time; no trail], look again more deeply [you are in charge of your time; any path can become your trail].) The action inquiry exercise has already begun as you read this, for you are already framing and advocating and illustrating and inquiring within yourself about it (or are you just advocating and developing a fixed attitude about the exercise?).

The fact that you do this exercise essentially alone and not at work helps to reduce the initial risk. It also helps to emphasize that these action inquiry exercises are entirely for you, not something you 'have' to do for work. Even more important, beginning with this exercise highlights the fact that action inquiry is, first and last, about generating a more vivid, embracing, non-verbal awareness that simultaneously senses its own limits. Whatever technical, verbal, or organizational skills you eventually improve, the source of continual quality improvement, in this action inquiry approach, is a more vivid awareness of what is at stake in each new moment and the courage to take an appropriate risk to enhance quality.

Exercise II

Now, let us begin, very gradually, to move your action inquiry experiments into your work environment.

As a second exercise, which we suggest you begin any time after you've 'got the rhythm' of the outdoors exercise, try an analogous awareness-jogging adventure *at work*. We are *not* suggesting a literal jog around the office. In a sense, we are suggesting no more than the well-known-and-often-scoffed-at advice to try managing-by-walking-around. But the exercise will be more fun if you think of it as planning and taking a half-hour vacation at work each day.

You can disguise your overall lack of goal orientation during this half hour by carrying with you several memos that you will deliver to people around the office, but don't forget that your purpose is to allow yourself to be surprised by people and things that you usually neglect or consider meaningless. On one day, during your 'vacation', you will perhaps pay more attention to the architecture than you did before, or perhaps to the different ways that people decorate their office spaces, or to the different pace and tone of the various work areas. On other days, you may start two or three conversations with co-workers you hardly know. Perhaps you will enter a small conference room, close the door, lie down on the floor, relax (or notice your fear that someone will walk in on you, or your difficulty in changing pace in the middle of the day). Feel the sensation in your feet and then follow the sensation all the way up your body. Or perhaps you may go sightseeing to a part of the plant you've never visited before.

By now, you may well be inwardly screaming: 'Why do these crazy things? Isn't this irresponsible? Who has time at work for a daily vacation anyway?' This is the tone of voice in which 97 per cent of the executives who have tried management-by-walking-around have talked to themselves after their first two or three tries, and why they've stopped doing it. Hopefully, though, the first exercise has begun to provide you with tastes of what spending time in this way can do for you. First of all, it can re-energize you for the rest of the day. Second, you will find that the changed pace causes you to think of creative solutions to problems that have been nagging you. Third, you will encounter people with whom you had to check progress on small matters, but hadn't managed to find time to call on them (and the serendipity of your meeting them in the hall is likely to generate a quicker, less defensive exchange). Fourth, others are likely to experience you as more open and accessible, simply because they see you moving around at a more relaxed pace than usual. Fifth, you will gradually begin to learn about all sorts of currents within the organization of which you were previously unaware and which influence how work gets done.

So, there are many potentially productive outcomes to this goalless exercise, but they must be welcomed as by-products rather than sought out directly if the exercise is to succeed in jogging your awareness. Again, the point is that a widening, dynamic awareness needs to surround our goal-oriented efforts if we are to learn how to improve our quality from moment to moment. But we are constantly sacrificing the dignity and long-term efficacy of such an embracing aware-ness for the short-term return we imagine we'll receive (our thirty pieces of silver) by totally subordinating ourselves to a particular goal.

At the end of the previous chapter we spoke of action inquiry being, simultaneously, a rehearsal and a perfor-mance. The performance is the goal-oriented outer action. The sense of rehearsal comes from the dynamic, widening awareness. So far, these exercises have emphasized cultivating the atmosphere of rehearsal in oneself. The next one, too, emphasizes inquiry more than action, and rehearsal more than performance.

Exercise III

Let us now bring the action inquiry exercises to business meetings you attend, but for which you are *not* the formal leader. In order to enhance your sense of initiative and awareness at these meetings, try periodically to unfocus your eyes slightly and gaze around at the group as a whole while listening more intently to the rhythm of the speaking. Intentionally unfocusing (or 'soft' focusing) your eyes can generate a marvellous kaleidoscope of feelings of self-consciousness, embarrassment and vulnerability; and it may take some time to convince yourself that no one else is aware of this change, although initially it may feel major and awkward to you. (Soft focusing is how great athletes, such as Michael Jordan, Larry Bird and Magic Johnson in basketball, generated 'full court vision' and thus saw opportunities and threats before others did.)

The idea is to pay attention not only to the content of what is said, but also, and even more closely, to the way in which people are speaking and gesturing. It is useful to keep some notes, dividing your page down the middle, with 'content' notes on the left and 'process' notes on the right. (Indeed, if you haven't done so already in relation to the first two exercises, you may wish to start an ongoing journal so that you can later review the pattern over time of your experiences, conjectures, insights, confusions and questions.)

Some questions on your observation of the meeting may include: Is the meeting well framed at the outset? Do people offer apt illustrations for their advocacies and can you see evidence that when they do so they have more influence with others? Are inquiries used as weapons, or as genuine ways of generating clarity and including more colleagues' perspectives?

As (probably over several meetings) you begin to get the 'taste' for following the conversation in this additional, more active way, you will also be developing convictions, based on real evidence, about group patterns that are inhibiting effectiveness (e.g. no one ever summarizes what was decided or makes sure that someone is taking responsibility for implementation).

You may now be ready for the fourth exercise, but before we move to that, notice that, again, as in the first two exercises, the emphasis of this action inquiry exercise is on actions that increase your awareness. This is always the first and primary objective when beginning to practise action inquiry: to enhance one's own awareness. The potential these exercises hold for enhancing awareness is illustrated in Appendix A, where you will find reports on the experiences of two people, one in Exercise 2 and the other in Exercise 3.

Exercise IV

The previous three exercises are hopefully beginning to establish a new atmosphere of widened awareness and rehearsal while you are at work. Now, we can try taking some specific actions while we simultaneously engage in this type of awareness-jogging for which you are cultivating a taste.

Take one or two initiatives per meeting that have nothing to do with your own agenda and nothing to do with the content of the discussions, but which attempt to help the group as a whole to manage its time well, to manage conflicts well, or to reach decisions. Often even the formal leader of the meeting takes very few of these group-focused initiatives, and everyone else may simply blame this leader for the boredom and the meandering, or for the stressful and jagged atmosphere.

Relatively low risk, constructive actions—often inquiries—can be both very visible and very much appreciated.

'The two of you obviously disagree on this. Can each of you offer us your strongest illustration on behalf of your view, as well as an illustration of the dangers in taking the other course of action?'

'If we continue discussing this item, we're not going to get to the rest of the agenda. Is that OK with the rest of you, or do you think we should check on how people would vote on this one and go on?'

The examples throughout this book provide many potential 'recipes' for how to interweave framing, advocacy, illustration and inquiry into more constructive and effective ways of speaking. It is so difficult to control our own form of speech that it is best to practise just one type of speech at a time at the outset. Keeping brief journals of your efforts can be an important method of seeing how quickly you can begin to make changes. At the same time, the effort to practise never ends. We have both been practising for years.

Certainly, this exercise alone is worth six months to a year of deliberate practice.

Of course, in practising these skills, you are welcome to go beyond meetings where you are not the leader to your daily interactions with peers, superiors and subordinates. We shall offer more exercises pertaining to you and the people you work with in the following chapters.

Conclusion

Ultimately, the sense of simultaneous rehearsal and performance to which these action inquiry exercises introduce you represents a new quality of awareness—a quality-improving quality of awareness—a continual, silent, impartial observation of your own performance amidst others. The manager experimenting with action inquiry treats each performance as a rehearsal, primarily dedicated to cultivating this ongoing, impartial observation. Each on-the-job dilemma comes to sound more and more like a call to both performance and rehearsal, to both effectiveness and inquiry.

The silent, inquiring observation that is at the core of action inquiry determines *when* the time is right for *what type* of explicit inquiry. But your choice to make one or more explicit inquiries does not foreclose the making of further inquiries. The essential characteristic of action inquiry is that it invites and welcomes true information relevant to an ongoing situation, even if that information seems to violate your preferences or assumptions about the situation. Some people initially imagine that the openness of action inquiry implies never coming to conclusions and acting. But this represents a misunderstanding of what we are advocating. Action inquiry occurs in the midst of action and is a search for timely action; it is not an academic kind of 'eternal' inquiry that occurs before or after or instead of action.

Action inquiry is a revolutionary process—so revolutionary that it revolutionizes revolution itself. In the past, revolutionaries have revolted against what they saw as institutionalized inefficiency, ineffectiveness or illegitimacy, with the assumption that they themselves were 'on the right side'. Then they typically established managerial styles and regimes that were just as closed and authoritarian as those of their predecessors, if not more so. (Think about the aftermath of the French and Russian revolutions or the aftermath of many corporate acquisitions.)

Action inquiry revolutionizes revolution by opening the 'revolutionary' to the possibility of transformation. Perhaps the inquiry will reveal that what needs changing is something about the actor, not about the rest of the situation. For example, the actor may need to change underlying assumptions, may need to begin inquiring into the other parties' assumptions and frames of reference, and/or may need to undertake a quest for legitimacy—all of which he or she may have habitually avoided previously.

It is this self-overcoming, self-transforming quality of action inquiry that accounts for its costs and its benefits. Action inquiry requires the risk and often the pain of personal developmental change. But on the positive side, action inquiry provides the operational 'handle' for shifting one's thought and action away from a pattern where underlying assumptions go unrecognized and unchallenged, where one's own frame of reference is a limiting, confining boundary, and where self-interest and mistrust prevent any effort to attain legitimacy.

Because action inquiry aims at no narrow self-protection and is ever alert to incongruities among purposes, strategies, actions and outcomes, it can restructure situations for long-term quality improvement. Personal development by the individual manager can spark transformation in others.

In the next chapter we examine more closely what personal development means and the part it plays in the leadership of continual quality improvement.

PART TWO

HUMAN DEVELOPMENT, TRANSFORMATIONAL LEADERSHIP AND CQI

5 Frames and personal development as foundations for CQI

So far in this book we have introduced continual quality improvement and action inquiry as though they occur in particular moments in time. For example, in introducing the notion of 'framing', we have focused on the importance of making clear the overall 'game' you believe you are playing with others at a meeting or in a one-to-one conversation, and testing whether you are all in fact in the same game. This *explicit* framing can improve the effectiveness of even the briefest exchange. Here is a company president speaking by phone to her special assistant: 'I'm assuming you are handling the Jones contract. Let me know if you need assistance.' The president makes her *frame* (her assumption) explicit and *advocates* that the special assistant seek her support, if necessary, to ensure that the job gets done. If the president's assumption is wrong, or if the assistant has been stymied by the project but has so far just pushed it to the back burner, it is in the assistant's interest to respond, now or in the near future, 'What? I've never heard of the Jones contract.' Or, 'I thought Paul was taking care of that.' Or whatever the truth is, if it is incongruent with the president's explicitly stated assumptions. Many of the day-to-day frustrations of work life can be avoided by such brief frame-and-assumption testing comments.

Now, in this chapter, we want to illustrate the other extreme of the *framing* spectrum. We wish to discuss the central and usually *implicit* frame that bounds each of us during any given period of our lives. It is this implicit frame that most severely limits our effectiveness. We shall make the greatest leaps in the continual quality improvement of our own actions when we become aware of these limits and begin to experiment beyond them. If we can become aware of these overarching frames in others and in ourselves, we can reduce unintentional conflict and misunderstanding and can even help ourselves and others to transform beyond the limits of our present assumptions.

As the chapter proceeds, we shall describe four different frames, the *Opportunist* frame, the *Diplomat* frame, the *Technician* frame and the *Achiever* frame, any one of which may characterize your overall approach to managing for a decade or even your entire career to the present. Developing a hypothesis about your own overall frame and those of your colleagues can help you to relate more effectively to them and to challenge yourself to experiment with thinking and acting outside your current 'box'. Each successive frame we describe is 'larger' than the prior frame in that it includes all the possibilities of the prior frame together with a new set of alternatives. Moreover, whereas the four frames do not recognize themselves as constructed frames and do not recognize that different people operate out of different frames, persons working from a fifth frame, the *Strategist* frame—which we shall describe very briefly at the end of this chapter and in more detail in the next chapter—become increasingly aware of the omnipresence of different frames when people interact. They therefore become more and more committed to the explicit testing of framing assumptions during particular encounters, such as the very brief exchange between the president and her assistant cited above. Later in the book (Chapters 11, 12 and 13), we shall describe still another frame, representing further development beyond the Strategist frame.[1] This entire book is intended to help you move developmentally towards these latter frames, if you choose to undertake such a journey.

We think you are most likely to enjoy learning about the first four frames by listening in as business people tell stories about diagnosing their colleagues and themselves. Of course, as you read these stories, you can also begin diagnosing your work group or the colleagues from other departments with whom you interact most often in your daily routine. By the time you reach the end of this chapter, perhaps you will also have an initial diagnosis of your own current developmental frame.

We suggest that on separate sheets of paper you list the three to seven work associates with whom it would be to your greatest advantage to work more effectively. You should also write your own name at the top of a sheet. Then, as you read the chapter, note which characteristics from each frame you associate with each person, reminding yourself with a few words of a particular occasion when he or she displayed that characteristic. (Section 4 of Appendix A 'Analysing Developmental Frames' illustrates one person's experience in identifying colleagues' frames.) You should find that each person displays one particular frame predominantly. Although that person will occasionally act in ways characteristic of the earlier frames, he or she should rarely show signs of the next frame (unless that person happens to be in developmental transition towards that stage) and will almost never exhibit characteristics of the frame two beyond. Remember, however, that you are not making a scientific judgement, but only an estimate; and the point of your estimate is not to be right or to pigeonhole yourself or your colleagues, but rather to help you to test whether your developmental hypotheses lead you to choose more effective actions as you work with them.

Table 5.1 offers you a sense of how one's world grows larger and more complicated at each succeeding frame. Table 5.2 offers a summary of the attitudinal and behavioural characteristics associated with each of the first six successive frames. You can refer back and forth from the stories to Table 5.2 as you read. Our story-tellers are managers or professionals who were learning about frames and developmental theory at the time they wrote their diagnostic stories.

Table 5.1   Governing frames at six successive developmental stages

Stage	Name	Governing frame	Focus of awareness
1	Opportunist	Needs, interests rule impulses	Outside world, effects
2	Diplomat	Expectations rule interests	Socially expected behaviour
3	Technician	Internal craft logic rules expectations	Internal logic, thought
4	Achiever	System success in environment rules craft logics	Interplay of plan, practice and effect
5	Strategist	Principle rules system	Synthetic theory of system–environment development over time
6	Magician	Process (interplay of principle/action) awareness rules principle	Interplay of awareness, thought, action and outside world in Eternal Now

Table 5.2 Managerial style characteristics associated with six developmental frames

Stage	Name	Characteristic
1	Opportunist	Short time horizon; focus on concrete things; manipulative; deceptive; reject feedback; externalizes blame; distrustful; fragile self-control; hostile humour; views luck as central; flouts power, sexuality; stereotypes; views rules as loss of freedom; punishes according to 'eye for an eye' ethic; treats what they can get away with as legal; positive ethic = even trade.
2	Diplomat	Observes protocol; avoids inner and outer conflict; works to group standard; speaks in clichés, platitudes; conforms; feels shame if violates norm; sin = hurting others; punishment = disapproval; seeks membership, status; face-saving essential; loyalty to immediate group, not 'distant' organization or principles; positive ethic = nice, cooperative.
3	Technician	Interested in problem-solving; seeks causes; critical of self, others based on craft logic; chooses efficiency over effectiveness; perfectionist; accepts feedback only from 'objective' craft masters; dogmatic; values decisions based on merit; sees contingencies, exceptions; wants to stand out, be unique; positive ethic = sense of obligation to wider, internally consistent moral order.
4	Achiever	Long-term goals; future is vivid, inspiring; welcomes behavioural feedback; effectiveness and results oriented; feels like initiator, not pawn; appreciates complexity, systems; seeks generalizable reasons for action; seeks mutuality, not hierarchy, in relationships; feels guilt if does not meet own standards; blind to own shadow, to the subjectivity behind objectivity; positive ethic: practical day-to-day improvements based on self-chosen (but not self-created) ethical system.
5	Strategist	Creative at conflict resolution; recognizes importance of principle, contract, theory, and judgement—not just rules, customs, and exceptions—for making and maintaining good decisions; process oriented as well as goal oriented; aware of paradox and contradiction; relativistic, aware that what one sees depends upon one's worldview; high value on individuality, unique market niches, particular historical moments; enjoys playing a variety of roles; witty, existential humour (as contrasted to prefabricated jokes); aware of dark side, of profundity of evil, and tempted by its power.
6	Magician	Disintegration of ego-identity, near-death experience; seeks participation in historical/spiritual transformations; creator of mythical events that reframe situations; anchoring in inclusive present, seeing light and dark, order and mess; blends opposites, creating 'positive-sum' games; exercises own attention, researches interplay of intuition, thought, action, and effects on outside world; treats time and events as symbolic, analogical, metaphorical (not merely linear, digital, literal).

62

Recognizing frames

To help you recognize the frame that applies to you and to each of the associates you listed, we continue now with the stories. We shall accompany them with further comments to clarify the nature of the frames.

The Opportunist frame   An independent contributor at a large firm gradually diagnosed one difficult co-worker, Charles, as an *Opportunist*:

> We are both at the same job grade, although he has been with the company longer, and I have been on the current team longer. When he first joined our team, he would stop by my desk 3 or 4 times per day to ask for work-related advice and design tips. Initially, I was very flattered and found his asking for my technical expertise very ego-satisfying and a boost to my self-confidence.
>
> After weeks and months of more frequent and lengthy stops at my desk, I felt as if he was deliberately manipulating my time. I would work through lunch or stay late to make up for the lost time, initially resenting him, then funnelling my resentment towards a system that promotes people on seniority. I now realize that I was externalizing blame rather than recognizing my own cowardice and inability to act. I did try some experimentation, picking up the phone when I saw him heading in my direction, or asking to see the research he had done and where he was stuck before offering help. When he sensed that I was going to make him work a little, he began asking someone else on the team for help.
>
> Some typical comments made about him by his colleagues include, 'I have gotten to the point where I cannot even say "Good morning" to Charles for fear of hearing the intimate details of his personal life for close to half an hour' and 'Ron, I don't know how you put up with sitting next to him. I sit three desks away from him and I still find it difficult to tune him out.'
>
> With the benefit of hindsight, I now think that my spending time trying to help him did him more harm than good because he has since been transferred to another team and has been denied a promotion. He has confided to me that his manager told him he should concentrate more on his work and less on seeking help and on his personal and social life.

Before you read on, try listing on a sheet of paper what you sense to be the distinguishing features of Charles's frame. What assumptions does he seem to be making about himself, about others and how to relate to them? What does he assume about how to be effective? How does he assume an ethical person should behave? What other patterns do you see in Charles, based on Ron's description?

Themes and patterns you see in Charles's *Opportunist* frame:

. . . .

. . . .

. . . .

Based on developmental theory and research findings, people holding the Opportunist frame try to make things work by manipulating them unilaterally or by making the most advantageous trades possible. Charles flattered Ron by asking him for advice in exchange for his time and technical help. The Opportunist manager is typically a tactful manipulator who may even use courtesy as a ploy, but still views the world as a one-against-all jungle fight. Charles's approach to the jungle is to go to the person who will give him the most for the least cost. He drops that person as soon as the exchange proves unprofitable in the short run. He gives little regard to what others may think of him or to the damage his immediate actions may be doing to longer term relationships.

As a basis for a management style, the Opportunist frame counts only short-term, visible costs and benefits. It appreciates only the financial and power aspects of organizations, not the structural and spiritual aspects. It does not value helping managers and organizations to transform and develop. Studies of managers have found that only 0 to 5 per cent hold the Opportunist frame.[2]

For the Opportunist manager, it is axiomatic that one must 'play one's cards close to the vest', since others are doing the same. The Hobbesian equation 'might makes right' holds, and the Golden Rule is recast as 'he who has the gold rules'. The Opportunist is severely limited by this frame. Whereas managers at later stages can choose to act opportunistically on particular occasions, a manager who is bounded by the Opportunist frame *has* to act opportunistically on every occasion.

The Diplomat frame   A supervisor in the housekeeping department of a large manufacturing company gives the following description of his superior:

> In my opinion, Phil, my boss, is at the *Diplomat* stage of development. He seems incapable of making decisions on his

own and he has even intimated to me that he feels he is a pawn or figurehead and not really in control of his areas of responsibility. Phil is very aware of protocol and observes it meticulously. He is risk averse. He avoids conflict at any expense. I think this is the major reason he feels like a pawn. He has given up so many battles that the idea of fighting doesn't even occur to him.

Phil is my immediate superior. It is commonly held among my peers (Phil's other subordinates) that he is ineffective in his position. He seems to accept, without resistance, anything that comes from higher up in the chain of command, and this often affects our department in a negative way. Here's an example: we (the housekeeping department) are at the point of entry to the Facilities operational area, which employs over 400 people. I am the first supervisor that newcomers are exposed to. In the recent past we have had numerous temps whom I never got to meet until the night they started. Some of these people are 'political appointees'. They have been recommended by vice presidents or members of the board of directors. I realize the world is imperfect and that favouritism occurs, but I believe I should be involved in interviewing all incoming employees. I further believe that Phil could at least object to the more blatant cases where political appointees are given regular full time status (which entitles them to full benefits) while we have people who have been here for months as temps waiting to move up to full time.

Phil has shared with me on occasion things he would like to see happen in our department or has agreed with me about some recommendation I have made to him. But all too often, those discussions end with, 'That will never fly', or 'The higher managers won't like that'. He will then try to convince me not to make waves and to accept 'the way things work here'. I have no wish to make waves, but I hope I will never become desensitized to the point where I will just accept things that seem so wrong.

Again, before reading on, try writing a brief synopsis of Phil's frame. Based on his subordinate's description of him, what do you consider Phil's guiding assumptions to be?

Themes and patterns you see in Phil's *Diplomat* frame:

. . . .

. . . .

. . . .

The Diplomat frame focuses attention on other people: family friends, work associates, the work group, the organization, the nation. Phil's focus is clearly on his superiors. For the Diplomat, the values of others take priority. Their definitions of appropriate behaviour are the best guides to action. Behavioural skills—the right moves or words at the right times—are seen as critical for gaining membership, meeting others' standards, and observing the correct protocol. From this frame, value is defined not by oneself, but by others. Some thing or some action has value if it sells, if it influences others, or if high-status persons treat it as valuable.

Like the Opportunist frame, the Diplomat frame has its bright side, but also its dark side. While the Opportunist frame can illuminate paths to adventure which the Opportunist manager embarks on courageously, it can also show the way towards the more shadowy realms of deception, manipulation and unwillingness to accept responsibility.

Likewise, the Diplomat frame has a dual nature. Sometimes, calling someone a Diplomat implies that he or she has the exquisite sense of tact that permits both honesty and agreement about the most difficult issues, enhancing the self-esteem and dignity of all parties in the process. In this same positive vein, the diplomatic manager can provide loyalty and goodwill that functions as organizational glue. At other times, the implication is that the Diplomat avoids and smooths over all potential conflict, masking both true feelings and objective data in an effort to maintain harmony at all costs. Thus the Diplomat can become alienated from associates who, like Phil's subordinate, are disillusioned by Phil's dismissal of their concerns and suggestions.

Diplomat managers do not seek out negative feedback about themselves. Quite to the contrary, they attempt to deflect it. They equate negative feedback with loss of face and loss of status. To tell them that it is constructive because it can help them achieve their goals does not make sense to them. No goal is as compelling to them as the implicit rule against losing face. This aversion to feedback helps to explain why the Diplomat , like the Opportunist, is 'locked into' his or her frame and is blind to the possibility of other ways of behaving.

The Diplomat manager is as unable to criticize others and to question group norms as to criticize self. We see this in Phil, who will not try to correct the apparently unjust handling of 'political appointees'. An organization led by a Diplomat will be inhibited from adapting to changing competitive realities or to discovering and creating new strategic opportunities. Subordinates will feel a sense of stagnation and disillusion. They are likely to lower their aims and effort and may even falsify information such as sales or production records in order to 'look good'.

Studies of managers have found that less than 5 per cent of senior managers hold the Diplomat frame. By comparison, 9 per cent of the junior managers studied, and 24 per cent of the first-line supervisors in these studies, hold the Diplomat frame. These data suggest that the Diplomat style limits one's chances for promotion.

The Technician frame   The same supervisor who described Phil offers this description of Larry, a fellow supervisor:

> Larry is a *Technician* in my opinion. He has unquestioned technical expertise in his area and believes himself to be unrivalled in this area as well as in administrative recordkeeping. He is a perfectionist, even going so far as to criticize one of his employees about his technique of decorating the office Christmas tree.
>
> Larry is very conscientious, has a high sense of obligation to moral standards, and feels this differentiates him from the rest of the group. He strives to outperform everyone around him and is not against pointing out the faults of others. He is almost as unforgiving of his own mistakes, so I guess that's fair. He values decisions based on merit as long as they fit within his guidelines. He would, however, prefer to make all the decisions himself. I work closely with Larry, and find that sometimes he will take over a project we are both responsible for and complete it all himself, which makes me look bad and, worse, puts me in a weaker role in the group.
>
> He is ambivalent about receiving feedback. He has shared with me a feeling that feedback is not required for him and that it is, in some instances, even irritating to him. He seems to be sure that he knows everything he needs to know to do his job. I am impressed with his planning and organizational skills. He has been a great help to me and I do not want to sound too negative about him, but he is extremely dogmatic. His word is law and is not subject to discussion. 'My way, or no way' is Larry's credo. Even though we are peers he seems determined to maintain a position of total dominance. I have tried to be patient and wait him out, but so far he seems to be unyielding.

When (and if) managers develop beyond the Diplomat frame, they begin to see other people's preferences as variables in a wider situation rather than as determinants of their own actions. Studies of various groups of managers

---

The themes and patterns you see in Larry's *Technician* frame:

. . . .

. . . .

. . . .

---

have found that between 38 and 68 per cent hold the Technician frame—always the largest proportion of managers in each group surveyed. For the Technician, the guide to action becomes logic and intellectually determined objectivity, discovered and arrived at independently: the one, provable 'right answer'. This certainly seems true of Larry based on his colleague's description of him.

Technicians no longer identify with what makes them the same as others in the group. They identify more with what makes them stand out from others in the group, with the unique skills that they can contribute. Without any discussion, Larry takes over projects for which he shares responsibility with a fellow supervisor. Technicians depend less on others' judgements of quality, and more on their own. In fact, because they so sharply differentiate themselves from the group, they frequently defiantly and dogmatically oppose all forms of authority other than that of their chosen specialty or 'craft' and their 'craft heroes'.

Technicians focus almost exclusively on the internal logic and integrity of their area of expertise, often setting perfectionist standards. They are seldom good team players because of their dogmatic demand for perfection. Again, Larry serves as a prime example. His logic is the only logic. He appears not to place a high value on feedback. While the Diplomat seeks the approval of others, the Technician subordinates the need for peer approval to the need for self-approval for having done a job well.

On the bright side, the Technician's admiration for a job well done can evoke in subordinates a striving for praise earned through perfection. But this same emphasis on perfection produces the Technician's darker side. The manager holding the Technician frame, placing primacy on rational thought, will expect strict adherence to a well-defined code of professional and moral conduct. There are no *degrees* of excellence—only good or bad, perfect or imperfect. Such high expectations of subordinates and frequent criticism of a job poorly done can produce a culture of competition and stress.

The Technician, too, may fall victim to this self-generated stress. In Chapter 2 we described Anthony, a young manager who for two full years dedicated his full efforts to becoming an expert in a very complex method for comparing company benefit programmes. Anthony testified to the anguish, both physical and mental, of his 'perfectionist nature': 'I would find myself obsessing about minutia in an effort to rationalize every last variation in my results.' Anthony's successful experiment with action inquiry gave evidence that he had begun to develop beyond the Technician frame—an accomplishment not every manager achieves.

The Achiever frame

Joanne, the manager we meet next, is new to the *Achiever* frame. Like Anthony, who took on the task of helping the senior managers of a consulting firm's branch office change their roles, Joanne is breaking the constraints of the Technician frame and is beginning to understand and experience things in a new way—the way of the Achiever. The length and detail of her story, as well as its fresh, up-beat tone, seem to reflect that newness. Look for themes again, and make notes about them.

> My job as market research manager for the magazine requires that I be a problem solver and 'perfectionist'. It is part of my daily routine to delve into why things are the way they are—digging, analysing, and presenting the results. Comments that people make about me include, 'You're really good with numbers', 'I don't know how you can understand this stuff'. These are comments that a Technician would love to hear. I am now finding this frame very constraining. I would prefer to be less detail conscious and be more involved with the overall picture, working towards long-term effectiveness rather than short-term efficiency.
>
> Steve, the marketing director, had confided in me that he was interviewing for a different position within the company and, if he were to accept, it would be fairly soon. It was vital that I display more of the characteristics of the Achiever stage of development in order to be seriously considered for the position of marketing director. I developed a plan that included a number of experiments.
>
> My first action upon hearing this news was to have a discussion with Steve and ask his advice on the best way to proceed. I said I was very interested in eventually becoming the marketing director. Steve expressed confidence that I could do the job, but his response also confirmed what I already knew—I

needed to become more visible to upper management—in general, take a proactive role in increasing my communication with these people.

The next major action that I took was to rewrite my job description. Jim, the publisher, had asked us to send him our job descriptions so he could start thinking about the division of responsibility (now that the marketing director position was unfilled). On Steve's suggestion, I rewrote my job description and included responsibilities of the marketing director that I am interested in taking on. I clearly stated in my letter that 'I'm not sure that I've adequately expressed my abilities and interest in the past and am taking this opportunity to do so'. I also told him that one of my priorities was to continue to improve my written and oral communication skills.

By taking this action I was letting Jim know that I was making efforts to change my behaviour. The letter itself was unprecedented for me. I also opened myself to some self-examination and opened the floor for criticism. My hope was that Jim would realize my level of commitment and assist my development.

While there was no direct response to my letter and rewritten job description, over the past few weeks, Jim and the national sales manager have sent me copies of presentations that they liked and have called to solicit my opinion on other presentations. Recently, Jim has asked me to take on the development of the general presentation. I adamantly expressed interest in this project in my letter.

An ongoing action is to maintain daily contact with Jim, the ad director, and the national sales manager. While this is not always possible, I've hardly missed a day without touching base with these three people at least once. While this sounds like a small and trivial thing, it is actually one of my most effective experiments. I used to go an entire week or two without speaking to the publisher. By taking this initiative, I've created a 'chain reaction'. My calls to them have started conversations that have prompted them to call me more often. During these conversations I've been able to convey my knowledge on different subjects—which in some cases has led to being given responsibility for certain projects or keeping track of certain matters. Another result is that my name comes up often in discussions between these people and other upper level managers in the company.

Another effective action that I took was to volunteer for a project with which I previously had no involvement. We needed to develop a new rate structure for buying advertising space in our magazine. The project had an almost impossible deadline, but I was able to meet it. It involved working several nights until 9 p.m. and on two weekends. I felt it was important for this project to go as smoothly and quickly as possible. If there had been delays and mistakes, Jim might not have entrusted it to me again. This was an area he might not have thought I could help with. If I hadn't taken the initiative, he still wouldn't know it.

The next major action I took was to schedule a meeting with Jim to discuss my compensation. In essence I wanted to ask for a raise, but I also wanted to convey that I was confident in my abilities and the contributions that I make and have the right amount of aggressiveness to be successful in marketing. This meeting was my best opportunity to properly apply framing, advocating, illustrating, and inquiring in my conversation. By thinking about these conversational elements, I was able to turn a potentially difficult and tense conversation into a positive and productive meeting. We discussed my reasoning and his and were able to make each other see the other's view on a few issues. He agreed that I was not adequately compensated for my contributions.

In conclusion, I am very satisfied with the progress I've made. While no decisions have been made to promote someone to the position of marketing director, I feel I've made significant progress towards the goal of being that person.

My frequent contact with the publisher and others in the company has helped me to move fully out of the Technician stage and into the Achiever stage. I receive criticism in a much more productive manner and have changed my focus from short-term satisfaction to long-term effectiveness. The most personally felt progress that I've made, however, is my ability to be an initiator and no longer a pawn.

The themes and patterns you see in this manager's *Achiever* frame:

. . . .

. . . .

. . . .

The Achiever is passionate about accomplishing goals. Whereas Joanne heretofore has concentrated on digging into the inner workings of things, mastering the numbers and presenting the answer, the Achiever frame is wider. It focuses not just on how things work on the inside, but on how to be effective in one's wider surroundings and on how to help the organization be effective in its environment. As Joanne moves from Technician to Achiever we see her attention expand beyond digging into research data. She conveys her 'knowledge on different subjects' and takes on new kinds of projects, such as recommending a new rate structure. She advocates a promotion for herself from the more technically oriented position of market research manager to the more entrepreneurially and managerially oriented role of marketing director, typical of the Achiever's focus on functions that help the organization carry out its established strategy.

Much more than those who hold the prior frames, the Achiever pays attention to differences between his or her points of view and those of others, and places a value on teamwork and on agreements reached through consensus as aids in carrying out pre-established goals. The Achiever welcomes personal feedback and seeks mutuality in relationships with co-workers. In Joanne's case, her associations with other managers are on the rise as she assumes the Achiever frame. She observes the sharp increase in her frequency of contacts with other managers, noting that her initiative in this area is even beginning to cause 'chain reactions'. She exchanges 'reasonings' with her boss on the subject of her salary, emphasizing not just that she got her way, but that mutuality was achieved. Increasingly, she appears to be seeking and valuing feedback.

There can be a flip side, a darker side, to the Achiever's way of handling feedback, however. Bluntly, the feedback had better fit within the Achiever's already-established scheme of things (his or her frame), or it will be rejected. You have probably known examples:

> The project manager asks you along with managers from several other departments to attend a meeting in order to give your department's inputs and comments about how the project is being run. Many changes are suggested, but the project manager accepts only those that are consistent with the basic approach she is already using.

> A friend phones you one evening excited about a new business venture he hopes to launch. He tells you his plans and asks your advice. He asks, in addition, that you invest money in the enterprise to help get it started. You think his plans are not sound. You suggest to him several key questions you feel he should explore before proceeding. You tell him further that you do not have the money to invest. He is extremely upset with both your responses. He ends the conversation by saying you and he are no longer friends.

In both these cases the Achiever seeks feedback, but when it is given it becomes clear that the Achiever's effort to achieve is made in terms of his or her own pre-established framework. The Achiever is not prepared to question the validity of the frame itself and possibly reframe his or her approach in the midst of action. In Joanne's case, the thing she emphasizes in describing her associations with others is the impact she had on the others: she *'created* a chain reaction'; she conveys *her* knowledge; she convinces her boss she is not adequately compensated.

The Achiever's orientation towards subordinates is complex. On the one hand, the manager at the Achiever stage values and encourages creativity among subordinates and is able to delegate significant responsibilities to them. On the other hand, however, the Achiever's inability to question his or her own limited conception of the organization's larger goals prevents any serious consideration or acceptance of alternatives that deviate from the official mission.

You are undoubtedly aware of many examples of the thought and action of the Achiever. In our studies of managers, taken as a whole, Achievers represented 35 per cent of the total.

A summary of four frames and a look ahead Now we shall revisit the four frames we have considered in this chapter—Opportunist, Diplomat, Technician and Achiever— with one more story. Art is a manager in a business owned by his family. In his story, Art describes transitions he has made through each of the four frames. This affords us a review, but also highlights in a remarkably vivid way something we glimpsed in Joanne's story: the potential people have for acquiring successively larger frames. Art presents himself as having accomplished at least four such transformations, with a fifth possibly underway. The last two paragraphs of his story provide a look at two further frames, the *Strategist* and the *Magician*, which are developmentally beyond the Achiever frame. When you reach that point in Art's story, you can look for new themes—*post-Achiever* themes. Art's story:

> When I was 15, I worked in my grandfather's store and I evidenced some Opportunist tendencies. I would do things that made me look good at the time, but had poor future consequences.
>
> At 19, when I was in college, I worked for my father who had bought a large car body repair franchise. My managerial behaviour was diplomatic: I wanted everyone to like me and I avoided confrontational situations. Due to the nature of the

people who work in that industry I could not, and did not, remain a Diplomat for long. Our employees generally had alcohol, drug, emotional, behavioural, social, and/or legal problems. Many were in and out of court and jail and could not handle their finances from one week to the next. In retrospect, this put most of them clearly as Opportunists.

I remember the turning point from a Diplomat's to a Technician's mindset, though I had no name for it at the time. The incident was the first time I had to fire someone. After that, my focus was on driving the employees to do the job right. I was very organized, methodical and procedural, instituting procedures in our shop that were recommended for use across the country. I hated anyone to try to tell me that there was a different way to do something other than the 'perfect' way I was already doing it, though I often would try new ideas after work when nobody was around. I also welcomed and enjoyed people asking me about problems they could not figure out.

I came to a brick wall using this strategy about 1983 when we could no longer find any new employees because of the low unemployment rate. I was not able to fire anyone for not following the rules because there was no one to replace them.

I found evidence subsequently of the Achiever style. Rather than adhering to the strict procedures, I decided on the goal to have the jobs done right and that there could be many ways to achieve that goal. I learned quickly the value of flexibility, working with an alcoholic who would often disappear for several days or weeks, a paranoid individual who put a mirror on his tool box so he could see if anyone was watching him, a person I would call hyper, who would run through the shop jumping over cars, climb walls, swing from pipes, coming up behind people to startle them, and an employee who, when I asked how he did such a good job, replied that he would just get high and work. Previously, I could easily have fired any one of them, but I learned that each was useful in his own way. At this time, I also sought out critiques on what I did and if there were ways that I could do better. I watched others to see what I could learn from them and found that everyone had something I could learn from.

In 1984 I started doing arbitration, and I think this introduced me to the Strategist's sense of multiple frameworks and the interaction of process and task. The first brief would seem so convincing, then the other brief would change my mind, and then the oral presentations would again change my view of the whole case. It was also interesting experimenting with different ways to resolve problems that leave each side feeling as if they had their say and accepting my decision as fair and reasonable. In dealing with customers and employees, I now use these same techniques.

The next precipitous event, which may be a glimpse of the Magician stage, happened when a customer was yelling about something to do with their car. It was also during the busy season. I had 15 employees, 75 cars, hundreds of inventory items, and customer inquiries to handle. I remember that while the person was yelling I felt that I was above the situation looking down. I figured out what I should do to correct the situation and then went back down. After this incident, I could do this as needed, separating myself from the circumstances and calmly determine what I should do to control the situation. After several times, I was both amazed and scared of being able to do this. . . .

Art himself identifies some of the themes of frames beyond the Achiever when he refers to his 'Strategist's sense of multiple frameworks and the interaction of process and task' and to the Magician's experiencing an interplay of detachment from, and committed action in, present circumstances. This is not our first encounter with such themes. In Chapter 2 we met Jennifer, the leader of the 'We Create Quality' project, who wanted to revive that project but spoke with special energy about her vision of the project as a means of transforming the process by which her department members worked with each other. She also shared Art's ability to detach and reflect during conversations in which a certain colleague produced an 'outburst.'

We shall explore these post-Achiever frames in more detail in the chapters that follow, but in the meantime, we hope you, the reader are beginning to become as fascinated and delighted as Art at the possibility of acquiring new frames yourself. If you have written on that sheet with *your* name at the top the frame that you think represents your own, along with a list of some of your own characteristics which typify that frame (or if you do that writing now) you will have taken the first step in the developmental process. Perhaps you will observe, like Art, that your list includes characteristics of more than just one frame, suggesting that you are already in a transition from one frame to the next.

By knowing where you are in the developmental sequence, you can proceed to begin thinking about and experimenting in action with themes that characterize the next frame beyond your present frame, as Joanne and Art are doing. You may also be able to help those work associates whose frames you identified to do the same—an undertaking to which we shall give special attention in Chapter 7.

For now, we return to the doorway that Art has opened, and enter a new realm, the world of the post-Achiever frames. These frames, starting with the Strategist, differ from the four frames we discussed earlier in ways that are vital to you as a manager and to your organization. Recent research indicates that people at the Strategist stage and beyond are substantially more effective in their organizations, and at transforming their organizations, than those whose frames precede the Strategist frame developmentally. Because of the importance of this developmental move beyond the Achiever stage, we aim the spotlight in the next chapter on the Strategist frame to show how its themes differ from those of the Achiever and to show the kinds of performance the Strategist frame enables.

Notes

1. The frames correspond closely to adult developmental stages identified by Robert Kegan, Lawrence Kohlberg, Jane Loevinger, Robert Selman, and others. See, for example, R. Kegan (1982) *The Evolving Self*, Cambridge, MA: Harvard; L. Kohlberg (1969) 'Stage and Sequence: The Cognitive and Developmental Approach to Socialization Theory and Research' in D. A. Goselin (ed.) *Handbook of Socialization Theory and Research*, Chicago: Rand-McNally; J. Loevinger (1976) *Ego Development: Conception and Theories*, San Francisco, CA: Jossey-Bass; and R. Selman (1980) *The Growth of Interpersonal Understanding*, New York: Academic Press.

2. Studies of the numbers of managers holding the various developmental frames include J. Davidson (1984) 'The effects of organizational culture on the development of nurses', Chestnut Hill, MA: Boston College School of Education, doctoral dissertation; Aaron Gratch (1985) 'Managers' perceptions of decision making processes as a function of ego development and of the situation', unpublished manuscript, New York: Teachers College, Columbia University; Robert E. Quinn and W. R. Torbert (1987) 'Who is an effective transforming leader?', unpublished paper, Ann Arbor, MI: University of Michigan School of Business; Salathiel Smith (1980) 'Ego development and the problems of power and agreement in organizations, Washington, D.C.: George Washington University, doctoral dissertation; W. R. Torbert (1983) 'Identifying and cultivating professional effectiveness at one professional school', paper presented at the annual meeting of the American Society for Public Administration.

6 Strategists in action: managerial and organizational learning

In Chapter 1 we said that continual quality improvement has at its centre a process of learning. We said further that this learning process is not a mechanistic, automated feedback process producing continuous change, but instead is a bumpy, sometimes upending kind of learning that brings to individuals and to organizations a widening and deepening of vision and a new capacity for learning and improved performance.

To bring about this not-always-pretty, but truly transformational learning, a special form of leadership is required. We have already seen several examples, all from persons who began taking leadership without being labelled as a leader by anyone else. In Chapters 2 and 3 we saw Jennifer using action inquiry to make her department more collaborative and to revitalize its quality improvement programme, Anthony breaking out of his technical specialist role to spearhead a redefinition of roles in his organization, and Jane interrupting a company president's habitual way of thinking (and her own) to form a new lending relationship for her bank.

These examples, and several of the others portrayed in the previous chapters, reveal a form of leadership in which the leader learns as he or she prompts others to learn. It is a leadership that generates individual and organizational learning concurrently. This leadership produces learning on-line, in the moment, through action inquiry. Furthermore, it is a type of leadership thought and action that is intimately linked with the later stages of managerial development, starting with the Strategist frame that we began to describe in Chapter 5.

The Strategist frame

The *Strategist* frame is not as frequently encountered as the prior frames, comprising just 10 per cent of the managers we studied. Eighty per cent of all Strategists were found to be at the most senior levels of management.

The Strategist frame is a frame that sees other frames as valid, relevant and usable. This frame thus brings into view the possibility that people's differing frames—however disparate, unique and internally inconsistent they may be—can be understood as valid from their own differing points of view. The Strategist is attuned more deeply than managers holding any of the prior frames to the uniqueness of persons and situations.

The Strategist realizes that all frames, including his or her own, are relative. With this realization, the Strategist, unlike the Achiever, is open to the possibility of 'reframing' his or her viewpoint and purposes in a situation, and helping others to 'reframe,' consciously seeking and choosing new frames that accommodate the disparities, paradoxes, and fluidity of multiple frames.[1] Moreover, the Strategist senses that such frame-changes cannot be generated unilaterally either by external command or by internal effort. Instead, the exercise of transforming power is a mutual process in which all the participants are initiators and make themselves vulnerable to transformation in the service of greater organizational legitimacy and effectiveness.

The Strategist frame is not without potential shadows and turmoils. The ability to see multiple frames and to choose a new frame creating new meanings, may leave the person feeling virtually paralysed for moments before taking action. However, it is the ability to see many meanings simultaneously that can drive the Strategist to develop an encompassing frame that makes order out of chaos, rather than take the easy way out by simply adopting one of the earlier, simpler frames.

The Strategist's subordinates, who may be unable to view situations from such a wide perspective, may feel out of touch with their manager and with the organization. But the manager with the Strategist frame, having keen awareness of multiple frames, is well equipped to act to maintain institutional and personal connections to subordinates.

Research has shown that the Strategist's ability to accommodate diverse frames, to adopt new frames, and to collaborate with others in reframing is an essential element in leading organizational transformation, particularly transformation to the later organizational stages when the organization institutionalizes the ongoing inquiry processes that generate continual quality improvement. In a later chapter

(Chapter 8) we shall introduce the stages of organizational development.

Single-loop and double-loop learning

Organizations that transform through an ongoing process of collaborative inquiry have a special quality. Such organizations are not merely learning in the sense of acquiring new information or in the sense of 'getting themselves back on track'. These organizations, and their managers individually, are developing new ways of learning.

We can clarify what we mean by defining two kinds of learning and awareness: single-loop and double-loop.[2] For individual managers, these different modes of learning relate closely to the developmental progression of frames we have been discussing. Chris Argyris and Donald Schön are primarily responsible, through their consulting, teaching, researching and publishing, for showing managers and management scholars the usefulness of the cybernetic concept of *single-loop* and *double-loop* feedback and learning.

By single-loop feedback one learns that one's actions are not achieving a pre-established goal, and must then 'prove' that learning by adjusting one's actions to increase the likelihood of achieving the goal. According to adult developmental theory, single-loop learning does not occur consistently for persons who have not reached the Achiever stage of development. This means that single-loop feedback does not always register on every person to whom it is directed and, therefore, does not always generate single-loop learning and more effective action.

In double-loop feedback one learns that the structure of one's meaning-making, goal-seeking, status-maintaining system (in other words, one's frame) is problematic. Double-loop feedback enables individuals and organizations to learn through examining alternative policies and objectives from new perspectives rather than simply improve ways of functioning within present perspectives. Again, according to adult developmental theory, each stage change is a double-loop learning process, but the fact and the process of such double-loop frame changes remain implicit before the Strategist stage. Only as persons reach the Strategist stage are they likely to seek out explicitly, or register, or act on double-loop feedback which highlights incongruities and incompletenesses within one's meaning-making system.

Adult developmental theory suggests that it is at the Strategist stage that a person begins to develop the capacity for integrative awareness that is needed to work with people holding different frames, to redefine presented problems, to seek underlying issues, and to foster a manager's or an organization's transformation.[3] To persons at the earlier stages, ambiguity, paradox and exploration of implied, underlying meanings are likely to seem vague and a waste of time rather than being seen as clues to innovative agendas, genuine collaboration and new stages of development.

In this chapter we shall help you, the reader, to begin thinking in the Strategist mode—perhaps to begin rehearsing Strategist thoughts and actions as they apply to your own circumstances. We shall do this by illustrating leadership as practised by Strategists. We shall introduce you to several managers we met through our research who illustrate sharply the difference between the learning disposition of the Strategist frame and the relative 'disability' of the earlier frames to generate transformational leadership. We suggest you make some notes as you read and reflect on the Strategist frame. Which of the managers on the following pages remind you of yourself? Which are different from you and in what ways? What are some instances in your own experience where, from the Strategist perspective, you could have thought and acted more effectively? What might some of these thoughts and actions have been?

A research-based look at the Strategist

Research has begun to confirm that persons holding later stage frames tend to be more effective managers. Our own research specifically points to a link between the Strategist frame and the manager's tendencies to redefine problems and to propose collaborative rather than unilateral action in response to problems.

In one of our studies, we placed 49 MBA graduates in a simulated management setting known as an 'in-basket' exercise. They wrote responses to 34 letters, memos, reports and phone messages similar to those found in a manager's incoming mail. Because each subject responded to the same set of 34 items, we were able to apply statistical tests to show that persons at later developmental stages redefined problems and made collaborative action proposals in response to more of the items than did persons holding the Achiever, Technician or other pre-Strategist frames. We identified individuals' frames by their responses to the Loevinger Sentence Completion Test, a comprehensively validated test for identifying a person's position in a series of adult developmental positions corresponding to the frames.[4]

We were excited when we obtained such clear research

confirmation that two particular types of managerial behaviour, redefining of problems and undertaking collaborative
action, were indeed more characteristic of managers holding
the Strategist frame than of those holding developmentally
earlier frames. But we wanted to know more. The results of
our in-basket study whetted our appetite for learning how
Strategists performed, not just in an exercise setting but in
their everyday at-work situations.

To find out more about Strategists in action, we performed
a follow-on study, interviewing nine men and eight women
who held a range of positions mainly in service industry
firms, including five financial institutions, two research
firms, two hospitals and two consulting firms. Four of our
interviewees were in manufacturing firms. All held advanced
degrees, mostly MBAs; nine held managerial positions,
including one chief operating officer and three functional
area heads; four were in specialist or individual contributor
positions (such as financial planner or loan officer); and four
were consultants. Fifteen of the 17 were in their 30s, with a
median age of 36 and a median length of work experience of
ten years.

Ten of these individuals had attained the Strategist stage
according to the Loevinger measure. (One was in fact
measured at a later stage called Ironist.) For purposes of
comparison, the other seven held developmentally earlier
frames. Five of these seven were Achievers, the other two
being Technicians. We separated the transcribed interviews
into two groups, Strategists and pre-Strategists. Because our
primary focus was on how those who have attained the
Strategist frame differ from those who have not yet reached
that stage, we referred for simplicity to all seven of the pre-
Strategists as Achievers, and to all of the other ten as
Strategists.[5]

We discovered that there were indeed important differences in the ways the Achievers and Strategists thought,
spoke and acted at work. We found the differences to be
particularly striking in three major arenas: their ways of
exercising leadership, their relationships with their superiors
and their ways of initiating action when proposing ideas or
programmes. We shall examine each of these in turn.

As you read each of the stories narrated by these managers,
you may wish to try to recall what you thought and how you
acted in a similar situation. Was your approach that of the
Strategist? If not, see if you can 'try on' the Strategist frame,
and make some notes about how you might think and act in
that or a similar situation.

When Achievers and Strategists spoke about leading, their contrasting frames showed clearly. Achievers saw leadership as cultivating and moulding subordinates to their own way of thinking. In some cases, they acted as mentor, in others as law enforcer or watchdog representing their own bosses.

Bill, an Achiever, shows this way of thinking as he describes his relationship with a low-performing member of his staff who, according to Bill, 'did not do a lot of work, tried to coast, and this was obvious to everybody in the group'.

> It was a series of specific conversations where I'd tell him, 'You're missing the boat here. You've got a job to do and I want to make sure you get the job done. . . . I don't think it's fair to the others, who are working very hard and aren't being rewarded any more than you are.'
>
> At various times we would come to a head and I'd threaten to fire him. Then he would buckle down and get it done for a little while. I would give him specific objectives and certain reward systems for him.
>
> He had a good relationship with my boss. I made it clear to him I thought he was taking advantage of that, and I told my boss the same thing. My boss agreed. He said, 'I'm out of it', but he never really was. This went on for six months, and that guy is now in my position. That was a very disappointing situation. I think I could have taken greater control; just fired him.

Bill says his problem lay in not taking a stronger stand and, in retrospect, this may be true. But at the time he could only have known this to be true by taking a wider perspective, as a Strategist would be likely to do, encompassing the points of view of all three actors. Only if he had understood that his boss was not really going to act and that the subordinate did not really share the productivity objectives would 'a stronger stand' have made sense at the time.

And what would the stronger stand have been? To the Achiever the stronger stand would have been to fire the subordinate at some point prior to the time that the subordinate took over the Achiever's position. To a Strategist, . . . well, you, our reader, are the person who wishes to practise the Strategist frame, so . . . what *would* have been a Strategist's approach to this situation from the outset? We invite you to outline your approach, on paper, prior to reading the following examples of Strategists approaches to subordinates. . . .

The Strategists' interviews provide several examples of much more patient efforts to work with a subordinate's frame, questioning it rather than dismissing it. Susan, a hospital marketing manager, describes a conversation with a subordinate whose performance had recently slipped:

> I wanted to crack her shell, because she is real tough. You can see the strain behind Francine's eyes, but she says, 'I'm fine.' I attempted to approach her by really sharing my feelings about the situation, not so much demanding that she open up, but saying I'm feeling concerned, I'm concerned about you. And I said, 'I need you to know that a lot of people are wondering what's wrong. Is something wrong?' That kind of conversation. It wasn't the first time we had had it.
>
> She finally said in a very matter-of-fact way, 'It really upsets me that everyone came to you to tell you they were bothered by my behaviour, and not to me.' So I said, 'In the future, I promise you, if people come to me I will tell them to go to you.' So she said, 'Thank you.' Her behaviour has improved tremendously.

Susan describes Francine's perspective ('I'm fine') and the incongruity between her perspective on herself and how she enacts herself ('You can see the strain behind her eyes'). Susan engaged Francine not by trying to enforce or mould her, but by offering her own and others' points of view ('a lot of people are wondering what's wrong') as points of departure for inquiry. In Argyris and Schön's terms, Susan undertakes double-loop learning by designing a situation in which the other person can be the origin of causation, in which the task is controlled jointly and in which the other has room to make choices and take risks. She chooses to hear the vulnerability in Francine's comment ('I'm upset . . . ') and shows that she is vulnerable to influence in response. Developmental theory suggests that such mutual vulnerability is a key stage in transformational change. Susan reports major change ('Her behaviour has improved tremendously').

The Strategists expressed a fascination with varied, potentially opposing frames (their own, their subordinates', other managers', their clients'). Rather than choosing one among these perspectives as authoritative, they sought to find a way to operate effectively amidst this variety. In this integrative awareness, the Strategists differed from the Achievers, who spoke more as though they had opted for a choice among dichotomies, for example by taking the role of law enforcer or watchdog, or by undertaking to 'mould' a subordinate.

Relationships with superiors

The data on relationships between Achievers or Strategists and their superiors were perhaps the most unexpected and counter-intuitive of our study. The conventional view is that the boss has the power so you must do what your boss says.

In fact, however, Achievers and Strategists in our study neither accept this frame nor operate from it. Both assume that it is possible, legitimate and even necessary to influence what the superior believes, wants and does. Frank, a consultant, shows the strength of the Achiever's urge to bring his 'superior' (in this case a potential client who was a corporate CEO) to see his framework. Frank believes he succeeded in getting the CEO to see his point:

> The CEO opened his mouth and let one of the vice presidents have it. He said, 'Surely you don't mean so-and-so.' He said, 'That's absurd; you can't run a business that way.' I said, 'Let's explore it. How do we know we can't run a business that way.' And the CEO and I had a fifteen minute dialogue, and by the time that ended he began to see what I was talking about. The other people present told me they saw that I wasn't going to be intimidated . . . nor would I get into his hip pocket.

Frank and the other Achievers saw clearly the difference between their own view and that of the superiors. Like Frank, the other Achievers were not afraid to advocate their views to their superiors. At the same time, like Frank, they implicitly held the rationality and effectuality of their own view to be beyond question. The end of Frank's story is that the CEO did *not* hire him to consult, an outcome that Frank does not attribute to any possible learning he may be able to do, but rather to his not having had enough time with the CEO.

In contrast to the Achievers, Strategists were more likely than the others to speak in terms of their perceptions rather than in terms of unquestionable realities. The Strategists would frequently discuss how they had revised and sharpened their definitions of themselves by juxtaposing their perceptions of self against their perceptions of their superiors. Sharon, a team leader in a consulting firm, provides a striking example as she discussed her differences with her boss, who was not, Sharon explained, the type who is accustomed to candid discussions of differences with his subordinates.

> I was working with a manager that I knew had a style very, very different from mine. I knew if I was going to make manager this year, it was crucial that I get this guy on my side, that I make him see I was ready to be manager.
> He was called the assassin. He was known for picking people off in that critical year. I figured the only way I know how to approach this is to talk to him about it—be honest and get things out on the table that no one talks about. So I said, 'Steve, I am

scared to death of working for you this year because I know you don't promote people. I know you think I'm screwing up because it's different from the way you do things, but trust me. It will work. I know it.'

He was very task oriented. He wanted to look at budget analyses and all this sort of junk, and I keep telling him, 'Steve, there's six people on this project. I don't need to look at a written report to tell you what's going on.' I think that was the pivotal point for me in changing because I realized we had two different styles. His had worked for him for a number of years. I could learn from him, but I could never be that way. And that's when I realized my style was no less valid. My way was not the wrong way. I don't need to continue looking for 'the' answer.

I had several conversations with him about our differences. I don't think any staff person ever confronted him on his evaluations of them or his approach. I just kept pointing out to him, 'Steve, we're different but trust me. I have delivered everything on time, haven't I?' And he would have to say, 'Yes.' 'My project team is happy?' He said, 'Yes.' I said, 'See, it's not that I do it worse, it's that we're different, and it's not that I can't learn from you'. And I think he got a lot from me. And everyone told me, 'Sharon, what did you do to Steve? He gave you an "Outstanding". He stood up and supported you.'

Significant here is the way Sharon addresses the differences between her boss's frame and her own in conversations with him. In action inquiry terms, she combines assertion and illustration of her views with explicit recognition of the differences in frames and with inquiry in the process of testing and building her commitment to a style of working. She does this even with a subject previously considered unmentionable in her organization—her boss's evaluation of her. She does not refrain from discussing this subject when her principles demand that she discuss it.

According to developmental theory, the Strategist will recognize the importance of principle over accepted conventions and rules in deciding how to act. Thus principle becomes an integrating force providing central meaning among diverse views of reality. Principled choice can sometimes mean explicitly violating rules, even those established by a superior. This is illustrated by Roger, the newly appointed director of operations for a manufacturing firm. Operations was to be a new unit, formed by consolidating two existing departments. Roger felt he had to call his new staff together and begin working with them despite the fact that his boss had told him to wait and not tell the new staff members that they had been selected.

While I knew these people were going to be on my staff, my boss's process and the process defined by the company was don't tell an individual for sure, for definite that they're going to be here. So I had to play games. In reality, what I did was I violated rules all over the place. I couldn't handle it. I had to lie to my boss and the human resources manager and say to them that I didn't inform people when really I did. I couldn't do it any other way.

In the next section, we shall see how this situation evolved as we discuss the different ways in which Achievers and Strategists were effective in taking action.

Action initiatives: proposing and implementing ideas and programmes

In general, our interviewees were effective. Our Achievers as well as our Strategists got things done, met objectives and were making career progress. They suggested new ideas and moved them forward. As our earlier examples have already shown, however, there were differences.

When Strategists described how they took action, they conveyed a sense of the simultaneous validity of others' ways of looking at things and a sense of the uniqueness of the situation. The process of action was not generalizable, meaning that one often could not go according to the book. Let us return to Roger's story as he describes his work in forming his new management team:

I got everyone together off site and said, 'You're going to be on my staff.' My boss didn't like that. He found out afterwards that I had talked to these people. I was going to fail one way or the other. I was going to fail if I didn't talk to them, so I figured I'd be able to deal with my boss.

I had a team building meeting two days ago, all of these people in a meeting with a facilitator, again off site. I made an opening statement. I said, 'OK, you're the consultants. I've just hired you. I want you, as consultants, to satisfy your needs for information so that you can recommend to me a future business strategy.'

What that did was it opened the floodgates. I got asked every question. We got every issue exposed. I said at the end of this, 'I do not want any hidden agendas between me and you.' So I'm finding things out. They told me they thought my boss or my boss's boss told me what to do. I said, 'No, they don't. It is my decision and I am expecting you to push back on me.' They said that they hadn't because they felt if they had pushed back it wasn't going to do any good.

Roger goes well beyond the task, as defined by the organization, in order to achieve his own goal of forming an effective team. He shows the acceptance of paradox and contradiction, which characterizes the frames held by people at the later developmental stages, by his deliberate choice between 'failing' with his boss and 'failing' with his team (while really intending to fail with neither). He did not limit himself to a single process. When he finds he can't move forward in the team-building meeting using a by-the-book approach, he discards it, 'opening the floodgates'. His remarks make it clear that he sees his effectiveness as relating to stage setting—developing a new type of frame for an interaction or process to take place in which his own aims can be expressed, but which can also accommodate those of others.

The contrasting perspective of the Achievers with regard to action initiatives is provided by Ellen, a market analysis manager at a major computer manufacturer. Ellen describes her efforts, which she views as quite successful, at bringing together and leading a cross-functional team to design and market a new software package.

> It involved at least a half dozen organizations' representatives who sat around the table on a weekly basis designing this programme and coming up with something that both they and the customer who was piloting it were very happy with. I felt very good about that because none of those people reported to me, but they all saw the advantages of doing business this way. The customer benefited, their goals were met. We channelled it from a lot of people to a single organization and the single organization dealt with our point of contact for support and service. Administratively it just became a much cleaner and tighter way of doing business for us. It was one of the major achievements I've accomplished inside the corporation. It had a lot of impact inside and a lot of impact competitively on the industry.

As in Roger's case, Ellen is effective in putting together a team, but she sees it differently. While Roger stressed the importance of 'opening the floodgates' to learn things he hadn't known—'the hidden agendas'—Ellen emphasizes that the team members 'all saw the advantages and benefits of doing business this way'. What Ellen sees as important is that it is *her* solution and *her* way of doing business that gains acceptance. She sets up and monitors 'a clean, tight way of doing business'. Roger, on the other hand, relies on principles of fairness and valid information, since 'the rules', as defined by his boss and his subordinates, are in conflict. Ellen's effectiveness, like Roger's, involves coordinating the efforts of many different individuals, but does not, as she described it, involve double-loop learning—looking at or questioning her own frame of reference, process or ideology.

How Strategists think and act

Our interviews provided a basis for several summarizing statements about the managerial practice of persons who have moved beyond the Achiever frame to the Strategist frame. These statements may be grouped in the three areas illuminated by the interviews: leadership practice in working with subordinates, relationships with superiors and the taking of action initiatives.

Leadership practice

1. Strategists are more likely than Achievers to undertake double-loop learning, designing situations where others can be the origin of causation, where tasks are controlled jointly, and where others make choices and take risks.
2. Strategists make more frequent and more conscientious efforts than Achievers: (a) to understand subordinates' frames, inquiring about them rather than dismissing them; (b) to form an integrative awareness of these frames, including discrepant frames; and (c) to use them as a basis for synthesizing new shared meanings.
3. Strategists are more likely than Achievers to test the limits of their organizations' and their superiors' constraints and to create new spheres of action for their subordinates and for themselves.

Relationships with superiors

1. Both Strategists and Achievers see it as appropriate to influence their superiors beliefs, goals and actions.
2. Strategists, in influencing superiors, are more likely than Achievers to undertake a negotiation among initially diverse frames to create a new shared frame, while Achievers are more likely to assert their own view as being beyond question.
3. Strategists are more likely than Achievers to identify their perceptions as perceptions, rather than as immutable realities, and to discuss differences in perceptions explicitly with their superiors.
4. Strategists, more than Achievers, base their actions on principles rather than rules, even when those principles are at odds with rules established by their superiors.

Action initiatives
1. When their actions are inconsistent with their principles, Strategists are more likely than Achievers to notice the discrepancy and act to reduce it.
2. Strategists are more likely than Achievers to view their action processes as unique rather than generalizable and rule governed.
3. Strategists are more likely than Achievers to define their effectiveness as consisting of setting a stage—a frame in which their own as well as others' aims can be expressed—rather than ensuring that their own solutions and processes are adopted.
4. Achievers use their awareness of various points of view to design ways of gaining acceptance of their goals. They see implementation as a linear move towards the goal. Strategists, however, use their awareness of various points of view to question and revise their goals. They see implementation as an iterative process involving creation of new shared meanings, leading to the reframing of problems.

From Achiever to Strategist

These statements argue strongly that the capacities managers need in order to create settings in which they, their colleagues, and their organization as a whole can transform require a developmental shift of perspective beyond the Achiever frame to the Strategist frame.

The cases and exercises we present in this book suggest what is involved in making that shift. It is a shift that involves an unusual kind of learning. Most management training and organization development efforts teach managers new knowledge and skills that enable them to function better within their existing frame (single-loop learning). However, the developmental shift from Achiever to Strategist requires that one understands and questions what one has previously taken for granted (double-loop learning), as Roger did when he 'opened the floodgates' to let his team members expose their hidden agendas. Roger's inquiry led him to discover that he had held two implicit assumptions that were invalid: (a) his team members knew he was free from autocratic control by his boss and (b) they would 'push back' on him if they disagreed with him. Making this developmental shift also requires experimenting in action with new frames (assumptions about oneself, others, and one's situation) as Sharon did when she confronted her boss about the 'undiscussible' topics of his style and how he evaluated his people.

We are convinced that this developmental exposing of

implicit assumptions and this experimenting with a new frame is crucial not only in helping individuals become leaders, but also in the process of continual quality improvement in organizations. Organizations as a whole, and groups within them, frequently share frames in common that limit their effectiveness and tend to persist. Quality improvement can succeed or fail depending on whether frames change.

Jean Bartunek and Michael Moch describe in detail a 'quality of work life' (QWL) intervention in a manufacturing organization where it was vividly clear that successes during the project, where they occurred, were due to the ability of people to replace an old frame with a new frame.[6] The old frame, widely shared in the organization, assumed that management should be paternalistic. People who developed a new frame assumed that the relationship between employees and management should be collaborative. Ultimately, the programme failed because the new shared frame never took hold sufficiently and the organization slipped back into the old frame.

In another case reported by Robert Krim,[7] a senior manager in a highly politicized US city government undertook a QWL improvement programme with explicit attention to frames. He used the same frame definitions that we presented in Chapter 5 to understand himself, the other key players, and to form an agenda for the quality improvement programme. A Strategist, he used his ability to understand frames that differed from his own, as well as to understand the limited validity of his own perspective, and gradually came to the realization, while he continued in his city government role, that he regularly 'deauthorized' himself in critical situations. Perhaps because his Strategist perspective was relatively rare, major players criticized him as 'lacking political instincts'. However, he made effective use of his understanding of colleagues' frames and also saw many possibilities for reversing deteriorating situations by examining them from new perspectives, employing double-loop feedback to test alternative goals and policies. He also struggled to overcome his 'self-deauthorizing' tendency. After two years, the programme had grown in size and appeared to be successful. None of the other six municipal QWL programmes in that US state survived more than a year. Nationally, fewer than one-third have survived as long as two years. Now, another six years later, this city manager has developed a separate not-for-profit consortium to help improve city services, and this new, larger organization has become a national model. Thus, the manager has very much ended his self-deauthorization, creating one organization and indirectly influencing many others.

This case supports our contention that the manager's frame is central to his or her effectiveness. It offers further evidence that it is the leader who has attained the Strategist frame who brings to the arena of action (a) a realization that persons and organizations differ from one another in the frames through which they interpret events, (b) an ability to examine his or her own, as well as the frames of others, and (c) a willingness to set a stage where new shared ways of making meaning can develop.

Conclusion

As research continues to show that managers who have attained the Strategist frame are more effective than those holding earlier stage frames in leading organizational improvement, you as a manager, and as one who trains and mentors managers, are afforded a compelling new perspective.

If the Strategist perspective is new to you, as it is to a great many people, we hope the reflections and notes you made while reading this chapter have helped you to begin to anticipate the Strategist frame and to rehearse Strategist actions. By exercising in this way, you can begin to develop the wider vision that enables personal autonomy as well as the kind of collaboration with others that produces a self-renewing organization. Shifting your frame is vital to your own effectiveness. Moreover, your nurturing of later stage frames in others is vital to your role as a catalyst in the process of transforming other individuals and your organization. It is to this role that we invite your attention in the next chapter.

Notes

1. The ability of individuals to accommodate diverse frames as an essential ingredient in organizational transformation is discussed in W. R. Torbert, 'Leading organizational transformation', in R. W. Woodman and W. A. Pasmore (eds) (1989) *Research in Organizational Change and Development*, Vol. 3, Greenwich, CT: JAI Press, pp. 83–116; and W. R. Torbert (1994), 'Managerial learning and organizational learning: a potentially powerful redundancy', *Management Learning*, **25** (1), 57–70.
2. Single-loop and double-loop learning are discussed and illustrated in detail in C. Argyris (1981) *Reasoning, Learning, and Action*, San Francisco: Jossey-Bass; C. Argyris and D. Schön (1974) *Theory in Practice: Improving Professional Effectiveness*, San Francisco: Jossey-Bass; C. Argyris and D. Schön (1978) *Organizational Learning*, San Francisco: Jossey-Bass; M. Rein and

D. Schön (1994) *Reframing*, New York: Basic Books; D. Schön (1983) *Reflection in Action*, New York: Basic Books.

3.   Research results showing a link between managerial effectiveness and developmentally later stage frames are reported in B. Hall and H. Thompson (1980) *Leadership Through Values*, New York: Paulist Press; K. Merron, D. Fisher and W. R. Torbert (1987) 'Meaning making and management action', *Group and Organization Studies* **12** (3), 257–74; S. Smith (1980) 'Ego development and the problems of power and agreement in organizations', unpublished doctoral dissertation, School of Business and Public Administration, George Washington University.

4.   Further information on the sentence completion test we used to identify our interviewees' frames may be found in J. Loevinger (1979) 'Construct validity of the sentence completion test of ego development', *Applied Psychological Measurement*, **3** (3), 281–311, and in J. Loevinger and R. Wessler (1970) *Measuring Ego Development*, San Francisco; CA: Jossey-Bass. Our research using an in-tray exercise to examine the relationship between managers' frames and their managerial behaviour is reported in K. Merron, D. Fisher and W. R. Torbert (1987)—see note 3.

5.   In our study of Strategists and pre-Strategists, we asked our interviewees to select two recent incidents to describe in detail, one where they felt they had been effective, the other where they felt they had been less effective. We occasionally asked questions for clarification, but mainly left it to the interviewees to organize their responses. The transcribed interviews were separated into two categories: pre-Strategists and Strategists. A different research assistant analysed the transcripts in each category, locating themes and exploring how common each theme was within that category. Then, the research assistants traded transcripts and each searched for the previously identified common themes (themes clearly illustrated in more than half of the transcripts in that category) among the transcripts in the other category. It turned out that no themes that were common among the Strategists were also common among the Achievers, and vice versa. This research is reported in D. Fisher and W. R. Torbert (1991) 'Transforming managerial practice: beyond the Achiever stage', in R. W. Woodman and W. A. Pasmore, *Research in Organizational Change and Development*, Vol. 5, Greenwich, CT: JAI Press, pp. 143–73. The present chapter is adapted from this article, and contains excerpts from it, with the permission of the publisher.

6.   J. M. Bartunek and M. K. Moch (1990) *Creating Alternative Realities at Work: The Quality of Work Life Experiment at FoodCom*, New York: Harper Business.

7.   R. M. Krim (1986) 'The challenge of creating organizational effectiveness: labor-management cooperation and learning strategies in the public sector', unpublished doctoral dissertation, Department of Sociology, Boston College.

PART THREE

TRANSFORMING GROUPS AND ORGANIZATIONS THROUGH ACTION INQUIRY AND CQI

7   Developing a CQI group

Through the past six chapters, we have been talking with you about taking a continual quality improvement (CQI) approach to your own practice. Of course, your own practice in an organization involves you with other co-workers, so a large part of what we have discussed has concerned how to diagnose colleagues as well as yourself and how to experiment with acting differently in the presence of your superiors and subordinates. But the focus has consistently fallen on how we can all *improve our own practice*.

In this chapter, and in the rest of the book, we shift our focus in a subtle but important way to the questions of *how to construct a group or organization that is committed and capable as a social unit to improve its members' practice*. We say that this shift in focus is subtle but important because we are not shifting the focus *away from* the individual to the group and we are not shifting the focus simply because we think it's a good idea to cover these topics. We are shifting the focus first to the group scale and then to the organizational scale of constructing a CQI practice because that is what you and any other individual who goes very far in your own practice of CQI will want and need to do. In other words, *we are continuing to focus on how you, the individual, can conduct action inquiry, but now the arena of your action inquiry can begin to expand* beyond your exercise of leadership in changing your own practice *to include your exercise of leadership in changing a group's or organization's practice*.

As early in this book as the extended examples of Jennifer's leadership to make her group a 'We Create Quality' group and Anthony's leadership in helping senior management redesign the team coordinator roles, we have seen how a person's earliest efforts at action inquiry can have group and organizational effects. But now we are going to focus on how you can have not just an *effect* on a group or organization, but how you can help *construct* groups and organizations where

CQI is built into the skills, norms and roles of all the members. In Chapter 6, we saw how Roger, as the new director of operations, was combining two departments into one and intentionally violated his boss's rule in order to begin building a more effective group. Similarly, you may need to violate the rules of your boss—whether that boss be inside you (your current governing frame) or outside you—when you begin to take the lead in constructing CQI groups.

Perhaps the simplest way to begin is to ask you who you can imagine would benefit from working with this book and its exercises in the manner you have been doing until now. If you manage a group of subordinates, you may think first of them. On the other hand, you may think of two, three or four people you like and respect who seem to have an interest in these issues, but who are spread around the company. Or you may think of some childhood friends, or college classmates, or neighbours who work in entirely different companies and industries and with whom you would enjoy meeting for an evening once every two or three weeks. At these meetings you would hear about each other's challenges at work and could consult one another about action inquiry approaches to those dilemmas.

But don't take this all too earnestly. Look back at the Strategist qualities outlined in Table 5.2. These are the human qualities that are useful in creating something new, rather than just reproducing more of what you already know—and humour plays a big part in the new.

Guess what? We are already in the midst of a new level of action inquiry exercises. This chapter offers you one exercise, with many subparts and several stories to illustrate directions you can take. The point of this exercise is to *take responsibility for trying to form a CQI group over a period of six months to a year*. As we have already suggested in the prior paragraphs, you do not need any managerial authority at your job in order to start trying to construct such a group, and the group you construct does not need to be from a single organization.

There will be three progressively more demanding measures of the success of your effort. The first is whether you persevere to the point of actually getting a group to meet together. The second is whether you and others can create and execute different group roles that generate enough interest and learning among the members that they continue meeting with the group and experience new successes at work. The third criterion of success is whether any of the group members reach the point you are now at—namely, the point of trying to construct their own action inquiry group.

Don't underestimate the difficulty of this exercise; and don't give up, defeated, when your first or second efforts to construct such a group founder or fail. It is difficult to create and sustain a group for which there is no obvious necessity, for which there are no external rewards, in which no one has any unilateral power or authority, and which is dedicated to doing something that each member will find difficult to do. Your powers of framing, advocating, illustrating and inquiring will be put to the test from the first conversation you have with a friend or colleague about creating such a group. And although it will be easier for you to gain initial compliance if you are proposing this activity to your immediate subordinates, with such a group you will face the ongoing dilemma of how to cultivate truly internal commitment on their part, rather than merely external compliance.

Here is one of the many points where humour can help. Because humour can be light and attractive, rather than heavy and pushy, it more easily invites others' internal commitment. (We are speaking here of Strategist-like, developmentally provocative humour, not the hostile humour of the Opportunist, or the Diplomat-like repetition of prefabricated jokes.)

The difficulties of generating sustained collective internal commitment to CQI meetings are no mere impediment prior to success. These difficulties represent the essential challenge at the heart of CQI practice. This challenge is to transform oneself, the relationships and groups one belongs to, and the organizations one works for to a pattern of activity in which *mutual, internally motivated* interactions predominate over *hierarchical, externally motivated* interactions. So, in facing these difficulties and in gradually developing a larger and larger repertoire of effective responses to the dilemmas of constructing CQI meetings, you are directly facing the true challenge of CQI at the group level.

We have some vivid memories of our own early efforts to construct CQI meetings (though we did not so name the meetings at the time). In one case, one of us thought he had gained a group's commitment to such work, only to learn later that his advocacies had seemed coercive to the other members and that his inquiries seemed to seek agreement rather than true responses. Although this incident was a depressing failure at the time, the learning that it engendered became seminal for his entire subsequent career and personal life. Such is the upside-down, inside-out, transforming process of action inquiry.

Now: before we try to assist you as you experiment with

constructing such groups, let us make one more important point. In the previous few pages we have been detailing the difficulties of successfully creating a CQI group. This, we believe, is the only responsible way to talk with you about making the commitment and taking the risks involved. In the same way, a start-up company seeking investment capital is obligated to detail the threats that may result in the loss of the investment. Despite these threats, people still invest if they see promise in the enterprise. In the present case of inviting you to create a CQI group, we want you to focus less on the outcomes of the activity, which may be more or less successful, and more on the developmental challenge and sheer fun of bringing a small group together.

For example, giving the group its own nickname can be an enjoyable activity, as can inventing unique names for the leadership roles you develop. In one CQI group in which we participated over a period of five years, a very dutiful woman agreed to act as convener/secretary for a year. Fearing that she would turn this role too into a drudging duty, we named her Queen of the group and pledged to serve her. The pleasure we all derived from this title lasted throughout the year and evoked some inspirational pieces of writing and meeting structures from her. At the end of the year, a man took over the role of convener—as it happens, a gay man. More gaiety followed, and soon we had all happily agreed that he, too, would reign as Queen. By the time the next man—this time straight—took over as convener, the title of Queen was once again inquired into, and once again proved resourceful enough to cover his case creatively as well!

We are not going to offer a series of predefined rules and guidelines for you to follow slavishly as you construct with a few others something like a CQI group, because to do so would obviously contradict the entire spirit of this process. Moreover, your own and your group's particular circumstances will alter what is practical and what is inspiring. On the other hand, we have found that *a sure recipe for failure in constructing CQI meetings is to approach them as totally unstructured rap sessions*. In such circumstances, the meetings are not very attractive to begin with to anyone who hopes to accomplish something real and useful. Furthermore, once the meetings begin, trivial conversation about the weather or the most recent football match is likely to drive out serious conversation.

So, we shall offer you a variety of ideas for structuring CQI meetings that can become resources for the structures that you and your group eventually construct together. Indeed, one of the central aspects of the ideas we shall be giving you is the notion of structures that are self-reforming. For example, you can organize your group's meetings in sequences of four-meeting cycles. Each successive meeting of a given cycle can focus on:

- Visioning
- Strategizing
- Implementing
- Assessing.

By the four titles alone, you can see that each new cycle of four meetings can begin with a revisioning and restructuring of the meetings based on the assessing that occurs at the end of the previous cycle of four meetings.

The first cycle of four meetings

During the first cycle of four meetings, group members can discuss the early chapters of this book together (e.g. reading about and beginning the action inquiry exercises described in Chapters 3 and 4 in preparation for the Implementing meeting).

Visioning

During the first Visioning meeting, group members can address together such questions as:

1. What is each person's long-term career vision, in the context of his or her vision of the good life? (The group can return to this topic in its second round of meetings, when group members have read Chapter 13 of this book, which offers a vision of the good life that you can test against your own.)
2. What is each person's short-term vision in his or her current job (or job search!) about the skills that need to be developed in order to become more effective?
3. What is each person's vision of action inquiry and CQI from his or her initial reading of this book or prior experience, and what initial criticisms does each person feel about the approach we offer here?
4. What is the vision and sense of commitment or scepticism each participant has with regard to this set of meetings on which the group is embarking?
5. What are some good analogies for the kind of activity that these meetings at their best represent?

Let us briefly offer three such analogies. Each deserves fuller discussion than we shall offer here, so your group may wish to elaborate on them. One analogy for these voluntary, CQI meetings is rehearsal for a theatrical production. What part is each person playing? How can each play his or her part better? Does the group need a different sort of character to make the play more interesting? Should members switch roles, or try out ways of acting that are opposite to their habitual manner? Would a change of scenery help? Who and how many feel empowered to interrupt the play (the rehearsal) to offer feedback and suggest starting over again?

A second analogy for these meetings can be World Cup football. World Cup football shows the importance of artful, accurate passing. Persons in meetings would be so much more effective if they recognized that each time they speak they are in effect receiving and passing the conversational ball. There are (virtually) no formal breaks in football, but there are many pauses and changes of pace in good football and good conversation. Can we take charge of the pace, or does the pace force us? With its blending of rugby, ballet and jujitsu, World Cup football comes as close to symbolizing the real-time power of balance in motion that we all blindly, haphazardly and ineffectually seek in our ongoing lives. In life and in conversation, as in World Cup football, genuine scores are few and far between, and scoring depends on a peculiar alchemy of vigilance, continual effort, skill honed to pure grace, rank opportunism, selfless teamwork and sheer accident. What rules changes would help to make soccer a game that men and women, skilled or unskilled, could play together in a way that was fun and challenging for each? What rules changes (or changes of implicit norms) will make your group meetings more enjoyable and more challenging 'games'?

A third analogy for your CQI meetings can be mountain climbing. What is the purpose towards which the group is aiming? What is the feeling of a 'climbing' conversation by contrast to a 'level' or 'downhill' conversation, and how can a group cultivate a steady, climbing pace? What equipment and provisions are necessary for the different kinds of climbs? How does one read the weather and the terrain and adjust to changing conditions?

All three of these analogies, and many others, can help group members envision together what their distinctive and shared purposes are.

Strategizing

At the second meeting of the first cycle—the Strategizing meeting—the following sorts of questions can be addressed:

1. What implicit or explicit strategies is each member currently following to achieve his or her long-term and short-term visions? Put differently, what developmental frame seems to each group member to describe him or her best, and can other members offer illustrations that confirm or disconfirm this tentative diagnosis?
2. What limitations do other members see in each member's strategies, and what alternatives can they suggest?
3. Based on the cases of Jennifer and Anthony in Chapter 2, what group leadership roles are different members willing to play in order to accelerate one another's learning within the group?

This last question encourages everyone in the group to participate in leading and restructuring the group's practices. A great many different leadership roles can be constructed and enacted, depending on members' preferences and developmental priorities. For example, you have probably served as the Strategizing leader (see description below) for the group during the first two meetings, and you may wish to continue in this role for the final meetings of the first cycle. Leadership roles can be traded or reconstructed (or reconfirmed) during the Strategizing meeting of each succeeding cycle.

In the context that we are suggesting here, the simplest set of four leadership roles corresponds directly with the four types of meeting. Thus:

- *The Visioning* (or revisioning) *leader* is responsible for introducing alternative visions or framings for action; for thinking 'outside the box'; for clowning and devil's advocacy; for introducing creative new ways of exploring topics (role playing, myth making, analogizing, meditating); for discussing the 'undiscussible'. . . .
- *The Strategizing* (or agenda) *leader* organizes and manages the group's meeting time, as is being discussed throughout this section. . . .
- *The Implementing* (or processing) *leader* pays special attention to how effectively members are speaking during the meetings (e.g. interweaving framing, advocacy, illustration, inquiry), how effectively they are exercising their leadership roles, and how effectively they are implementing their on-the-job action inquiry strategies; in addition, this leadership role models and encourages the offering of feedback to one another in a timely fashion during the meetings. . . .
- *The Assessing leader* develops measures that systematically test members' perceptions of one another; or their reaction

to each meeting; or their managerial stage of development; or their effectiveness in their new on-the-job initiatives, as perceived by their colleagues. In addition, this leadership role organizes part of the Assessing meeting of each cycle in order to present, and generate discussion about, the resulting data. . . .

As we have said above, these are only four of many possible leadership roles. If the group with whom you are working consists of your subordinates in an ongoing work group, some members can become leaders for specific projects that involve subgroups of the entire group, or their subordinates.

Implementing

At the third meeting of the first cycle—the Implementing meeting—the following sorts of questions can be addressed:

1. In what ways does each member regard himself or herself as acting differently at work or in general because of this group's meetings? What obstacles are members encountering in their efforts to experiment with new behaviour both in the group and outside it?
2. What is each member's experience in trying the experiments proposed in Chapter 4 of this book?
3. What feedback do members have about one another's behaviour and enactment of their leadership roles in this group to date?

In addition, members can role play one another's difficult on-the-job dilemmas. It is often fun and instructive for the member presenting the dilemma to role play his or her primary 'antagonist' in the situation, while several other members take turns experimenting with alternative strategies for acting more effectively in the role of the person who presented the dilemma in the first place.

The Implementing leader may wish to record on tape parts of your meetings and then play back short sections at the Implementing meeting so that members can really hear themselves speaking, and so that the group can focus on actions that seem to have been especially effective or ineffective, analyse them together, role play new actions, and then become more vigilant about that type of speaking in the future.

Assessing

The Assessing meeting of each cycle is as straightforward as the word sounds. It concerns questions of *how* to assess one's progress in understanding and implementing action inquiry and CQI and of *how much* improvement one has actually made during the period assessed. We suggested above some of the different types of measures a group may use in describing the Assessing leader's role. The 'trick' here is that the Assessing leader has a relatively low profile role during the first three group meetings of each cycle, but a relatively high responsibility for doing some 'homework' between meetings, in order to present the group with some measures to choose among, helping the group to commit to measures that will be truly useful. The Assessing leader also needs to analyse the data generated and think carefully about how feedback on the measures can be presented at the Assessing meeting in a way that leads to insightful conversation and future payoffs.

In general, it is best to start by collecting and feeding back data that is close to members' direct experiences and not comparative. From this point of view, 'Who was most effective during the first three meetings?' is not an appropriate question initially, since it requires high levels of inference and is comparative. By contrast, asking each group member to describe as concretely as possible two ways in which each group member has been effective and two ways in which each group member has been ineffective can provide useful feedback to each member and can lead directly to new quality improvement goals. An enjoyable question is: 'What kind of animal does each group member remind you of?'—with an illustration to support the answer.

Whatever the measures show, the point is not to prove anything to anyone, but rather to create fruitful conversation. If most people agree that Tim is quiet and mouse-like, this does not prove that Tim is too quiet. It simply shows that everyone else in the group perceives him that way. This properly raises a number of questions. Does Tim think he is 'too quiet'? Is he being more quiet than usual? Does hearing this feedback motivate Tim to want to contribute more? And so on.

Assessment measures should also be connected to group goals and group member goals. Some assessment questions can relate to the particular quality improvement goals of each member. If the group is a work group, then the Assessing meeting provides opportunities to amend the current appraisal and reward systems that the work group has been using.

Assessing also includes more than measuring. It can include the choice of several illustrations from the group's early meetings to convey the overall atmosphere that is developing in the group. Or, each member can be asked what metaphor best captures his or her overall feeling about the group ('These meetings are like fireworks', or 'This group labours like a great sea turtle crawling up on a beach to lay her eggs'). A well-functioning group would be one where the kind of excitement about trying new behaviour expressed by Joanne and Art in Chapter 5 would be generated.

In later cycles, the group may wish to experiment with more comparative data, in addition to the concrete data just described. For example, the Assessing leader may wish to propose something like the Overall Group Contribution Assessment form shown on page 105.

The comparative nature of this sort of measure is obviously potentially more confronting of group members. If handled with continuing action inquiry, such confronting information can motivate additional insight and learning. It also provides good practice for handling performance appraisal meetings at work, which often include a comparative element ('Why did Susan get promoted instead of me?').

As the foregoing possible scenarios for each of the first four meetings hopefully illustrate, the different meetings at best take on significantly different flavours and cadences. Also, the different leadership roles cultivate significantly different leadership skills. The bare outline of possible questions and activities that we have offered is meant to stimulate your imagination rather than to constrain your actions. There is a great deal of room for improvisation in this structure. For example, moving through all four types of activities may require more than the four meetings suggested.

The proposed structure also introduces the likelihood of tension at times—tension between the leadership initiatives of different members, as well as, within each member, tension between participating in the current topic of discussion and remembering his or her leadership responsibility. Just as the action inquiry exercises in Chapter 4 introduced a kind of jogging that jogs one's awareness, so this group structure is meant to create an awareness-awakening environment.

We suggest that you plan to hold meetings once every two or three weeks. More frequent meetings too easily become a burden and do not allow enough time for on-the-job experiments in between. Less frequent meetings too easily result in a loss of momentum and continuity. If your group consists of six persons, you may want to suggest that

Overall Group Contribution Assessment

This form asks you to rank order group members' contribution over the prior three meetings to the objectives of the group, on several dimensions.

   The number 1 represents the most positive possible contribution on each dimension (no one may merit that); the number 18 represents the most negative possible contribution (again, no one may merit that). No ties are allowed (though the averaging of everyone's ratings may result in ties or near ties). *Include yourself in the ranking* and *circle your name* (this permits you to learn during the feedback how closely aligned your self-perception is to others' perceptions of you).

   How you cluster the group as a whole and how large the gaps are that you leave between particular rankings will offer additional information on how you have perceived the group's overall effectiveness and the relative effectiveness of different members.

Leadership initiatives	*Feedback about in-group action*	*Useful stories/ job advice*	*Experiments with new behaviour*
1	1	1	1
2	2	2	2
3	3	3	3
4	4	4	4
5	5	5	5
6	6	6	6
7	7	7	7
8	8	8	8
9	9	9	9
10	10	10	10
11	11	11	11
12	12	12	12
13	13	13	13
14	14	14	14
15	15	15	15
16	16	16	16
17	17	17	17
18	18	18	18

subgroups of three have lunch at least once between each of the group meetings. These luncheon meetings can serve as occasions for more in-depth consulting to one another around possible creative action inquiry initiatives on the job or with friends.

The second cycle of four meetings

The next set of four meetings we leave open to your design, or the design of the new Strategizing leader. In general, these four meetings may follow specific, three-month action projects by each member through the four phases. For some members, this action project may already be the attempt to start their own set of CQI meetings. At the same time, or alternatively, each member can commit to experimenting with very specific types of behaviour at the meetings themselves (e.g. someone who receives the feedback that he or she is experienced as loud and overbearing may experiment with discovering gentle, quiet actions that are effective).

In all these meetings, and in further cycles of meetings, you are practising action inquiry in a new dimension. No longer just a self-improvement effort, your action inquiry practice now contributes to the improvement of others, as theirs does to you. You and they are taking responsibility for the group's development. Now CQI gains impetus and power by becoming the shared purpose of a group. Groups are the 'building blocks' of organizations and are themselves small-scale organizations. Thus you have begun to move quality improvement beyond individual scope towards organizational scope. In the next chapter, we address the parallelism between personal and organizational development.

As you continue reading into the following chapters, you will find additional material for further cycles of these CQI meetings. For example, as this book gradually shifts focus again from action inquiry at the scale of group leadership and group development to action inquiry at the scale of organizational leadership and development, so too can the focus of your CQI group meetings shift from the individual scale through the group scale to the organizational scale. In Appendix A we have provided further action inquiry exercises (and a description of one group's experiences in starting up a CQI group); thus, in short, there are plenty of action inquiry exercises to perform.

In fact, probably only a small minority of our readers were inspired and found the time right to start such a CQI group as soon as they began reading this chapter. Some additional percentage of you is feeling appropriately informed about and challenged by this whole arena of exercise and self-development now as you complete the chapter and have a somewhat clearer picture of where such exercising can lead. Perhaps you will start a CQI group during the next month.

Many of you, however, are probably still weighing whether it is worth the effort to engage in this sort of work and play. By all means, go ahead with your reading, if that is your preferred level of engagement at the moment. We simply invite you not to forget that, after you finish your reading, you can cycle back through the book and try the personal exercises suggested in Chapter 4 and the group level exercises suggested in this chapter.

Constructing effective personal action and effective groups is a very high form of artistry, which, like all artistry, requires unending practice before it becomes 'natural' and before one becomes spontaneously creative in that art form. Good luck!!!

8 Developing a learning organization

One way to characterize what we have begun to explore together in the last chapter is to say that we are beginning to practise how to create a learning organization.

Of course, the word 'organization' is a little overblown for the small groups formed to encourage the practice of continual quality improvement (CQI) that we have just been discussing, but we should remember that one of the larger organizations in the world began from just such humble beginnings. We are referring to Alcoholics Anonymous and all the other 12-step groups that the AA approach has since spawned. Alcoholics Anonymous began as a conversation between two persons who wished to change their practice.

Alcoholics Anonymous is a learning organization in the sense that it supports individual persons in reforming their lives when they are almost hopelessly addicted. Alcoholics Anonymous is a good example of a learning organization, in that it demonstrates how eager the individual member must be for transformation in order for transformational and developmental change to occur. Granted, we cannot directly generalize from Alcoholics Anonymous to the organizational situations most of us inhabit at work and in our leisure. We rarely inhabit organizations in which everyone shares the same intense motivation to transform in a particular direction, and in which there is no other order of business but personal transformation.

We also recognize that Alcoholics Anonymous is not focused on *organizational* learning and transformation—on creating a learning organization—but rather on *individual* learning and transformation. But, for our present purposes, the example of Alcoholics Anonymous is very useful as a pointer in the direction of a kind of organizing that encourages both personal and organizational transformations along the path towards CQI and a learning organization.

When we first introduced the process of action inquiry at

the personal level, we described it primarily as a manner of speaking with others that integrated *framing, advocacy, illustration* and *inquiry*. When we first introduced the process of action inquiry at the group level in the previous chapter, we spoke of it in parallel terms as a process of integrating *visioning, strategizing, implementing* and *assessing*.

As we continued to explore action inquiry at the personal level, we examined the transformational learning that can occur as persons move through developmental stages towards an action inquiry that is increasingly all-encompassing. Again paralleling that movement, we present in this chapter a way of understanding organizational development as a sequence of stages. A given stage may characterize a given meeting or project, or a whole organization over many years. Thus, you can become as subtle as you wish in analysing overlapping and mutually influencing developmental processes in your organization. Within the organization's overall frame, particular projects or divisions may represent leading or lagging developmental tendencies. Similarly, the CQI group that you start may transform from one stage to another after a single meeting, or after an initial cycle of four meetings.

As a group or organization evolves towards the later stages it increasingly approaches the true character of a learning organization. And, as our later illustrations of organizational transformations will show, the more the transformational process from one stage to another is structured like a temporary learning organization, and the more it encourages the brief recapitulation of the early stages of development as substages within that transformation, the more likely it becomes that a genuine and successful frame-change will occur for the organization.

As Table 8.1 shows, these two stage theories of development at the individual and the organizational scale are directly analogous to one another. (You will note that we show an early childhood stage—the Impulsive stage—and a late adulthood stage—the Ironist stage. We made little mention of these stages in earlier chapters, since we found no managers in our large samples at either of these stages.)

Table 8.2 describes the unique characteristics of each stage of organizational development in a little more detail. We shall offer a few comments on each stage, in order to highlight the personal–organizational parallels in Table 8.1. We shall then give some concrete illustrations of particular meetings and of whole organizations moving from one stage to another. Organizations very often halt along the path to

Table 8.1   Parallels between personal and organizational stages of development[1]

Stage	Personal development	Organizational development
1	*Impulsive* Impulses rule reflexes	*Conception* Dreams about creating a new organization
2	*Opportunist* Needs rule impulses	*Investments* Spiritual, social network and financial investments
3	*Diplomat* Norms rule needs	*Incorporation* Products or services actually rendered
4	*Technician* Craft logic rules norms	*Experiments* Alternative strategies and structures tested
5	*Achiever* System effectiveness rules craft logic	*Systematic Productivity* Single structure/strategy institutionalized
6	*Strategist* Self-amending principle rules system	*Collaborative Inquiry* Self-amending structure to match dream/mission
7	*Magician/Witch/Clown* Process (interplay of principle/action) rules principle	*Foundational Community* Structure fails, spirit sustains
8	*Ironist* Intersystemic development rules process	*Liberating Disciplines* Widen members' awareness of incongruities among mission/ strategy/operations/outcomes and skill at generating organizational learning

Source: W. Torbert and D. Fisher (1992) 'Autobiographical awareness as a catalyst for managerial and organizational development', *Management Education and Development* **23** (3), 184–98. Reprinted by permission of the publisher.

becoming learning organizations when they reach what could be frame-changing opportunities and challenges. Instead of transforming, they defend their current culture and structure and tend to rigidify. Hence, it is important to get a feel for the sorts of leaderly initiatives that can generate organizational transformation.

Table 8.2 Characteristics of each stage of organizational development[2]

Stage	Name	Characteristics
1	Conception	Dreams, visions, informal conversations about creating something new to fill need not now adequately addressed; interplay among multiple 'parents'; working models, prototypes, related projects, or business plans developed; critical issues—timeliness and mythic proportions of vision
2	Investments	'Champions' commit to creating organization; early relationship-building among future stakeholders; peer networks and parent institutions make spiritual, structural, financial commitments to nurture; critical issues—authenticity and reliability of commitments; financial investment appropriately subordinated to structural and spiritual investments
3	Incorporation	Products or services produced; recognizable physical setting, tasks and roles delineated; goals and operating staff chosen; critical issues—display of persistence in the face of threat; maintaining or recreating consistency between original dream and actual organizational arrangements
4	Experiments	Alternative administrative, production, selection, reward, financial, marketing and political strategies practised, tested in operation and reformed in rapid succession; critical issues—truly experimenting—taking disciplined stabs in the dark—rather than merely trying one or two preconceived alternatives; finding a viable, lasting combination of strategy and structure for the following stage
5	Systematic Productivity	Attention legitimately focused only on systematic procedures for accomplishing the predefined task; standards, structures, roles taken for granted as given, usually in deductive, pyramidal terms; marketability or political viability of product or service, as measured in quantifiable terms the overriding criterion of success; reality usually conceived in dichotomous, competitive terms— win/lose, rational/emotional, leader/follower; critical issue: whether organization 'remembers' analogical concerns about congruity from mission to strategy to operations to outcomes during this period of emphasis on deductive systems
6	Collaborative Inquiry	Explicit, shared reflection about corporate mission; open interpersonal relations with disclosure, support and confrontation of apparent value differences; systematic personal and corporate performance appraisal on multiple indexes; creative resolution of paradoxes—inquiry/ productivity, freedom/control, quality/quantity; interactive development of unique, self-amending structures appropriate for this particular organization at this particular historical moment

The parallelism between personal and organizational development

It is not immediately obvious just how the individual stages in Table 8.1 parallel the organizational stages. Let us start with a brief comment on the parallelism between the *Impulsive* stage of personal development and the *Conception* stage of organizational development. Just as very young children are highly imaginative and express many impulses (e.g. to become an artist, or a nurse, or a professional athlete) that they do not necessarily pursue in later life, so adults frequently fantasize with friends about organizations they would like to create (e.g. to market a baby stroller that could be folded up and would have made today's visit to the city easier), but seldom follow up. In retrospect, when one in every ten thousand or so such conversations eventually evolves into a major organization, as Alcoholics Anonymous did, and as the idea to create a fold-up baby stroller did, the founding of the organization can be traced back to such incidental or passionate or calculating conversations.

The parallelism between the next three stages of personal and organizational development is less obvious. When we described the Opportunist, the Diplomat and the Technician in Chapter 5, we were not describing children in the normal process of development, but rather adults in organizations who are still motivated by early stage logics. Therefore, we can see the rigidities and limitations in their effectiveness quite easily. By contrast, when we discuss organizations at these three early stages (*Investments, Incorporation, Experiments*) in this chapter, we shall describe them in their natural developmental process (i.e. in their 'childhood') at those stages, so the constructiveness of that stage will be more obvious than its shortcomings (see Table 8.2). Let us now, however, describe the similarities between persons and organizations at each stage. Both the person at the Opportunist stage and the organization at the Investments stage seek resources from the environment and capabilities with which to manipulate the environment. At best, an 8–12-year-old child who is at the Opportunistic stage has parents who are making inspirational and social network investments on his or her behalf (e.g. offering the child an integrative faith of some kind and exposure to good teachers). Similarly, wise organizational founders and wise venture capitalists will be concerned with the inspirational resonance and profundity of the organization's mission and mentors, as well as the social, professional and business alliances that can support the organization during its Investments stage. On the other hand, if the organizational founders are themselves still arrested at the Opportunist stage of development, they will act as though tangible financial resources are the only significant resource needed. The organization may appear very successful in terms of financial backing in the short term, but the lack of network resources and inspiration will result in lower commitment by all stakeholders and will stunt its development in the longer term.

Given some resources and capacities to work with, a person at the Diplomat stage during the early teenage years and an organization at the Incorporation stage are both learning how to operate successfully according to the rules of their social milieux (which we call 'peer groups' in the case of teenagers and 'markets' in the case of for-profit companies). In both cases, there are many difficult moments, and neither the young teenager nor the young company may have the persistence to succeed. Or, both may lose their 'honour' (sense of self-respect based on loyalty to a constructive mission) in their eagerness to conform to the demands of their milieux.

Failure to meet the demands of the larger milieux may result in a person's life-long membership in a semi-illegitimate, dependent underclass. In the case of an organization, failure usually means outright economic failure or a very contingent survival in a small local niche. Success in meeting the demands of the milieu at the price of one's 'honour' also has a significant dark side: it makes development to further stages much less likely.

Persons who are able to 'break the mould' of their immediate social milieux begin to seek out something more consistent to subordinate themselves to than the helter-skelter, conflicting demands of the others about them. They are seeking a more purposive way of organizing their life and a more objective way of measuring their relative success at doing so. The many different human activities to which one may apprentice oneself, which have craft logics, craft masters and (relatively) objective methods of measuring success, suggest themselves. The teenager who says, 'I like track better than soccer because in track you are measured by your actual time in the event, whereas in soccer it's whether the coach likes you' is expressing a growing attraction to the Technician stage logic of doing well in terms of objectively measured standards and rejection of the Diplomat stage logic of doing well those things that will gain another person's approval. (Of course, the statement may also contain a significant degree of defensiveness and unfairness to the soccer coach.)

In any event, this movement from Diplomat to Technician

stage logic parallels an organization's movement from Incorporation to Experiments. The Technician's experiments towards excellence in any given craft involve a relatively narrow-gauged series of 'stabs in the dark'. An organization transforming towards the Experiments stage at best conducts such experiments in all realms of its business, from the way in which it conducts its accounting (typically moving from the cash to the accrual method and from manual, paper records to computer systems) to the very fact of engaging in proactive marketing rather than simply servicing clients who come through the door.

These brief and relatively abstract portraits begin to suggest the parallelism that exists between the two models of development.

Organizing business meetings with a sensitivity to developmental process

Having developed a little feel for the possible parallelism of the individual and organizational scales of development, we can now get a glimpse of how the social process in which we are engaged comes into focus once we apply developmental theory to all scales of social development. In principle, we can view each new project or new product, each new team or task force, each new agenda item, meeting or series of meetings as a developmental process. When we try to do this, we quickly realize two things: first, that there are multiple developmental processes which influence one another, either interrupting, inhibiting or encouraging development at the scale we have originally focused on; and second, that human and social development does not proceed along the smooth path that Table 8.1 implicitly suggests. Both of these facts make observing and encouraging development towards CQI and a learning organization more difficult. Both of these facts also make the theory seem much more realistic.

Let us offer a brief example of an executive who, without ever having thought of himself as using developmental theory, in fact manages meetings in a manner that parallels the early stages of organizational development we have just been reviewing.

This senior vice-president of a Fortune 100 electronics firm has an undergraduate mathematics background, with an interest in the Pythagorean theory of the octave as the organizing structure for colour (the seven colours of the rainbow), for sound (the musical octave), and for human activities such as meetings. Of business meetings, he says (with our organizational stage names in parentheses):

The first note 'do' is the leader's vision for the whole meeting. It has to be both crisp and inspiring. It's got to surprise people just a little—jog them awake, make them reconsider what they came in prepared to do. [*Conception*—generating a surprisingly creative new vision]

'Re' is the first response, the first chorus from the group. The leader has got to allow for this if he wants a creative, committed meeting. How he choreographs that first response determines how far the meeting can go. [*Investments*—helping others to join and own the issue]

'Mi' is the first concrete decision of the meeting. If it's taken early on and makes sense to everyone, there's a general loosening up, and the rest of the meeting is likely to fly. [*Incorporation*—something being produced; the vision becoming real]

A lot of meetings end there, but if you want to go further, you've got to realize there's a big interval between 'mi' and 'fa'. The leader can best bridge this interval with a new structure for the meeting. 'Fa' is primarily the group's note again, so the leader's structure should be something that brings out the chorus, something like breaking into subgroups on different issues. [*Experiments*—exploration and testing of many implications of the vision] (*He goes on to discuss the rest of the 'meeting octave'.*)

. . . But the actual meeting can also be viewed as the middle part of the octave ('fa', 'sol', 'la') between the two intervals. In this larger perspective, the pre-meeting preparation is the first part of the octave and the post-meeting follow-up is the final part.[3]

This final paragraph of the executive's vision of how meetings are best conducted points to the very notion of overlapping or nested developmental processes that we introduced above. You are welcome to compare back and forth between Table 8.2 and the executive's description of each musical note in a well-run meeting to see the degree to which they parallel one another. But our point is less that there is a perfectly precise parallel, and more that this illustration brings to life the general sense of how a meeting can be viewed developmentally (not to mention how much more interesting and productive business meetings in general would be if more executives were this imaginative in managing them!). Our point is also to give you further support in imagining how to organize the small meetings for practising CQI that you may be starting since reading the previous chapter.

In this spirit, and to continue the exercise of imagining how to 'see' developmental theory at work on different scales of social organizing, we present in Table 8.3 a guide that one senior management team uses to help its members to manage particular agenda items at their senior management meetings (each item is typically scheduled for half an hour or 45 minutes). This guide is *not* explicitly modelled on developmental theory, and the individual stages of development are therefore not as obvious as in the previous example. But the guide does use the *framing/advocating/illustrating/inquiring* language introduced in earlier chapters, and you should be able to follow a general developmental path in the sequence of handling a particular agenda item.

Table 8.3   Agenda item management at meetings

When you are preparing and presenting particular agenda items at senior management meetings, consider the following steps:

1. Divide the time between a diverging, including period and a converging, concluding period.

2. The diverging period will typically include the following sub-steps:
   (a) framing the overall flow of activity you intend for this period and framing what the issue is;
   (b) testing/inquiring whether this way of framing meets others' expectations and the demands of the issue;
   (c) presenting your advocacies and illustrations about what to do;
   (d) eliciting others' counter-advocacies and illustrations.

3. The converging period will typically include the following sub-steps:
   (a) framing the kind of decision necessary and the decision-making process you propose;
   (b) testing/inquiring whether this sounds appropriate or anyone has an alternative procedure to suggest;
   (c) poll the group quickly, making clear this is not a vote, but is for information purposes;
   (d) test with members who are going to be critical to the implementation if they are on board or have any amendments;
   (e) attempt to state a consensus of the group and test whether everyone can buy in;
   (f) explicitly develop an assessment process that someone not in agreement can implement, in order to bring the issue back for reconsideration if the current solution is not working;
   (g) test for CEO's buy-in, or wish to impose his/her solution;
   (h) have formal vote if consensus is not forthcoming.

4. Check proposed procedure with the relevant agenda advocate.

5. Possibly seek coaching from CEO or consultant prior to meeting.

Can you follow the stages of development in the foregoing agenda item management process shown in Table 8.3? Step 1 provides the overall Conception for the manager using the guide, and step 2(a) represents the Conception stage of the given agenda item during a meeting. Step 2(b) addresses the question of how to gain other members' Investments. Steps 2(c) and 2(d) attempt to develop a specific solution or procedure with regard to the agenda item—the Incorporation stage. Then, steps 3(a), 3(b), 3(c), and 3(d) represent Experiments around reaching a decision. Steps 3(e), 3(g), and/or 3(h) get the job done—*Systematic Productivity*. And finally, Steps 3f, 4 and 5 look forward to a process of *Collaborative Inquiry* which may restructure the approach and the decision. The fact that step 3(f) is slightly out of sequence suggests that it may function more effectively as the final step.

From Incorporation to Experiments Let us now change step again and look more closely at two examples of whole organizations moving from one stage to the next. Each example is intended to illustrate how the consultant who intervenes creates a temporary learning organization with a great deal of feedback and creative decision making, as a vehicle for encouraging organizational transformation and reframing. Each example is also intended to illustrate how each later developmental logic comes progressively closer to institutionalizing CQI and to establishing a learning organization that challenges and transforms not only its members' assumptions, logics and practices, but also the organization's systems, structures and standard operating procedures. However, since the transitions we illustrate in this chapter do not go beyond Systematic Productivity, the organizations we present here will not reach the stage of explicitly and self-consciously encouraging CQI. Such explicit and self-conscious work typically begins during the transition from the Systematic Productivity stage to the Collaborative Inquiry stage, a transition to which we devote the next two chapters.

Like the other brief cases presented in this chapter, this one is meant to help you to imagine, as you think about your company or department or work team, what stage of development currently characterizes it, and what kind of sustained action commitments may be warranted to help your organization to transform.

Let us begin here with an organization that is, from our point of view, undergoing the transition from Incorporation to Experiments. Before you begin reading this case, take another look at Table 8.2 to remind yourself of the characteristics of the Experiments stage of organizational development. Then see if you recognize these elements in the case as you read it.

The case[4]
A small, but rapidly growing company has recently become geographically dispersed because of two acquisitions of other small companies by its president. The president asks a consultant to design a two-day quarterly retreat for the 40 managers who constitute the top three layers of management in the organization. 'The people equation is the most difficult, recurrent, and intractable issue', says the president, 'and we need our managers to have new core competences that include recognizing and taking responsibility for the impact their actions have on one another and for the organizational values that their actions are creating.' The president proposes a lecture/discussion of the consultant's theory of managerial and organizational development and some skill-building sessions.

The consultant interviews six members of the organization by phone and returns to the president with a plan for the two days that interweaves managerial and organizational learning in ways which, if successful, will directly transform the organization. Instead of pure skill-building sessions, the consultant proposes (and the president agrees after some concern about the risks) that the staff meet in four cross-functional/cross-locational groups of ten to develop new ways of organizing in the four areas that the interviews have indicated are of greatest concern: (1) budget development; (2) recruiting and training; (3) internal communications; and (4) meeting management. Senior management is asked to be prepared to make binding decisions with regard to the proposals before the end of the retreat (and such decisions are in fact made at the actual retreat). Thus are inquiry and productive action integrated at the retreat. We can also see that this procedure will result in organizational learning and change. The meeting processes arranged for the retreat and described below show how individual, managerial learning is interwoven with organizational learning.

Each of the groups of ten is to be managed through five leadership roles, and each leadership role will be held by two members. The two persons with the most influence over the ultimate implementation of any changes in that area serve in the 'Expert and follow-through' leadership role. The other four leadership roles are 'meeting leader', 'decision clarifier and codifier', 'process facilitator' and 'clown' (whose express function is to make 'outside the box' comments, use humour, and turn suggestions inside-out in order to see whether they are thereby improved). Members are to be assigned roles that their fellow group members judge are most developmentally provocative for them. (For example, the president later finds himself assigned a 'clown' role, and plays it so well that several extravagant stories about his performance quickly make the rounds!)

Without reproducing here any of the detailed supports provided, the schedule in outline calls for an initial presentation/discussion, led by the consultant, that connects the managerial and organizational development theory presented in this book to the history and dilemmas of the organization. The consultant suggests that the three independent sites have been operating at the Incorporation stage, and that the new multi-site company will require a frame-change and a lot of experimenting on everyone's part, such as this retreat as a whole involves.

Next, the conference splits into the four topic areas. In each case, one subgroup of five is to develop a set of proposals in one hour, while the other subgroup of five observes their role-mates and gives five minutes of feedback at the end of the first half hour and again at the end of the hour. After a short break, the observers and the actors switch roles, with the same feedback arrangements, and the new actors produce a *different* set of proposals for the same concern (e.g. budget development). After another short break, the entire group of ten develops an agreed-upon proposal. These organizing processes provide individual managers with an unusual amount of immediate feedback about their leadership choices, while at the same time increase the likelihood that divergent views on the organizational issues are developed, considered seriously, and resolved.

The next morning, each of the four groups makes ten-minute presentations to the other 30 managers, followed by five minutes of discussion, concluded with written feedback from all 30. The groups are given half an hour to digest the feedback they have received. The entire group then reconvenes for two-minute comments by their (senior management) 'follow-through' leaders on how their proposals have been influenced by the feedback and what they are committing to do, beginning the following day, in the office. The consultant next leads a discussion debriefing the entire exercise and then leaves the room while the management group develops feedback for him.

At the end of the actual meeting, the feedback to the consultant included suggestions such as 'needed more leadership for group assignments at outset', as well as positive comments such as 'great to see branch participation without corporate interference', 'meetings in this organization will never be the same again', and 'progression of programme was great and lack of structure strengthened learning'. On a scale of 1–7 (where 1 meant 'time wasted', 4 meant 'as good as an average quarterly retreat', and 7 meant 'best quarterly retreat ever'), the 40 participants rated this retreat 6.5 on average. Major changes in all four areas of concern followed.

Comment

As you can probably see without any additional explanation, almost every activity at the retreat represented Experiments stage organizing on the part of the participants. Everyone experimented with new meeting roles, none more so than the president in his clown role. Everyone experimented a great deal with giving and receiving feedback, from the determination of what role each was to play through the feedback to the consultant at the end. Moreover, all four efforts to create new organizational structures in the four areas of concern represented disciplined stabs in the dark. The methods of rapid group decision making were new to the organization as well.

What may be less obvious is that the organizational characteristics of the retreat as a whole represent a distinctive 'logic of practice' that is more ironic and subtle than the Experiments stage logic. You may have noted that the structure for the retreat was quite complex, yet the participants claimed at the end that 'the lack of structure strengthened learning'. This kind of paradoxical structure, which widens rather than restricts participants' freedom of action, is called 'liberating structure' or 'liberating disciplines'. You will see that 'Liberating Disciplines' is shown at the bottom of Table 8.1 as the most advanced form of organizing we can imagine. Neither it nor the prior stage of organizing, 'Foundational Community', is described in Table 8.2 because they are so uncommon. We shall not consider 'Foundational Community' in detail until Chapter 12, and we shall introduce 'Liberating Disciplines' in Appendix B. But you now have one small, time-limited example of an organization that simultaneously learns *and* produces results *and* generates personal learning by its members—*all at the same time.* Such an organization, and only such an organization, truly deserves to be called a 'learning organization'. Our example suggests that an invited consulting intervention is more likely to generate an organizational transformation to the degree that the consulting intervention itself represents a temporary, late-stage learning organization.

From Experiments to Systematic Productivity

Now let us turn to an example of an organization transforming from the Experiments stage to the Systematic Productivity stage. Again, we shall have the opportunity to glimpse an invited consulting intervention structured and enacted in a late-stage, learning organization manner. Before reading the case, look again at the descriptions of the stages of development in Table 8.2. Prepare yourself to look for evidence of this organization's movement from Experiments to Systematic Productivity, but this time be ready to watch the developmental unfolding of the transformation process, led by a consultant and an executive vice-president. Notice how this process became a temporary learning organization, recapitulating the early stages of development *en route* towards helping the organization change its overall frame.

The case
This company has become quite complex in terms of legal structure during its Experiments stage, in an effort to maximize the entrepreneurial freedom and initiative of every member of its senior management. As a result, the corporate structure shows a not-for-profit parent company and an umbrella for-profit subsidiary containing seven subsidiary companies. Each of the seven vice-presidents of the for-profit company serves as president of one of the subsidiary companies. Each subsidiary president has developed his own profit-sharing formula with the umbrella company, based on whatever chips he has to work with and hard bargaining. Each such bargain is viewed as relatively illegitimate by other members of the senior management 'team'. The vice-president and chief financial officer of the umbrella for-profit company is the only woman among the ten senior managers, the only person who is widely trusted, and the only person who is not president of a separate entity.

This jerry-built structure that reinforces cowboy individualism rather than developing any coordination or team spirit is outflanked, in a desperation move, by the president of the umbrella for-profit, who negotiates the 50 per cent sale of the whole company in order to raise new and absolutely necessary capital. The new 50 per cent partners agree to grant the company operating freedom, but demand careful accounting of revenues and costs and a return on their investment proportionate to the net revenues of each subsidiary. This apparently minor demand, along with the new capital controlled by the president of the umbrella for-profit, gives him new forms of effective control over the presidents of the subsidiaries. But it simultaneously increases their distrust of him.

A consultant who works with the developmental theory presented in this book is hired to assist the senior team in a retreat which is explicitly intended to restructure the company internally to fit its new ownership status and capital structure. From the first luncheon with the entire senior management to determine whether every member can accept the consultant, the consultant is aware of the high level of tension and distrust. One member recommends that the consultant pay for the opportunity to work with the group, rather than being paid, since he has not worked in this industry before and will therefore be learning. The consultant earns a round of laughter by parrying with the comment that he thought the mark of a good consultant was how much he can charge to learn. After a slight pause, he continues by saying nonchalantly that at least he has learned how to talk to more than one person at a time without causing instant distrust—a trick which he understands most of them have not yet mastered. This generates another round of laughter, and the consultant is hired.

The consultant proposes that he begin with a round of one-on-one interviews, followed by feedback from him to each individual. At the retreat, each member of senior management will be asked to discuss the feedback he or she has received and to set two goals for personal behaviour change, before restructuring of the organization is discussed.

The interviews with, and feedback to, each individual permit the consultant to develop some trust with all the members, while simultaneously letting them know how others view them and where there is collective agreement about the future of the organization, without allowing any dysfunctional group dynamics to occur. It is during these interviews that the consultant begins to see that the chief financial officer is the person with the best relationships in the group and the one who focuses most impartially on the welfare of the organization as a whole. During the feedback to individuals, he explores how willing each member is to acknowledge others' issues with him and to set significant personal change goals which they will share with the group as a whole. He also explores how willing all are to cede some of their autonomy to a more centralized organizational structure, characteristic of the Systematic Productivity stage of organizing.

In particular, the consultant probes members' reactions to the suggestion (which he says emerged from the initial interviews) that the chief financial officer be promoted to executive vice-president of the umbrella for-profit corporation. This suggestion is widely agreed to, either because persons genuinely trust her and respect her competence, or because they see her as a buffer between themselves and the president of the umbrella corporation.

During the first day, the retreat is highlighted by astonishingly revealing comments from each member, along with commitments to change aspects of behaviour which others would never have predicted they would acknowledge, much less change. This only happens, however, after the consultant is initially challenged about why the group should start with 'touchy–feely' behavioural issues before dealing with the 'infinitely more important' structural and financial issues. The consultant responds that the group is, of course, free to redesign the retreat as it wishes and that he would not usually lead with such a personal activity, but trust in the group is so low that he is personally convinced that no lasting progress can be made on the 'objective' issues without a new kind of spiritual investment by each member. This challenge and response seems to bring the stakes into focus for everyone.

During the second day, the retreat is highlighted by a series of consensual agreements. The first is to promote the chief financial officer to executive vice-president. The second is to centralize accounting and budgeting. The third, which provokes the longest argument, is to dispense with the separate stationery that has highlighted the president of each subsidiary and to substitute a single version of corporate stationery that lists all the vice-presidents on the team as, first, senior vice-presidents of the umbrella for-profit and, only secondly, as presidents of their own subsidiaries.

It is difficult to stress strongly enough how essential the new executive vice-president's overall style and specific actions are to the success of this day and the later success of the reformed company. As soon as she receives her mandate from the group, she proposes the importance of centralizing accounting and finances. Because of her past record of trustworthiness, reasonableness and competence, the group comes to agreement on this without undue difficulty. Then, when the stationery issue becomes divisive, she adroitly highlights what an important symbolic issue it is and says that she views the decision as a vote of confidence or no-confidence in her ability to make the newly centralized organization work.

The consultant continues in an occasional coaching relationship to the new executive vice-president. Six months later, the consultant meets with her and the senior vice-presidents for a one day retreat. Three months after that the senior vice-president who had been least willing to accept the leadership of the executive vice-president takes a position with another company. She, in turn, takes over the presidency of his subsidiary as well as continuing to serve as executive vice-president of the umbrella for-profit.

In twenty-four months, the organization has generated enough net revenues to be able to buy itself back from its 50 per cent partners, and the president of the umbrella for-profit and the executive vice-president have married one another.

Comment

In this case, we see that each subsidiary corporation, true to the Experiments stage, had become a distinct, almost completely decentralized experiment, with very little trust or cooperation between the parts. So little trust or cooperation, in fact, that the consultant chooses to maintain the decentralization in the early phase of his relationship to the company, while he builds trust with individuals and discovers the one member with good enough relationships to serve as the hub of the more centralized organization needed for the Systematic Productivity stage. So little trust and cooperation, in fact, that the consultant designs a retreat format that asks each person to offer a gift to the group (their willingness to make a behavioural change) before the group tries to make any collective decisions. The consultant puts heavy emphasis on sharing the developmental theory as a new vision (recapitulating Conception) of what the next stage in this company's history ought to be, and in particular to legitimize the notion of greater corporate centralization that has previously been anathema to virtually all the members. The consultant also puts heavy emphasis on the inspirational gifts (recapitulating Investments) that members need to offer (in this case, each member's commitment to a behavioural change), in order to develop the trust necessary for more interdependent work. Finally, the consultant puts heavy reliance on creating a very specific structure with a heavy reliance on one person (thereby recapitulating Incorporation as a substage of the organization's transformation). The executive vice-president's experiments over the next year represent the Experiments substage of this company's transformation to the Systematic Productivity stage.

As previously mentioned, this case is meant to help you to imagine the stage of development that currently characterizes your company or department or work team, and the kind of sustained action commitments that may be warranted to help it to transform.

Conclusion

The next two chapters continue this conversation. There, we shall move to the challenge of helping an organization transform from the Systematic Productivity stage to the Collaborative Inquiry stage, the transition that parallels the move we examined in Chapter 6 from the Achiever to the Strategist stage on the personal scale. Just as few managers develop to the Strategist stage, few organizations develop to the Collaborative Inquiry stage. Yet this is the first stage at which the organization begins to develop an explicit, ongoing learning capacity that can truly support continual quality improvement.

Notes

1. W. Torbert and D. Fisher (1992), 'Autobiographical awareness as a catalyst for managerial and organizational development', *Management Education and Development*, 23 (3), 184–98. Reprinted with permission of the publisher.
2. A full chapter of description and illustration for each stage is offered in W. R. Torbert (1987) *Managing the Corporate Dream*, originally published by Dow Jones-Irwin, Homewood, Illinois. The book is now available from William R. Torbert, copyright holder, Carroll School of Management, Boston College, Chestnut Hill, MA 02167.
3. This quotation originally appeared in *Managing the Corporate Dream*. See note 2 for full reference.
4. This case originally appeared, in slightly different form, in W. R. Torbert (1994) 'Managerial learning, organizational learning: a potentially powerful redundancy', *Management Learning*, **25** (1), 57–70. Adapted by permission of the publisher.

9 TQM programmes and the ongoing paradox of generating organization-wide Collaborative Inquiry
written in association with Barbara Davidson

In the previous chapter we have already followed a number of the steps through which any organizing process evolves if the objective is to create a genuine learning organization. Ultimately, a genuine learning organization truly encourages the practice of continual quality improvement (CQI) among all its members and is actively open to re-examining and transforming its own assumptions about its environment, its shape and its strategies.

But, even though the previous chapter describes five steps along the path towards a learning organization—Conception, Investments, Incorporation, Experiments and Systematic Productivity—there is a very significant sense in which an organization only reaches the *threshold* of becoming a learning organization after these five steps. Most organizations, like most persons, evolve through each of these early developmental transformations by a process of more or less traumatic trial and error that is never named, never explicitly recognized as a transformation of assumptions, and never undertaken with the intention of eventually establishing a learning organization.

Occasionally, an organization is shepherded through one transformation or another by executives or consultants, as illustrated in the previous chapter.

Even idealistic, mission-driven companies and not-for-profit organizations are, during their development to the Systematic Productivity stage, typically based on the assumptions:

(a) that *the mission is known*; and
(b) that the *organization's challenges are*:
    (i) *to find the right structure and strategy* to accomplish the mission, and
    (ii) *to overcome external competition or external political blocks* to accomplishing the desired outcomes.

Not until the next developmental transformation—between the Systematic Productivity stage and the Collaborative Inquiry stage of organizing does the purpose and process of establishing a learning organization typically become self-conscious for the organization. (This may happen in the form of a TQM programme. This chapter and the next address the process by which this transformation occurs.)

The motivation for developing beyond the Systematic Productivity stage towards the Collaborative Inquiry stage comes from a dawning recognition that the organization's mission is actually a mystery that requires continual re-searching and reformulating if members' actions are to become truly mission-oriented. At the same time some organizational members may begin to appreciate that there are inevitably systematic gaps between the espoused mission, values and strategies of organizational members on the one hand, and their actual patterns of practice on the other.

Therefore, there is not only *a mystery about what an organization's mission really means,* but there is also *a mystery about how to recognize and correct* the *incongruities* that tend to grow between espoused directions or priorities and actual practices. In other words, what motivates organizational transformation beyond the Systematic Productivity stage is the growing recognition among some members who are willing to take leadership responsibility that it is not only the changing external environment that creates new problems for the organization, but its own way of operating.

Ever since the 1950s in the United States, this kind of dawning recognition has led to a variety of organizational and managerial education ventures: T-groups (sensitivity training groups); the whole field called OD (organizational development); to QWL programmes (quality of working life) TQM (total quality management); and, most recently, process re-engineering. The developmental theory we have been discussing can help us to understand why these approaches so quickly become disappointing fads. One reason is that, in order to become marketable on a larger scale, each innovative approach to Collaborative Inquiry develops through its own distinct stages until it reaches its own Systematic Productivity strategy and structure. Because the specific innovative strategy and structure are different from the client company's strategy and structure, it may help that company to make one significant adjustment in its manner of operating.[1] *But any such prestructured intervention does not transform the whole company into a Collaborative Inquiry stage learning organization that continues to research its mission and correct incongruities among mission, strategy, operations and outcomes.*

A second, related, reason why these well-known managerial education ventures fade after sometimes having an initial impact on the organization is that only organizational members who have transformed to the Strategist stage (or beyond) fully appreciate the value and the logic of the Collaborative Inquiry process, because (as shown in Table 8.1) the Strategist and Collaborative Inquiry stages are logically parallel. Therefore, only managers at the Strategist stage and even later stages are able to implement Collaborative Inquiry on a continuing basis. As we have seen earlier, only about 10 per cent of managers are found at this stage, and more than half of the managers we have measured are placed two or more stages before the Strategist stage. Thus, the task in helping an organization transform to the Collaborative Inquiry stage is not only to transform the structure of an objectifiable social entity, but also to transform the consciousness of many of its members. We do not know what proportion must become Strategists before the organization can reliably be expected to maintain itself at the Collaborative Inquiry stage, but we are convinced that the proportion of the senior management team that is operating at the Strategist stage makes a disproportionate difference. Since each developmental transformation can take several years, and since the person developing must first discover the internal motivation to seek beyond his or her current frame, it would seem astonishing to us if a company could increase its proportion of Strategists from 5 per cent to, say, 20 per cent in less than five years.

Very few companies have the vision, the will, or the resources (to provide the leadership and to contract for the scale of consulting support necessary over that long a period) to evolve to the Collaborative Inquiry stage. Consequently, the training processes that are developed for the company's employees typically aim to instil Achiever/Systematic Productivity skills. These may be useful in the short run, but they will not generate transformation beyond the Achiever/Systematic Productivity stage.

One way of highlighting the radical difference between the reality of the Achiever/Systematic Productivity stage and the reality of the Strategist/Collaborative Inquiry stage is presented in Figure 9.1, in which the horizontal line represents the limited Achiever awareness, whereas the horizontal and vertical lines together represent the added dimension of awareness that the Strategist begins to cultivate. (This additional dimension of awareness is fully internalized during the transformation beyond Strategist to the Magician/Witch/Clown stage that we shall introduce in Chapter 11.)

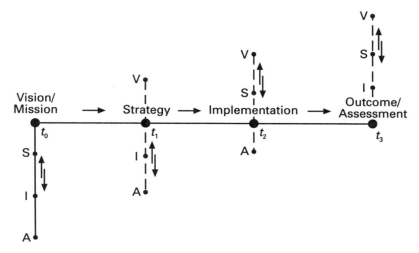

Figure 9.1 Achiever sequential awareness vs. later-stage simultaneous (and sequential) awareness. The horizontal line from t_0 to t_3 represents Achiever sequential awareness; vertical lines at any point in time represent later-stage simultaneous awareness

The horizontal line in Figure 9.1 represents the episodic sequential thinking of the Achiever: first a vision and mission is conceived at the organization's founding (though it is not necessarily recorded and codified); next, through a process of experimentation, the organization evolves a workable strategy; the strategy is then implemented; and, finally, one measures the results and finds whether the organization is successful. The Achiever may enact this sequence without conceptualizing its sequential nature, much less recognizing that multiple microscopic re-enactments of this process occur within the larger sequence.

The Strategist begins to appreciate first that there is a nameable, systemic, historical dynamic to action and that sensitivity to timing can make one's actions more effective. The Strategist is able, in effect, to 'see' the horizontal line of history because he or she cultivates at least moments of 'vertical' experiencing during which he or she escapes identification with the horizontal and can take a point of view on it. Thus, the Strategist is able to systematize 'horizontal' history and also to get indications that reality is not only sequential, but is also, in an even more profound sense, 'vertical' or simultaneous. You can 'test' these two different types of awareness by imagining yourself in the following situation:

You are a member of a CQI group at the earliest sequential phase of visioning. Even at this early phase, the participants are involved in some sort of actions with one another. You may articulate a demanding, attractive, marketable vision, but you do so as the second half of a statement, after first having put down the idea of a potential partner who can make a major capital contribution to the enterprise. Disillusioned, the potential partner withdraws from the project. So, there is strategy, implementation and outcome even at the time when Visioning is the central task, and thoughtless, habitual strategizing and acting can jeopardize the very best of visions.

But suppose your awareness had been of a different sort—represented in Figure 9.1 by the vertical line—which, from moment to moment, spans these four simultaneous realities, making you capable of 'seeing' when your action and effects become incongruent with your mission and strategy? Only such an awareness of incongruity permits us to self-correct in real time at the moment of incongruity. Only a person exhibiting such self-correction and CQI personally will be trusted over the long run to lead the process of generating a self-correcting, CQI process organizationally. For example, what if, as the potential partner is walking out the door in a huff, you say, 'Jane, will you forgive me? I can be so competitive at the moment when I'm struck by what I think is a brilliant idea. Maybe it's not such a brilliant idea, and there was in fact nothing wrong with yours either. But I need you and the others to help ride herd on me at moments like this. Will you stay, so we can find out what *does* make sense and do something exciting together?' By becoming self-critical and vulnerable, based on a non-defensive, simultaneous awareness of several different 'layers' of experience, you can self-correct.

Strategists begin to have occasional glimpses of this vast region of simultaneous awareness and thus are more likely than Achievers to initiate self-corrective action. As persons evolving towards the Magician/Witch/Clown stage of development, Strategists are seeking ongoing contact with this 'pulse-of-life' awareness. Only at the Magician/Clown/Witch stage does simultaneous experiencing become more or less continual.

As you have probably seen, this entire book is attempting to help you to begin cultivating this kind of four-fold, simultaneous awareness—whether we speak of framing/advocating/illustrating/inquiring, or of visioning/strategizing/implementing/assessing, or of jogging our awareness through the variety of action inquiry exercises.

From Experiments to Collaborative Inquiry

Now that we have suggested in general terms what the project and the difficulties of transforming towards the Collaborative Inquiry stage of organizing are, let us gain a more concrete sense of what can be involved by following one company's evolving from Experiments through Systematic Productivity towards Collaborative Inquiry over a five-year period.

This company is an HMO (health management organization) that we shall call Sun Health Care, headquartered in the south-east of the US. Founded 13 years ago, Sun's growth really took off about five years ago, showing first respectable and then enviable retained earnings while growing at twice the average rate of the industry as a whole. The organization has been involved in a continual quality improvement programme for the past four years. In the following pages, we shall introduce you first to the recent history of the industry as a whole, next to the overall history of Sun, and finally to the internal actions within the company that generated those results. In the next chapter, we shall be able to see how the personal development towards Strategist-like actions of certain key individuals is currently interacting with the company's development to the Collaborative Inquiry stage.

Brief history of the industry

HMOs were created in the US as early as the 1930s, but their popularity soared during the early 1980s, as the lower cost alternative to skyrocketing health care costs. In 1987 and 1988, the HMO industry was hit with large losses as a result of underpricing to gain market share, excessive medical and administrative costs, poor management and undercapitalization. Two-thirds of the HMOs in the US lost money in 1988. In 1989 the industry began to recover. Loss margins shrank to 0.4 per cent from 3 per cent the year before. At the same time, an industry shakeout was beginning: although overall enrolment rose by 12 per cent between 1988 and 1990, the number of plans decreased by 7 per cent, including the highly visible bankruptcy of Maxicare in Los Angeles which left thousands of enrollees without coverage.

Between 1990 and 1992 the industry returned to profitability, increasing premiums and reducing costs. Enrolments grew at 8 per cent and the number of plans decreased by 3 per cent. Quality improvement initiatives gained momentum despite some poorly managed attempts and some physician resistance. Service options were widening, and new alliances emerged that turned complementary service providers into full service organizations. Consumer surveys showed mixed reactions to HMOs. Doctor revolts hit the two largest plans in Sun's state: one revolt caused the CEO to resign, partly due to a new compensation system that tied physician pay to productivity; at the other HMO, complaints about slow payments and lack of attention to physician demands forced the resignation of three top executives.

In November 1992, Bill Clinton won the presidential election with a campaign promise to control health care costs and ensure universal access. With the anticipation of govern- ment mandated health care reform, the framework of the entire industry was put into question. It was clearly going to change in one way or another. Physicians showed an increased interest in entering into affiliations. Hospitals seemed eager to buy or form health care organizations, not only to contain costs, but also to position themselves as part of larger networks that could potentially become regional health care providers under the new national system. Employers were increasingly limiting the number of health care choices they offered, seeking out plans that showed evidence of cost reductions and high-quality service.

History of Sun

Sun had produced a small profit even in 1988 when many HMOs suffered considerable losses. From 1989 to 1993, Sun's enrolments grew over 20 per cent annually on average, more than double the industry average, through increased penetra- tion of its original service area and expansion to contiguous regions. At the same time, its net worth grew to twelve times the 1989 level. In 1993, an impartial consumer satisfaction survey showed Sun as having tied for first place nationally in terms of consumer satisfaction. A national industry ranking of overall performance showed Sun to be the smallest and youngest HMO among the top ten, and an employee climate survey conducted by a large firm specializing in such surveys showed Sun to have made the most significant improvement from one year to the next ever found by that firm.

The natural question is: 'What happened within Sun between 1989 and 1993 to produce the balanced and positive results just enumerated?' In 1989 the president decided that senior management should develop a formal strategic plan because the organization's size and growth seemed to warrant it, because he wanted the senior group to act more as a team than as division directors, and because he wished to influence his two boards of directors (a corporate board and an independent physicians' board) to think more strategically.

Internal action   After interviewing a number of consultants who might help the senior management to develop its first formal strategic plan, the president engaged one who emphasized the significance of developing a mission statement that recognized the importance of clients and employees as well as of physicians and profits. This consultant also emphasized the significance of helping the senior management team to evolve, not just to the point of planning together, but to the point of implementing the plan together effectively and of continuing to work together in a strategic manner. In other words, the consultant was advocating the simultaneous (or 'vertical') development of visioning, strategizing, and implementing. (It may not come as a surprise to you to learn that this consultant is measured as beyond the Strategist stage of development.)

The plan that evolved included objectives related to profits, enrolment growth, cost control, expansion analysis, employee development and quality improvement. The company also hired a new manager to create an internal training department.

Equally important, the process of developing the plan included study, feedback, and discussion of the senior team's views about each other's performance and relationships. The president learned that he could improve the levels of initiative, shared understanding and commitment to follow through among team members by managing the team meetings in a more collaborative fashion. The team members became aware that one member whom they had somewhat isolated because of his many initiatives was not so much a self-serving rate-buster as they had inferred. In fact, the president said he wished other team members would act more like him. To a significant degree, this vice-president could be viewed as a model member of a more peer-like team where not just the president but all team members could legitimately take initiatives. These changes in the way the president learned to lead the senior management team, and in the kind of membership behaviour that was valued, prepared the team to be effective in implementing the new strategic plan.

Overall, then, the company appeared to be transforming away from a more informal, decentralized form characteristic of the Experiments stage of organizing. Until the development of the strategic plan, the company had operated without an explicit mission that embraced its major stakeholders, without a strategic plan, without an organized senior management team meeting process, and with vice-presidents who saw themselves pre-eminently as departmental heads. Now, the company was evolving towards the Systematic Productivity stage of organizing—towards a more focused form. It is important to note that, contrary to the usual experience that greater focus disempowers participants because their jobs become narrowly and bureaucratically defined, *this way of vertically aligning mission, strategy and action process empowers an organization.*

Indeed, the process of developing the strategic plan, much like the interventions described in the previous chapter, also portrayed a form of Strategist/Collaborative Inquiry quality. As the consultant left the organization upon completion and adoption of the plan, however, the shared leadership structure for the senior management team soon fell into disuse, with the exception of the president's ongoing efforts and successes at guiding meetings in a more collaborative manner. The senior management team thus 'settled into' a strategically directed Systematic Productivity manner of operating, and the still-later-stage aspects of the consulting intervention receded from view.

After the consultant left, the quality programme initiated by the company as one of its newly adopted strategic objectives combined departmental operational studies and work redesign and based both on TQM principles. Although an external company was initially hired to support this process, the new manager of training and employee development led the way in taking full ownership of the process into the company, transforming the prefabricated work redesign methodology into a training process suited to this particular company and to the departmental redesign teams, as well as to the cross-functional new product and cost containment teams.

Thus, although the senior management team and the company as a whole settled into a Systematic Productivity mode of operating, the president, in his effort to manage the senior group more collaboratively, and the manager of employee development, in his leadership and redesign of the quality improvement programme, both acted in more Strategist/Collaborative Inquiry-like ways.

At the same time, the company was offering doctors the choice of organizing themselves into joint ventures, which monitored their own costs with the incentive of having a share in increased net revenues. These joint ventures were offering doctors collegial review, better returns and lower costs. As a result, the percentage of the network organized into joint ventures grew rapidly, and those who continued as independent practitioners were faced with the ongoing question of the form of organization that would serve them best. Although management (and an increasing number of doctors) believed that the joint venture form was in fact the way to the future—combining greater efficiency, greater profits and peer control rather than third party control—management did not unilaterally mandate this choice for all the doctors, but instead created an ongoing choice-making situation. From a developmental point of view, this structure is a particularly interesting transitional form with elements of both Systematic Productivity and Collaborative Inquiry.

As each year passed, the senior management team was transforming the strategic planning process from a top-down, departmental process to a yearly, bottom-up, interdepartmental process. Each succeeding year's plan included more detailed objectives and accountabilities for interdepartmental dependencies. Performance measurements were identified and publicized throughout the company for member growth, member satisfaction and profit. And, as already summarized in the introductory history of the company, these measures showed results that everyone in the company could be proud of.

Jogging senior managers' awareness

Nevertheless, the senior management team was not entirely prepared for the degree of controversy that began to develop as more and more departments undertook reorganization. All of the reorganization plans highlighted the critical nature of *inter*departmental cooperation (Collaborative Inquiry between departments). But two of the seven vice-presidents and their departments were increasingly experienced as roadblocks to interdepartmental coordination and as less collaborative within the senior management team, even though both believed themselves to be strong proponents of the CQI programme as a whole and of interdepartmental cooperation. Their differences from the rest of the team were highlighted by the president's new, more collaborative style of running meetings.

One of the two was seen by others as too frequently 'oppositional' at the meetings, slowing down team decision making to an exasperating degree. The other was seen as taking an independent, 'cowboy' attitude and not contributing sufficiently to the senior team. Both were seen as encouraging an attitude of superiority, priority and entitlement within their departments, rather than an attitude of cooperation and service. The 'oppositional' vice-president had generated a great deal of irritation and resentment, and the president was considering firing her. The 'cowboy' vice-president maintained an independence, but as he stayed out of other people's way he was more tolerable, and the issues surrounding his performance were fuzzier. Also, he was a 'cheerleader' within his own department, commanding enthusiastic loyalty among many of his subordinates.

The two most probable scenarios in these circumstances would be either (1) for the president to continue struggling to work with both vice-presidents, perhaps strongly reprimanding and warning the 'opposer' and rapping the knuckles of the 'cowboy'; or (2) for the president to fire the 'opposer'.

At this point, however, the actual scenario departed from the probable because the president sensed that neither of those initiatives would be consistent with integrating action and inquiry, with exercising transforming power, or with generating an opportunity for developmental transformation on the part of either vice-president (not that the president used this language). The story of what actually happened is retold in detail over the next pages because it shows the president learning more about the Strategist/Collaborative Inquiry type of awareness and action that concerns itself with the vertical alignment of mission, strategy, action and outcome at a given moment, while dealing with senior managers who did not initially appear to share this concern. As you read, you can work on developing your own Strategist/Collaborative Inquiry awareness by observing the striking differences in thinking and action between the managers (including the president) who were acquiring this awareness and those who were not.

The president realized that the 'opposer' generated inquiry by her opposition, even if she often did not help such inquiry to reach closure in mutually agreeable action. Firing her could potentially send two negative messages to the company: (a) critical inquiry is not encouraged; and (b) persons who do not conform to the preferred managerial style will be dealt with summarily. Both these messages

would directly contradict the development of a transformational CQI culture. Moreover, lower level managers were
being asked to transform their managerial styles from
superior/supervisory assumptions to collaborative/facilita-
tive assumptions (supervisors' titles were literally shifting to
'team facilitator'). Thus, it would be consistent to offer vice-
presidents the opportunity to transform their styles (if, upon
further inquiry, they required transforming). Such an exercise
would also give the senior management group as a whole the
opportunity to learn how such transformation could be
facilitated on an ongoing basis. Thus, the President was
viewing the situation not only sequentially in terms of the
kind of team he wanted in the future, but 'vertically' in terms
of how he and the team could act in the present to become
the team he wanted in the future.

To help structure and conduct this new action/inquiry, the
president recalled the consultant who had assisted the
strategic planning two years previously. The initial investiga-
tion indicated that the 'opposer' had indeed lost the trust and
patience of all direct associates. Views of the 'cowboy', on the
other hand, were highly variable and not as raw.

What the 'opposer' did   The reactions of the two vice-presidents to the feedback
about their performance were different from what one might
have predicted. Accepting that she was not opposing effectively, even if opposition was warranted, the 'opposer'
agreed to 'surrender' ('surrender' was the word actually
used) her customary role. With the consultant, she crafted a
three-page plan of action for the next six months, which they
proposed first to the president and then, incorporating his
modifications, to the senior management team. Because of
the frankness of the problem-assessment, the clarity of the
proposed goals and coaching procedures, the commitment of
the vice-president, and the explicit evaluation process (which
put the burden of proof on the vice president), the team
agreed to make the necessary effort. In so doing, the senior
team was embarking on a (potentially) transforming Collaborative Inquiry adventure.

The early weeks of implementation of the plan involved
great efforts on the part of the consultant and almost all of
the senior management team because, despite her best
intentions, the vice-president repeatedly acted in ways that
others interpreted as oppositional. After about the fourth
concrete instance of immediate feedback, however, the vice-
president appeared to 'get' just what micro-actions worked
(in the sense that other team members saw them as positive,

good-faith experiments) and what micro-actions didn't work (in the sense that others saw them as more of the same old tendency to oppose). Thereafter, this issue was effectively resolved, although other aspects of the erstwhile-opposer's style still irked her peers on occasion.

What the 'cowboy' did   By contrast, the 'cowboy' resisted both the validity and the significance of the performance feedback about himself. People's perceptions were wrong, he felt, and his style was in fact optimal for the organization.

If this were true, the consultant asked, would he participate in developing a process with the consultant whereby other members of senior management could come to appreciate his efficacy and perhaps amend their own approaches? No, the 'cowboy' responded, that was their problem, not his.

Could he see how this response might evoke the evaluation that he was not collaborative/facilitative in his relations with his colleagues? To this question, he responded with some anger that he was being trapped.

Prior to a planned meeting between this vice-president, the president and the consultant, the vice-president met with the president on a separate matter: he intended to fire one of his managers for 'gross insubordination'. 'What is the evidence?' asked the president. The vice-president described a pattern of behaviour, based on hearsay, supplemented by a memo by this manager to the human resources department questioning the justice of a corporate decision. The president said this evidence was not unambiguous enough to justify firing. In fact, it was not clear the manager had done anything inappropriate whatsoever. He added that he believed other senior managers held a significantly different interpretation of the same events.

Then and there, the president called in the rest of the senior team for an impromptu meeting, and several of them confirmed that their information from several sources made it seem like more a problem of how the vice-president had acted than of how the manager had acted. The vice-president was not able to find a constructive way of using this feedback, later describing the event, during an interview with the consultant, as a humiliation at which 'I got my brains beat in'. The consultant interviewed both the vice-president and the manager he had wanted to fire, and found inconsistencies within the vice-president's own story and no basis for firing the manager.

The president continued to try to work with the vice-president, but the 'cowboy' became increasingly suspicious that his job was on the line. Several weeks later, the president asked this vice-president to perform a task which the vice-president quickly asserted he could do 'standing on my head'. The president responded in a pleased tone that this was good because it would increase the senior management team's trust in the vice president. To this, the vice president responded angrily that he should have received a major bonus for his previous year's work rather than being tested in this way and that they should discuss a separation package together. At this moment, both men had to part for other meetings, so the matter was left hanging.

The president related the event to the consultant over the phone, adding 'I'm sure he'll change his mind when he thinks it over'. 'What do you care?' the consultant responded, arguing that the president's suggested task for the vice-president, as well as his whole manner of treating the difficulty from the start, had been one that integrated action and inquiry, aligning his own strategy of acting collaboratively with his actual practice (e.g. when he called in the other senior managers for the impromptu meeting). By contrast, said the consultant, the vice-president's response was both uncollaborative and uninquiring, as had been his entire pattern of behaviour since the issue of his performance had first arisen. Whereas the president was continuing to search for convincing second-hand evidence that the vice-president was effective or ineffective, the consultant argued that the president now had a plethora of first-hand evidence (evidence from the 'vertical' dimension of what occurs in the present) that the vice-president did not integrate action and inquiry, did not collaborate well, and did not engage in CQI with regard to his own performance.

Whereas second-hand evidence is always subject to alternative interpretations, this first-hand evidence struck the consultant as more unambiguous because it offered a simultaneous view of the vice-president's vision (not becoming vulnerable to inquiry), strategy (alternating between compliance and angry rejection), action (non-collaborative) and outcomes (no signs of quality improvement). The consultant said that he did not wish to pressure the president towards agreeing with the vice-president's separation proposal if he was not comfortable with it. The question was how valid to regard, and how seriously to take, the relatively unambiguous first-hand data from the president's own interactions with the vice-president, in contrast to the relatively ambiguous second-hand data. The consultant urged the president to take 15 minutes of quiet, meditative time alone at the end of the phone call to see whether a clear conviction about the proper course of action announced itself.

Immediately following this period, the president asked the vice-president to meet again in order to work out the details of his resignation, separation agreement and announcement to the company. Twenty-four hours later, the vice-president was no longer working at the company. After his departure, a systematic pattern of misrepresentation about senior management decisions to former subordinates of the 'cowboy' was discovered and corrected.

What was the president becoming clearer about and more committed to during this experience? Perhaps that the true challenge of quality improvement is the challenge of generating not just *continuous, incremental improvement in outcomes*, but also *continual, simultaneous awareness of the vision, strategy and implementation associated with outcomes*. To engage in transformational improvement in real-time senior management encounters it is necessary to integrate action and inquiry and to exercise mutual, transforming power, as the 'oppositional' vice-president and the team had done with one another. She and the team transformed from a limited, limiting awareness of outcomes (the things she was complaining about and her status as 'opposer') to the simultaneous awareness of vision, strategy, implementation, and new outcomes needed to produce jointly the six-month plan of action. The particular outcomes of such exercises are, in principle, *not* predictable because they create conditions for learning that require self-transforming initiatives on the part of executives, as well as continual creativity under pressure by peers who are at once demanding and supportive. The logic of the Collaborative Inquiry stage of organizing can only flower and come to be trusted within a company if it is practised in micro-encounters, such as the difficult one just described.

At the outset of the inquiry regarding the two vice-presidents, none of the other senior executives, including the president, would have predicted that the 'opposer' could or would transform as radically as she did, or that the 'cowboy' would resist and resign as he did. Because of the action/ inquiry procedures, however, and the clear initiatives by both vice-presidents (one transforming, the other resigning), the outcomes united the senior team more strongly. Once again, however, the team as a whole did not adopt the Collaborative Inquiry logic as its general mode of operating.

Instead, as if relaxing after a difficult trauma, it returned to its Systematic Productivity mode.

The next challenge

The president all too soon gets a chance to test his growing appreciation for the invention of Collaborative Inquiry-type procedures with another vice-president whose performance appears problematic. Astonishingly, after nine months, the new marketing vice-president, the replacement for the 'cowboy', acquired through an expensive national search, appears to be generating some of the same problematic effects as his predecessor, despite significant differences in their overt managerial styles. Whereas the predecessor was relatively loud, enthusiastic and motivating, the new vice-president is relatively quiet and concerned with account-ability. Nevertheless, the new vice-president is similar to the 'cowboy' in that he says relatively little in senior management meetings despite repeated invitation, seems to under-inform his area about company-wide direction, and generates enough discomfort among his subordinates about the ethical nature of some of his actions for the president to hear about it.

The president is very careful not to prejudge the new vice-president on the basis of limited information, and also recognizes that the apparently close analogy between the predecessor and the current vice-president may point to an organizational issue rather than a personnel issue. As a result, the president invents a new Collaborative Inquiry procedure that is not merely a tactic for dealing with this problem, but is also a strategy for team-wide learning and change. He proposes that the entire senior management group create an executive development process for itself. The senior management team agrees, deciding to define together: (1) standards for the 'ideal' senior management team member, (2) developmental issues that the team as a whole faces and (3) a first-year set of developmental objectives for each member. At the same time, the president raises the specific issues he is aware of with the marketing vice-president and, together, they rehire the original consultant to work with the vice-president and the marketing managers as well as with the senior team.

Tables 9.1, 9.2 and 9.3 show, respectively, how the team came to define its 'ideal member', its 'ideal process' and the steps its current members could take to move towards the ideal. It may be of interest to you to think of the senior managers in your own organization as you read the descrip-tion of an ideal manager shown in Table 9.1. How many of

Table 9.1 Standards for 'ideal' Sun Health Care senior management team member

1. *Leadership*
   - Desire and ability to become strong leader, taking executive responsibility for entire company as it grows
   - Seen as a leader of the company (not just own department) both inside and outside the company
   - Seen as effective manager of own area who keeps it working harmoniously with corporate-wide objectives
   - Wants to teach others knowledge, skills, orientation and judges own success by the ability to develop one's managers
   - Demonstrates creative problem solving under pressure
   - Gets things done well

2. *Vision/mission*
   - Dedicated to Sun and the health care industry
   - Exemplifies in daily practice who we are (mission) and who we want to become (vision)
   - Able to motivate staff to share in our vision, philosophy

3. *Creative work ethic*
   - Strong commitment to: working hard; honesty; conveying energy, enthusiasm; quality improvement; customer orientation
   - Acts with highest integrity as well as sensitivity to the culture of the company
   - Prioritizing skills guided by mission and strategic objectives
   - Manages time not just efficiently, effectively, but also creatively

4. *Knowledge of what's* really *going on*
   - Broad understanding of industry
   - Understanding of all areas of Sun Health Care
   - Knowledge of technical issues affecting our business
   - Expertise in matters concerning own department
   - Keeps finger on pulse, knows what's *really* going on

5. *Implementation-focused strategic approach*
   - Able to weigh business options objectively: uses effective problem-solving tools; acts on behalf of the corporation, even if not popular in own area
   - Demonstrates leadership in the development *and execution* of strategies and business plans: contributes innovative ideas; strong-willed, persuasive, and also seeks out disconfirming data
   - Contributes to development and implementation of corporate priorities involving other departments; understands issues in other departments
   - Oriented towards cross-functional problem solving and sharing of information

Table 9.1 Standards for 'ideal' Sun Health Care senior management team member (*continued*)

6. *Artful performance in meetings*
   • Without usurping others' leadership, assumes leadership accountability in all meetings in which he or she participates: gives full attention to meeting; prompt at start of meeting and after breaks; carries out all assignments in a timely manner; willing to ask 'dumb' questions to assure understanding; respects the contributions of others; willing to clarify/elaborate on ideas; willing to compromise, or craft a better third alternative; eases tension in the group without diverting attention from significant differences

7. *Transformational interpersonal skills*
   • Develops interpersonal skills consistent with Sun, such as: caring; down-to-earth; teamwork; ability to change
   • Excellent communication skills: listening, speaking, writing
   • Effective team player: actions help achieve consensus; supports achievement of agreed-upon goals
   • Negotiation skills
   • Recognizes, manages and transforms conflicts into energizing new modes of cooperation

8. *A gravity-defying learning orientation*
   • Continual development of technical, business, managerial skills
   • Sees difficult challenges and stretch goals as a reason for being here
   • Thrives on notion that we defy gravity and will keep doing things people believe we can't achieve
   • Develops assessment processes for measuring own knowledge and leadership within own department
   • Physician executives learn business skills and business executives learn about medical thinking and the unique abilities needed to affect physician behaviour
   • Seeks new ways of understanding what customers want
   • Able to ask questions that keep you from being fooled for long

your senior managers meet the first five standards, which might be termed the 'ordinary' ideals we have for persons in executive leadership roles? And how many are in contention as examples of the final three, which are more extraordinary and paradoxical ideals? Would we even recognize such subtle forms of leadership as assuming leadership account-ability for a meeting 'without usurping others' leadership'? How does one 'ease tension in the group without diverting attention from significant differences'? Certainly, if such performances occur at all, they must be the manifestation of the sort of simultaneous awareness of self, group, task and purpose that we begin to cultivate as we move towards the Strategist stage and later.

But, as interesting as it may be to consider the eight ideal standards that the senior managers at Sun Health developed, perhaps it is even more important to emphasize that we are in no way suggesting that other senior managers pin these in front of themselves at their desks. What we are suggesting is that other senior management teams can gain clarity and inspiration by engaging in similar experiences. This one began by having each senior team member develop his or her own list of standards. These lists were then integrated and categorized, but without names for the categories. The subsequent discussion turned out to be both fun and touching, as members jokingly and truthfully vied to caricature how badly each other failed to keep their fingers on the organization's pulse. A number of the members also expressed their excitement at the idea of defying gravity and 'doing things people believe we can't achieve'. The president admitted that this had been a phrase he contributed and was delighted that it had evoked such a spontaneous, positive response from others. These are the 'moments of truth' that generate shared vision and commitment within a team. At best, Table 9.1 reminds the Sun senior team of those moments. If you are interested by the result, consider creating a similar list with your current team.

Table 9.2 shows the 'ideal process' that the Sun team created for its meetings. Again, the point is not to superimpose this process on any other team, but rather that a team can work to surface its current dilemmas (such as 'unfocused agendas') and transform them into objectives ('a focused, overall agenda') with defined leadership roles that support realization of the objectives.

Table 9.3 shows the kind of developmental learning objectives that senior team members eventually began setting for themselves for the following year within the frameworks just described. The striking thing (to us) about these personal objectives is that they are so clear and unequivocal about each member's 'flat sides'. This resulted from a good discussion of each member's initial draft of his or her objectives. As the following year progressed, each member reported twice on his or her efforts to meet objectives, and received both supportive and confrontive feedback from peers.

Table 9.2 Sun senior management team development agenda

As agreed by the team members, *the principal team development issue for this year is:*

DEVELOPING A FOCUSED, OVERALL AGENDA.

The team has further agreed to rotate the agenda development and meeting leadership function to a different team member every three months.

In addition, the team has defined six agenda categories, each of which requires creative and disciplined management. These are:

1. Updates
2. Open items
3. Visioning
4. Strategizing
5. Implementing
6. Assessing

The meeting leader manages the first two agenda categories, while four other team members serve as the 'advocates' for the remaining four categories. Each advocate is responsible for determining what items in his or her category deserve team attention and for coaching whoever is responsible for each agenda item. In addition, as particular agenda items are considered by the team, each advocate has a special responsibility for raising issues related to his or her advocacy area as appropriate.

In general, it is understood that there is a natural flow for particular agenda items from Visioning to Strategizing to Implementing to Assessing and from there to the Update or Open item categories, if further senior management attention is warranted.

In this initial sequence of events, we see how the president generates two whole sets of organizational learning processes (one for senior management, one for the marketing managers) as part of his response to the dilemma with the marketing vice-president. The president is clearly getting more of a feel for creating Collaborative Inquiry-type organizational learning opportunities.

After interviewing the vice-president and the six marketing/sales managers (see Table 9.4 for interview schedule), the consultant offers the vice-president feedback about the findings (including direct quotes, but no identification of particular speakers). The findings show, among other things, that the team meetings are viewed as being unimaginatively led by the vice-president ('Vice-president leads the meetings.

Table 9.3   Sample of individual senior manager developmental goals

1. *Consensus building*
   To accomplish this goal, I shall be implementing the senior management recommendations outlined during our discussion of my presentation. Specifically, if I experience opposition to a recommendation which I believe should be adopted, I shall explore with individual senior management members the source of their resistance and address those concerns directly. In addition, I shall try to identify those individuals who concur with my proposal and enlist their support in building consensus. Concomitantly, I shall reassess my recommendations in the context of the questions raised and restructure my position to reflect my reassessment. Finally, I shall solicit individual 'evaluations' of whether I have demonstrated a more effective ability to build consensus.

2. *Supporting and managing subordinate development*
   To improve my skills in this area, I attended a management self-assessment programme in which you are evaluated by your subordinates. I am currently reviewing these evaluations and I shall meet with the evaluator, discuss the issues raised, and request re-evaluations. Concomitantly, I plan to review relevant literature and possibly attend a programme on managing professionals. Finally, I shall be working with human resources on ways to foster employee development and to assess the effectiveness of my efforts.

3. *Communication at external meetings with potential strategic allies*
   In response to the observation that I speak infrequently at external meetings, I shall make a conscious effort to increase my input into these meetings, both to impart information and also to make known to an outside group the thinking of my department. If effectiveness at communicating appears to be a problem when I solicit team members' feedback after each such meeting, I shall seek out remedial courses.

They are one gigantic "to-do" list, with routine check-ins.' 'There are no discussion items at meetings, no strategy, no decision making, no discussion of relationships within the team.') The foremost challenge for the next six months is described as curing 'the lack of respect and lack of trust within the team'.

The findings also show that the performance of two members of the marketing management team is viewed as sub-par by three or more of the other members, and the vice-president is one of these two. Moreover, the vice-president is mentioned only once as one of the two most effective

Table 9.4 Managerial interview schedule

1. What do you see as the two or three most critical strategic/ business issues or managerial/process issues for your senior marketing management team to address in the next 3–6 months?

2. How would you describe the marketing management team right now—its overall climate, sense of direction, cohesiveness, performance, ability to manage conflict?

3. How and how well do management team meetings work? Who takes leadership? How well?

4. Do any two-person relationships within the team inhibit its overall efficacy?

5. Is the managerial style of any or several of the team members a recurring problem for you and the team? If so, describe the patterns as you see them.

6. What problems, if any, do you think others on the team have working with you?

7. All things considered, who do you see as the two most effective members of the team, not counting yourself?

8. What skills do you see yourself most in need of improving in order to increase the team's effectiveness?

9. Other than changes in yourself, if two of your wishes for the team could be granted, what would you most wish changed?

members of the seven-person team, and he is mentioned three times as a member of a relationship that *inhibits* the efficacy of the team. In addition, he receives one page of positive comments about his contributions to the team and two pages on perceived areas for improvement (e.g. 'has pressured more than one of us to misrepresent issues or our opinion to senior management and has himself directly misled them').

Perhaps because the feedback report contains no brief summary like the foregoing two paragraphs, but is, rather, spread across nine pages of quotations, the vice-president reviews the information with the consultant in a calm manner, with no indication that he views the situation as one of major concern. He accepts the recommendation that a half-day retreat with the marketing management team be used to create a shared-leadership structure for meetings and to get team input and buy-in to his own formulation of the developmental objectives for the next year.

At the time, the consultant is uncertain how to interpret the vice-president's calm, constructive concern during this meeting. Is the vice-president simply addressing the issues seriously? Does he not put together the pieces of evidence and therefore not yet appreciate the magnitude of his dilemma? Or is he playing his cards so close to his chest that he is hoping to evade the dilemma (there is a rumour he has been interviewing for positions outside the company)? In a sense, it doesn't matter which is the case because the president and the consultant are both committed to a process of confronting the vice-president with information and giving him new choices at each step, rather than in making untested inferences, or in manipulating a particular preconceived outcome.

In further phone conversations with the vice-president and the six marketing managers, the consultant develops an agenda for the retreat, attempting in his process and in the meeting structure itself to model the kind of co-leadership that is being proposed for future team meetings. Each hour of the meeting is co-led by the consultant and a different member of the team. The first hour is devoted to developing an improved meeting structure and shared leadership.

The three managers viewed as most effective by the team are all asked to assume regular leadership roles for the coming year, with the notion that these roles may be redefined and will be rotated year by year to support individual manager's developmental objectives. The vice-president will continue to take leadership with regard to strategic issues facing senior management and the company as a whole. The three new roles are: (1) agenda-manager, meeting-leader; (2) executive-secretary in charge of monitoring and appraising implementation of meeting decisions; and (3) team facilitator, in charge of coaching members who so request and of intervening in cases of conflict or blockage.

During the second hour of the meeting, the vice-president introduces the new senior management development process and presents his ten goals for the coming year. His goals reflect the feedback he has received from the consultant, but in relatively vague language. The discussion reorganizes these goals and consolidates them into a more concrete form. The managers take the opportunity to press the vice-president to be sure that he recognizes the pattern of difficulties that his style has repeatedly created.

Then, during the third hour, the marketing managers discuss creating their own individualized development agendas analogous to the new senior management process. In particular, the manager who has received the feedback that four members of the team experience his style as a recurring problem speaks up to express his surprise at the feedback and his desire to rectify the situation. A meeting is set for the following week among the consultant, the vice-president and two of the managers identified as having relational issues.

This first meeting appears to have been highly successful in terms of organizational learning, in that the team is re-energized by the new structure. But the managers are not sure how confident they can be that the vice-president is learning and will change. They point to several comments he has made that seem to minimize past problems.

The president, in turn, is shocked that the vice-president says nothing whatsoever to him about the meeting the first time they see each other afterwards, and is shocked again when they meet a day later and the vice-president says simply that the meeting was quite good and seems to have overcome all prior problems. The president, in a moment of consternation and inspiration, asks the vice-president to write down on a single page over the weekend how he has understood the feedback from the consultant and on what basis he believes that this single meeting has resolved all the problems.

On Monday, the vice-president meets, as previously scheduled, with the marketing manager who is to become the new 'team facilitator'. This marketing manager has served as team leader for several of the company's early cross-functional new product teams; therefore, together with the president and the manager of employee development, she is one of the members of the company most practised in the Strategist/Collaborative Inquiry action logic. The manager's explicit agenda is to increase the trust between herself and the vice-president, in order to increase the probability of success in her proposed role of team facilitator. The vice-president suggests that this manager is the only one who experiences the problems that she is describing. The manager, who has no knowledge of the president's request of the vice-president, responds by making an almost identical request. She asks the vice-president if he would be willing to write a short summary of how he understands the feedback he has received from the team through the consultant. For the first time, we see several of the players in an organizational episode—the president, the consultant, and the marketing manager in this case—all acting from a Strategist/Collaborative Inquiry perspective.

Within an hour of this meeting, the vice-president delivers

a short handwritten note of resignation to the president. A week later, after discussion with the consultant and the senior management team, the president appoints two of the six marketing and sales managers as acting vice-presidents for sales and for marketing and recommends that the two subgroups (sales and marketing) continue their common meetings with the new shared leadership structure. The marketing manager in the foregoing story becomes one of the two new vice-presidents.

Conclusion

Clearly, we cannot know whether the vice-president who just resigned learned anything valid through this entire process. On the other hand, the two managers who have accepted the promotions to acting vice-president are putting themselves into position for significant managerial learning. The president has also learned a great deal. He has learned, in a way that he can feel confident, that the vice-president was not prepared to participate actively in transformational learning. At a more abstract level, the president has learned twice-over now that difficult personnel decisions can be made in a way that is not unilateral but mutual. Moreover, he has learned that he can use a difficult dilemma like this to leverage a great deal of organizational learning.

What were the organizational learnings in this case? The president, the senior management team as a whole, the consultant, and the marketing management team developed a number of organizational learning processes for both the senior managers and the marketing/sales managers: (1) the set of 'ideal' standards for a senior manager; (2) a new senior manager development process; and (3) a new shared leadership structure for the marketing/sales managers. In addition, the senior management team eventually developed an analogous shared leadership structure for its own meetings (as shown in Table 9.2). As senior management team members struggle to understand and practise the full potential of their meeting leader roles, they are generating further leadership supports for themselves, such as the agenda item management guidelines in Table 8.3 of Chapter 8. Furthermore, several of the other vice-presidents are currently crafting shared leadership structures for their management teams.

Thus, this second case of ineffective senior manager performance shows us how the company's president is learning not only how to solve the presenting problem but how to use it to generate long-term Collaborative Inquiry stage structures. The president no longer has any formal leadership role within the senior management meetings. Instead, he is available as an information source and coach to the formal leaders. He feels liberated and empowered by this change, since he is now freer to represent himself as strongly as he wishes on either substantive, or procedural, or developmental issues. In other words, he wants to be as free as possible to move his attention among levels of awareness and reduce the likelihood that he will become sequentially limited within single levels. At the same time, he is pleased by the new level of leadership initiative on the part of the vice-presidents because both he and they are increasingly involved in outside-the-company negotiation of strategic alliances—brief meetings with virtual strangers who are often competitors—where every possible skill in agenda management and clear communication are at a premium.

We see that the senior management of Sun Health Care is beginning to experiment with Collaborative Inquiry types of management for its own affairs. In the next chapter, we shall describe how the senior management team is re-inventing itself yet again six months later, and re-inventing the company as a whole in a Collaborative Inquiry mode as well.

Note

1. For example, the 'breakthrough' stage in Juran's model of quality improvement. Juran, J. (1951) *Quality Control Handbook*, New York: McGraw-Hill. The real point is not to redesign once and create the 'perfect' design, but rather how to create the imperfect, stumbling, but self-redesigning process illustrated in this chapter and the next.

10 The quintessence of Collaborative Inquiry
written in association with Melissa McDaniels

Our experience at Sun Health Care confirms for us how peer-focused, Strategist-like leaderly action is critical for the evolution of a continual quality improvement (CQI) initiative towards full Collaborative Inquiry. In the previous chapter, we have already described some of the Strategist-like actions of Sun's president, its marketing manager who has been promoted to vice-president, its manager for employee development, and its consultant. In this chapter, we shall continue to document Sun's evolution towards the Collaborative Inquiry mode of CQI and the significant roles that the Strategist-like actions of these four play. We shall also try to show some of the 'rough edges' of this developmental process, so that Sun emerges less like a mythic fairy tale and more like an ongoing struggle among ordinary men and women.

The manager for employee development at Sun has remarkably illustrated the proposition that Strategists treat their superiors in a peer-like way (as we discussed in Chapter 6). He has proposed an entirely new organizational structure for the company to the senior management team. This new structure retains the existing departmental structure (in effect, the company's Systematic Productivity structure), while initiating a new system of cross-functional areas (which can become, in effect, the company's Collaborative Inquiry structure). The new, cross-functional structure includes all of senior management on different, internal policy 'boards', which develop and implement policies in areas such as training and the CQI programme. Here is how this manager analyses Sun's recent history and current challenge in the introduction to a document presented to senior management:

The implementation of TQM in organizations has been described in terms of stages:

Stage 1: Awakening
Stage 2: Activities
Stage 3: Breakthroughs
Stage 4: World Class.

This simple model can describe the progress of TQM at Sun.

Stage 1: Awakening
The rapid growth of membership and employees raised questions about how to manage this growth. Departments had no frameworks around which to organize and plan for their growth; thus, Senior Management commissioned an operations review of two major departments. At the same time, Senior Management had a desire to push down more of the operational management of the company to the middle management and the departments; thus, the methodology chosen for the operations analysis was consistent with the major principles of Total Quality Management. This philosophy and approach focused on controlling costs while at the same time emphasizing service quality.

In April 1990, design teams from Claim Services and Medical Services worked with an outside consultant, two internal consultants (one each for work redesign and training) and a management support team to complete the work redesigns. From this experience, a methodology was documented and developed into a training process so the rest of the company could continue with work redesign.

Stage 2: Activities
Two more years were required to complete work redesign in all the departments. In each case, the following general steps were followed:

1. Identify key processes
2. Gather the facts
3. Define the current situation
4. Analyse the process
5. Define the ideal process system
6. Alpha test and convene design walk through
7. Present to the Steering Committee for confirmation.

The results of this total restructuring of departments were new or enhanced work processes (standard methods) and new organizational designs. Frequently, these new designs resulted in work teams made up of individuals who had previously worked primarily as individual contributors. The departmental organization also was kept as flat as possible and cross training was stressed where appropriate.

During this stage, Senior Management developed a planning process that incorporated TQM as a primary business strategy and identified the need for a core competency in New Product Development. A new product realization process was developed and a first new product was introduced in 1991.

Stage 3: Breakthrough
Experience with work redesign and the use of cross-functional teams has led to the expansion of the use of this technology to resolve organizational challenges. Four new products have now been introduced, with several more in the planning stages. In addition, teams have redesigned the referral systems, identified and implemented medical cost controls, reduced the rate of abandoned calls, and have been working to redefine yet again the standard methods in most departments. Using what they have learned in training on CQI, problem-solving, and project management, employees are involved in a total of over 50 process improvement projects this fiscal year.

Significant breakthroughs are also coming as a result of our Employee Survey process. This data has enabled management to identify and respond to the areas of Compensation, Performance Management, and Appreciation and Recognition. New systems in these areas are now under development by middle management teams. Senior Management and middle management are now organized into work teams with specific roles and responsibilities.

Concrete performance improvements have also been achieved. Sun's goal for a 7.5% administrative cost was achieved in 1992–93 (down from 10% in 1990). The industry average is 12%. For 1993–94 administrative cost remains at 7.5% of revenue in spite of major investments in resources for the Medical Services department. Without these investments, administrative costs would have been less than 5%. Major breakthroughs have occurred in the medical cost control area such that our new rates for 1994 will reflect a 2% average inflation rate (down from 12% in 1992). This pricing structure will have major implications for our competitiveness in managed care markets.

Sun is on track to double its market share in five years (beginning in 1991). We have become the third largest HMO in the south-east, with the largest number of participating physicians, and among the highest customer satisfaction ratings in the HMO industry.

Stage 4: World Class
World Class describes an organization whose quality management practices are recognized as being among the best in class. Sun is planning to benchmark some of its practices (Training, Quality, Costs) against the best in order to achieve World Class status. In addition, Sun is being recognized both nationally and locally for its quality of customer service and its overall management and is being benchmarked by others.

World Class also refers to the expansion of quality initiatives to suppliers and even customers. Sun is piloting a process for

introducing TQM throughout a large network of medical providers and, in particular, to the management of its medical joint
ventures.

Finally, World Class suggests a sophisticated measurement
and information system to pinpoint both needs for and results
from quality improvement activities. External customer measurement has been intensified, that has improved internal measurement at the organizational and process levels, and the
Information Services function has been raised to a Vice-Presidential level.

The following set of recommendations focuses on developing a
system of cross-functional management that directly involves
Senior Management in the policy and prioritization process for
both our training and our quality process, putting company-
wide needs above the functional needs of their departments. . . .

This is the introductory section of a large book that the
manager for employee development hands to the senior
management team at the outset of his presentation to them.
He has already discussed his proposals at least briefly with
every member of the team and in great depth with several.
During the presentation, some of his diagrams are difficult to
follow. Moreover, there is some confusion about how he is
proposing to position himself in the 'new' organization (is
this just a sophisticated power grab?). It turns out that the
manager has left this detail for late in the presentation (he in
fact eventually offers several alternatives).

Despite these awkward moments, his overall prior track
record and his careful pre-presentation briefings result in
several senior management team members strongly supporting him at critical moments. Only a few months earlier
these same senior managers might well have had nothing to
say on this topic, or might have raised sceptical questions
without recognizing their effect of discouraging initiative and
innovation. Now, with the new level of committed interaction
that has come to characterize meetings since team members
have taken on added leadership responsibility, there is
animated discussion among them, with probing questions
responded to, not just by the manager, but also by various
vice-presidents. The manager is not left isolated, nor the fate
of his proposal determined solely by *his* rhetorical skills. At
the end of the allotted time some of the issues at hand have
not been clarified and resolved, but rather than delay action,
a subset of the senior managers volunteer for the cross-
functional quality improvement committee, which is to
continue to define itself and report back to the team as a
whole.

In addition to the fact that the manager for employee development is *measured* at the Strategist stage,[1] the foregoing events also point towards a Strategist-like action logic. From the outset of the foregoing episode, we see that this manager has the quality of confidence, interest and competence to create a synthetic vision for the future of the company and to advocate it to his formal superiors. The vision synthesizes theoretical ideas from a variety of sources with the actual history of Sun Health Care.

The manner in which he then intertwines process and content is also Strategist-like. He carefully prepares, not only in terms of the formal 'book' he presents to senior management, but even more in terms of the preliminary conversations he has with individual members. Also impressively Strategist-like are the multiple models he offers for his own future role, showing that he is vulnerable to influence and that he is open to a variety of framings of his role.

At the same time, the overall impact of his intervention encourages the senior management team to entertain, and to begin to participate in, an altered framing of the way the company may work better in the near future, as well as an altered framing of the way the senior management team may work together as a unit.

The president's restructuring proposal

There is no evidence that the manager's new model for the senior management team directly influences the president to think of new models of working together. Nevertheless, three weeks later, at the end of a meeting to begin developing the company's 1995 strategic priorities, the president, from his own perspective, and to the palpable though silent shock of the team, raises the same issue of reforming the senior management team.

With the swirl of partnership, merger and acquisition opportunities, he states that he would like to be able to meet with a smaller executive committee of the ten-person team in order to conduct ongoing strategizing, since the smaller team can be convened more easily, can devote more time to strategizing, and can presumably reach consensus more quickly. He suggests that perhaps a new role of chief operating officer (COO) needs to be created to monitor the internal affairs of the company. He asks everyone to consider this type of restructuring and to suggest other ideas.

Perhaps you can imagine some of the feelings you might have upon first hearing this proposal, especially if you were a member of a senior management team that was working with unusual harmony and effectiveness (the company is currently experiencing the most profitable quarter of its history). Are several members of this peer-like group going to be promoted and become the others' bosses? Am I going to be asked in the group to declare my preferences in these matters? Does the president already know who he wants on this 'executive committee'? Isn't this something that he ought to decide himself and then announce? Does he feel that some of us, including me, are not performing at the same level as others? Is my job on the line here?

In a demonstration of the trust within this team, all these questions are in fact voiced, if hesitantly, at the meeting. The president responds that he has not decided anything yet and has not matched people to his suggested roles. He is acting on the basis of the recent growth in size of the team and the knowledge that no other HMO of comparable size works with such a large team. He says he genuinely wants suggestions. He is willing to make the final decision himself, but wants it to be the best informed decision possible.

The consultant's restructuring proposal

After this meeting, the consultant, who has been present, independently develops a model for proceeding with this 'collaborative inquiry'. He foresees brief telephone interviews between himself and each senior management team member, followed by team meetings at which an overall summary of members' suggestions (without mentioning names of who proposes what) help to structure the discussion. Such a process permits all the relevant information to reach the table, rather than have members' fears that they are alone in their views potentially distort the information that is shared. (At the same time, one can ask whether the consultant is inserting himself between the president and the rest of the team in a way that retards the vice-presidents' development of greater parity with the president by expressing themselves directly to him.)

In a further move that may indicate untimely self-insertion, the consultant works through his own preliminary outline of a specific structure that may be the outcome of the foregoing process. This structure has the entire senior management team meeting together for a half day every other week, with two subgroups of equal importance meeting on a weekly or even more frequent basis. One subgroup is a four-person strategy committee for external strategizing, as requested by the president; the other subgroup is the quality improvement committee for internal operations that is part of the employee development manager's suggested structure. In this way, the

CEO's new structure and the manager for employee development's new structure dovetail together, and the two principal elements in an organization's capacity for world-class performance—its alertness and strategic relation to its external environment and its alertness and strategic relation to its internal environment—are given equal weight.

According to the consultant's preliminary model, each member of the strategy committee will represent one of the four aspects of the management process discussed in earlier chapters—Visioning, Strategizing, Implementing and Assessing—thus carrying forward a central structuring element with which the team is currently becoming familiar. The president can take the Strategizing role. Whoever takes the new COO role will sit in the Implementing chair within the strategy committee and will head the quality improvement committee (see Figure 10.1).

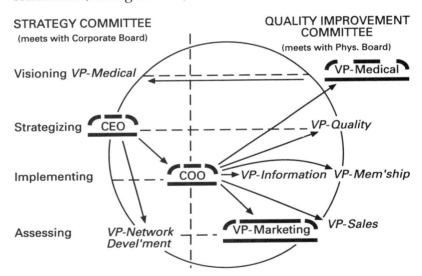

Figure 10.1   Sun senior management

The consultant imagines that one of the two doctors on the senior management team will sit on each committee and will quite appropriately represent the Visioning process at this time when the medical profession is per force engaged in revisioning itself. For, what is properly occurring during this transformational period in American health care if not a re-exploring of the relationships between the individual practice and the social institutions of medicine? What is happening if not a revisioning of medicine from a primary mission of curing illness to a primary mission of cultivating health?

What is happening if not a revisioning of medicine from a defensive effort to prevent death to a positive support in one's preparation for the challenges, fulfilments and special delights of old age and the facing of death?

The consultant foresees deploying one or two members of the quality improvement committee to each of the same four cross-functional managerial processes. Also, because the manager of employee development has been mentioned more than once as a possible vice-president, the consultant foresees his or her promotion to a vice-presidency and a role on the quality improvement committee.

Thus, we see, even before the consultant's findings and ideas are discussed, and even before the president's restructuring proposal is explored, how a collaborative inquiry about the appropriate vision for the future of the senior management team is being generated by three persons related to the company—the president, the manager for employee development, and the consultant. A striking aspect of these three initiators of restructuring plans is that only one of them is a member of the senior management team. Thus, the plans are emanating from very different perspectives: from a 'subordinate', from a 'superior', and from a 'bystander'.

The specific proposals are very different from one another, yet they also have much in common. All three proposals have Strategist-like qualities. All three visions are developed and presented with the invitation to a continuing conversation that will alter the initial idea in unanticipated ways as some kind of consensus is developed. Also, all three visions are so patterned that they are in fact mutually compatible, as the consultant's initial ideas illustrate. All three are patterned as uniquely crafted collaborative inquiries leading towards a uniquely crafted Collaborative Inquiry structure (although, as we shall see shortly, the senior management team itself is not at all sure at the outset whether the president has a Collaborative Inquiry structure in mind—an understandable uncertainty, given the hierarchical emphasis of his proposal).

Next steps

The president is at first hesitant about the necessity for the consultant's proposed process of phone interviews with the team members during the two days prior to the team's initial meeting on the topic. But he and then the senior management team agree to it after a little discussion. (The consultant does not discuss his specific model yet, and does not know whether it will ever become relevant.)

The phone interviews reveal wide agreement within the group that the fast growth of the company in the turbulent, unframed environment argues in favour of the president and a small executive or strategizing committee to devote approximately 75 per cent of its collective attention to strategizing and positioning the company. Team members also generally agree that it will benefit the company to have the president become more visible on the regional and national scene and be more exposed to different innovations that are currently occurring. They also believe that the organization will be better off if the president can reduce his attention to operational detail. Members currently feel that the president does not have enough time to mentor and coach them. Yet, at the same time, there is some concern that the group is so used to the president's leadership, even after the past six months of greater collective leadership within the meetings, that it will be difficult for members of the more operational group to accept another leader; they may try to circumvent that leader and still go to the president. Several members suggest that instead of one COO, three executive vice-presidents (EVPs) be appointed, each with one or two of the other vice-presidents as subordinates.

At the same time, members are concerned *not* to change in ways that jeopardize the excellent overall climate of respect, mutuality, collaboration and commitment that exists within the team at present. There is general agreement that if there is to be a COO then he or she should *not* be hired from outside because the learning curve to learn Sun's idiosyncratic culture is so demanding. Several are also concerned that the message of this restructuring to the managers in the company will be that senior management is adding a layer of hierarchy when it has been advocating the reduction of hierarchy; moreover, these members believe that the management level should also be restructured if senior management is to be changed; otherwise, the managers may feel betrayed.

Shadow issues

Another theme that emerges from the phone interviews can be introduced as an unarticulated tension between the 'insiders' and the 'outsiders' on the team. This may properly be categorized as a kind of 'shadow' issue for the team: one that is not clearly evident to the team's own members or to anyone who might observe the team 'from the outside'; one that causes ambivalent emotions, fear and denial even just at the mention of it. Such tension between 'insiders' and 'outsiders' had been a theme that was not publicly articulated two or three years earlier within the larger organization, the managers at that time being viewed as 'insiders' who had often been with the company almost since its inception, and the senior managers being viewed as 'outsiders' recently hired into the company at that level. At that time, only one member of senior management was an 'insider' who had been promoted from within the company.

Now, however, there are three clear 'insiders' on the senior management team who have been promoted from within (the original 'insider' plus the two new vice-presidents of sales and marketing). Moreover, the president, the CFO, and one of the medical vice-presidents have by now earned the status across the company as competent and loyal 'insiders' as well. The clearest outsiders are the three most recent additions to the team who have been hired into a vice-presidential role from outside the company.

In general—and it is important to the understanding of what is now being said to emphasize that the following statement has never before been explicitly stated within the company in this general way—the insiders view the outsiders as not well enough aligned with the quality improvement initiative and the general ethos of collaborative relationships within the company, and as relying too strongly instead upon hierarchical authority, delegation and expert knowledge.

Conversely, the outsiders view the insiders, in general, as somewhat less crisp (our summary word, not theirs) and less strategically oriented. The 'outsiders' in general lean towards introducing more hierarchy within the team (e.g. the 'three executive vice-presidents' model for restructuring).

This mild and unspoken disjunction between 'insiders' and 'outsiders' is made a little more prominent by two other overlapping disjunctions: the disjunction between the 'accountants' and the others, and the disjunction between two different buildings in which different members of senior management are quartered. The president, the CFO and the two newest appointments from the outside all share accounting firm backgrounds and work in the same building. One concern within the team is that, if there is a strategizing committee and it is composed predominantly of 'outsider/ accountants', and if there is a quality improvement committee which is composed predominantly of 'other-building/ insiders', *barriers may rise between these two, so far submerged, subgroups of senior management*. This development would compromise the enormous comparative advantage that the president is viewed as having almost single-handedly generated for Sun by his rare capacity for mastering both the insider, detailed, 'worm's eye' view of the company and the outsider, strategic 'bird's eye' perspective on the company in its competitive environment.

Another shadow issue for the team is the increasing workload and stress levels that have accompanied the recent growth of the company and the recent turbulence in the health care environment. Members acknowledge this concern in private, outside the meetings, but it is not discussed formally.

These issues—in their partially submerged and fuzzy character and in the consequent difficulty of articulating them and acting upon them—are characteristic of a type of issue that arises in the evolution from Systematic Productivity to Collaborative Inquiry. During the Systematic Productivity stage, a company takes its mission and its industry environment for granted as fixed (recall the discussion at the outset of Chapter 9). As it evolves towards the Collaborative Inquiry stage, a company questions its mission and environment, begins to recognize that it can shape both (not merely be shaped by them), and begins to be able to articulate the way in which taken-for-granted perspectives of individuals and subgroups within the company mould that shaping. Such 'implicit shapes' are, by their very nature, difficult and controversial to articulate explicitly, yet the failure to do so will prevent the company from evolving beyond Systematic Productivity.

The consultant follows the phone interviews by offering the above summary to the president and the senior management team. In addition, he offers the president the very specifically crafted alternative structure represented in Figure 10.1 to consider.

If you have been thinking that the consultant's model is incomprehensibly and ridiculously complex, then your reaction is similar to the president's. The president is initially cool about this model. It strikes him as too complicated to communicate easily and as unnecessarily unconventional. The paradoxical integration within the model of peer-like circularity, with horizontal division of functions between two committees, with the vertical division among the four simultaneous management processes, and with the almost hidden traditional, hierarchical lines of authority *does* make the model extraordinarily complex. The model displays Collaborative Inquiry stage logic, rather than the unambiguously pyramidal and deductive logic of the Systematic Productivity stage. But it may well do so in a manner that is, for all practical purposes, simply indigestible.

The president proposes yet another model in response. What about reconstructing the senior management team into *several* overlapping subgroups, perhaps one for each of the company's three primary strategies, with no COO or EVP layer?

And here we leave the process, for we have now followed Sun up to the moment of this writing. Moreover, the point of this story is more about developing a taste and a talent for the process that has just been described than it is about identifying any one particular outcome. Appreciating the significance of this kind of process is one sign of what we term the Strategist/Collaborative Inquiry breakthrough.

The Strategist/ Collaborative Inquiry breakthrough

In Chapter 9 we introduced the idea that the evolution from the Achiever/Systematic Productivity stage of development to the Strategist/Collaborative Inquiry stage of development involves a gradual augmentation of personal and organizational awareness from a sequential version of reality, wherein one is focusing on *either* visioning *or* strategizing, etc., towards an increasingly simultaneous experiencing of *both* visioning *and* strategizing, etc. Now, in the context of our discussion of insiders and outsiders on the Sun senior management team, and the more general notion of an insider's 'worm's eye' view and an outsider's 'bird's eye' view, we can describe the breakthrough to 'Strategist experience' as the developing ability to integrate the insider's (actor's) 'worm's eye' view and the outsider's (inquirer's) 'bird's eye' view—that is, to experience these perspectives as mutually necessary rather than as mutually exclusive. In this mode, as shown in Figure 10.2, you experience yourself as simultaneously seeing from both the inside and the outside; you experience yourself as simultaneously acting and inquiring; you experience yourself as simultaneously engaging in business-as-usual and in revisioning the business.

Now of course, the transformations from immersion in one perspective to the ability to alternate between one perspective and the other at different times, and to the continual reality of experiencing both perspectives simultaneously, are rarely as sudden and final as the word 'breakthrough' implies. (Indeed, one can interpret all of the developmental transformations between the Diplomat stage and the Magician/Witch/Clown stage as movements in this progression: from the Diplomat's total immersion in an insider's perspective, to the Technician's effort to find a formal, objective, outsider's perspective, to the Achiever's alternation between

I. Dichotomous, disconnected perspectives of different persons or institutions

II. Alternative perspectives for a given person or institution

III. As simultaneously experienced by a given person or institution

Figure 10.2   Three relationships between insider and outsider perspectives. Diagram III represents the ana-logic of the later developmental logics

the two, etc.) But the 'breakthrough' to both/and simultaneity *is* a *qualitative* change as the word implies and one that, according to current research, few human beings experience and even fewer experience continually.

The four Strategist-like actors who appear to be enacting the primary leadership roles in helping Sun's continuing evolution towards fuller realization of the Collaborative Inquiry stage at first glance appear to be at different points along an 'insider–outsider' continuum (see Figure 10.3). The president, who has been associated with the company the longest and has ultimate line authority within the company, appears to belong on the 'insider' extreme of the continuum. By contrast, the consultant who is not a full-time member of the company and is primarily retained to provide a more 'objective' outside perspective, seems clearly to anchor the 'outsider' extreme among the four. The new vice-president for marketing has line responsibilities in a staff function (marketing research), and has led the early cross-functional new product teams as well as currently serving as agenda manager for the senior management team. Thus, she fits towards the insider end of the continuum, especially in terms of the emerging Collaborative Inquiry structures such as the new product teams which she pioneered for the company, but with some 'outside' flavours such as the staff and inquiry emphasis in marketing research. The manager for employee development is in effect an internal consultant and trainer, and thus an outsider/staffer, though he too has line responsibilities for his department. Thus, he may fall slightly to the 'outsider' side of the centre of the 'insider–outsider' continuum, but clearly also has a very strong insider flavour as a full-time employee and manager.

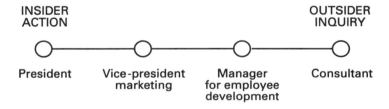

Figure 10.3   Four strategic players at Sun

This continuum clearly captures a significant aspect of the reality of the situation; but just as clearly, when we reflect on the matter, this is a single-visioned, outside-in, structural view of the situation. As we have already seen, there is another sense, which we regard as even more significant for the future development of Sun, in which all four of these organizational actors integrate insider/ outsider, actor/inquirer and business-as-usual/revisioning perspectives. And there is yet a third sense, we suspect, in which each of the four enacts the two different ends of the insider–outsider continuum in an unintegrated fashion.

Let us hear how persons at Sun who do *not* use the language of this theory speak about these four. Let us hear how their day-to-day colleagues speak of them and how they speak of themselves. Here is a senior manager speaking about the president:

> . . . (the president's) support and belief are absolutely essential. He has been a real leader, he has been willing to change. He had to change some things about the way he thought about planning, he has had to learn a new system. He has had to come out and be a much more visible leader than he probably would have liked or was his natural style. He has learned a lot.

In these comments, we hear how the president has become both more outgoing and more ingoing—how he has integrated more outgoing leaderly action with more ingoing self-revisioning inquiry. As we have already seen, other members of the senior management team regard the president as having an exceptional ability to integrate the insider, detailed 'worm's eye' view with the outsider, strategic 'bird's eye' view. On the other hand, if we were to speak of insiders as 'soft' and 'subjective' by contrast to outsiders who are 'hard' and 'objective', then the president clearly favours the outsider–objective perspective.

The other Strategist-like actor of the four who falls towards the insider end of our original bifurcated insider–outsider continuum is the new vice-president for marketing.[2] Of her, a colleague says:

> . . . the new product development process has been an enormous change effort, because it has meant substantial changes for the role of lots of managers and things that are going on in their departments. So (she) has had to be a change agent in that regard.

Here we hear this insider described not as a defender of the current culture and structure of the company—not as an agent of stability—but as an explorer of new ways of working, as an agent of change. Moreover, she is viewed as also being open to personal change:

> When (she) gets feedback from (the president) she knows just how to manage it, and how to deal with it within the group, and is not fazed by it at all.

In describing the manager for employee development, whom we originally place slightly to the outsider side of the bifurcated continuum, one of his superiors on the senior management team uses almost the same sort of language as we are using:

> and I think his role has changed in some regards from being a singular kind of outside consultant to being really an active participant; and that is a fine line that he needs to play here because he is a manager in the organization, and on the other hand he is an outside, you know, consultant, helping the managers develop, and playing both of those roles, depending on the project at the time. It is pretty tricky.

This theme of the trickiness of walking the tightrope that stretches in each moment orthogonally through the insider–outsider continuum is illustrated more concretely by the following comment:

> . . . he is very good at finding the pace that the other people in the organization actually learn at. And similarly, with the senior management, he is persistent about this, but he will not move ahead and get his head cut off for his troubles; he will really work patiently to bring senior management along on an issue. He is quiet, you know; he is not loud; he is not flamboyant; and I think those are important factors in his being successful as an internal change agent. If he were flamboyant, he probably wouldn't last.

This theme of the trickiness of walking the tightrope that stretches in each moment orthogonally through the centre of the insider—outsider continuum is echoed yet again in a comment about the external consultant:

> . . . to play the role he is playing in many cases, in the sense that he is a consultant (yet) he is also on our board . . . is a very tricky role for him.

Interestingly, the external consultant claims that he does not experience his simultaneous board membership and consulting position as the 'tricky' aspect of working with Sun:

> Over the past five years, I have become both a board member and a consultant at all three companies with which I currently work. Given the nature of the three organizations—one is a mission-oriented for-profit and the other two are market-responsive not-for-profits—and given my personality and style of working, I find that the board position highlights my long-term dedication to the mission of the company and that this emphasis balances my primary aim as a consultant of influencing senior

management's effectiveness in the near-term. It is also important that none of the board positions is itself lucrative and that I have an agreement with the president that I will relinquish the consulting role if a potential or actual conflict of interest is illustrated, or any time the president so wishes.

So, what's tricky for me now, after five years of association with Sun, is not so much balancing the board/consultant roles as it is dealing with the multitude of significant business relationships with persons and groups at all levels of the company. Although the company as a whole is my primary concern as a board member, and the efficacy of the president and the senior management team is my primary concern as a consultant, the person or group I am currently dealing with becomes, in a very real way, my primary client at that time. For me, the tricky trick is to act in a way which is true to my current primary client and to the other two primary concerns—the efficacy of the senior management team and the mission of the organization—at the same time.

In a sense, the external consultant is here talking about all the complex ways in which he is internal to the organization and balances multiple long-term relationships within it. However, this consultant's appreciation for complexity seems to blind him somewhat to the simple issues. We have already mentioned how his complex suggestion for restructuring senior management 'missed' the president, who was his primary client with regard to that issue. With regard to the foregoing quotation about what is really tricky for the consultant, *he* may not think balancing his board and consulting obligations is tricky, but a recent evaluation by the senior managers of the consultant's performance this past year shows that the senior managers are not fully open with the consultant because of his board role.

A fitting complement to this (partially mistaken) 'insider' sense that the 'outsider' consultant ascribes to himself is the 'outsider' sense that the internal consultant/manager of employee development talks about cultivating for himself:

You have to always stay fresh. You need to keep yourself fresh and your ideas fresh . . . so you kind of maintain the air that the external consultant brings, which makes you more . . . you get 'invited to the party' all the time because of that. I need some of both (internal and external consulting). I have told the company I need that; it is part of my education. It is a part of what makes me better. . . . The contact with the academic environment, the contact with other consultants, with other clients . . . re-energizes me. Now I can just bring all of that stuff back in here with a lot of intensity and enthusiasm.

Conclusion

This final quotation of this chapter nicely epitomizes the creative intuition that draws the Strategist/Collaborative Inquiry action logic beyond itself towards the myth-making action of the Magician/Witch/Clown/Foundational Community stage—towards continually reframing action—that we shall introduce in the following chapters.

The accent in the very first sentence of the quotation is on continual freshness—on experiencing freshly, seeing the situation freshly, feeling afresh, feeling inquiringly, reconceiving one's intent in the midst of action, experiencing the 'vertical' dimension of each next moment. And the treasure such self-refreshment brings to the organization is celebrated in the final sentence which describes the reverse of on-the-job burnout and organizational exhaustion that is so common in the demanding, globalizing, continually self-reconfiguring business and professional environments of the 1990s. If Sun senior managers could all refresh themselves at work as this manager advocates, then the shadow issue of workload and stress would be less prominent.

The overall response by the Sun senior management team to its accomplishments during the year in regard to becoming more collaboratively self-managing and in regard to supporting one another's professional development, with the help of the consultant, is strongly positive. On a rating of the consultant's work between −5 ('Detrimental'), 0 ('Sometimes useful, sometimes not worth the time') and +5 ('Of clear strategic value'), their average rating is +3.3. Members speak of 'Vastly improved management of the agenda and open items', of 'Team management actually working' and of how 'Getting to think strategically about one another's personal development (has been) good.' They speak of the consultant as 'Helpful with specific management problems' and as 'A good third party voice in discussions and decisions.' 'Suggestions concerning how to approach a particular problem were always right on target' and 'Helpful in controlling the emotional aspects' are additional positive comments.

Not every initiative was evaluated as successful, however. The majority of the team favours not continuing to work with the four Advocacy roles, named Visioning, Strategizing, Implementing and Assessing. From their point of view, the four ideas neither became clearly defined nor helped the team. As one of them put it, 'We got bogged down in form over substance.' Or, as another one wrote, more diplomatically, to the consultant, 'I did make every effort to understand the theoretical basis of your management theory. I must say some of the concepts are still difficult for me to comprehend.'

The president decided not to make any formal change in the team structure, but to name several members to an informal strategizing team. At the same time, the employee development manager persisted with his plan to create an internal 'quality improvement' board that includes other members of the team. These low-key, minor moves caused no ripples whatsoever, and taken some time after the initial inquiry are themselves well-crafted, strategist-like moves.

Thus the team is quietly evolving towards the Collaborative Inquiry stage, but it remains quasi-allergic to any discussion that veers toward 'process' or 'theory'. Also, we can see that some members tend to advise Achiever/Systematic Productivity solutions to dilemmas (e.g. 'make us finish what we start'). In fact, the consultant *had* supported a process of redefining the Advocate roles: a meeting had been held and agreements *had* been reached, and a member of the team had volunteered to bring the write-up to the team; but then the member had dropped the ball. Should the consultant have 'pushed' that member again? Perhaps so. But this is the subtle dance during the transformation from Systematic Productivity to Collaborative Inquiry, when the process or form of action comes to be seen as equally significant for the long-run effectiveness of the organization as the immediate substance and short-term outcome. The team seems to be about half-way there.

Before we move on to the next chapter, there is one last thing we would like to do. We wish to test whether the story of Sun Health Care seems to you to shed light on the organization(s) to which you belong.

- Do you see a need for a kind of CQI process within your school, or company, or church, or agency that not only 're-engineers' existing tasks and ceremonies, not only cuts costs, and not only makes the voice of your clients or customers more influential in shaping the products or services the organization delivers, but also revisions and reframes the organization as a whole?
- Does the idea of simultaneous action and inquiry at the organizational level make sense and seem desirable to you?
- Does the notion of personally integrating an outsider and an insider perspective seem feasible and attractive to you?
- Do you see why it is consistent with moving in such a direction that one begins increasingly to learn about one's 'rough edges', as this chapter has tried to inform you about the 'rough edges' of the process at Sun?

If you have been working with a CQI group for some time now—either one created within your organization or one created in response to Chapter 7 of this book—is it perhaps time to engage in a collaborative inquiry about reframing it?

If your CQI group has been working within the over-all Visioning/Strategizing/Implementing/Assessing struc-ture presented in Chapter 7, is it perhaps time to try something entirely different, as the Sun senior management team has decided to do?

Notes

1. Seven managers and senior managers at Sun have volunteered to take the sentence completion form we have used throughout our past 15 years of developmental research (for detail, see Appendix A of W. R. Torbert, (1987) *Managing the Corporate Dream*, Homewood, IL: Dow Jones-Irwin). The manager for employee development is scored at the Strategist stage.
2. The new vice-president for marketing is measured by the process described in note 1 as transitioning from the Achiever stage of development to the Strategist stage of development.

PART FOUR

THE ULTIMATE OBJECTIVES OF ACTION INQUIRY AND CQI

11 The 'chaotic' action awareness of transformational leaders

'You need to keep yourself fresh and your ideas fresh', the manager of employee development at Sun Health Care tells us. It sounds like an attractive idea, doesn't it?

A simple idea—an obvious idea—and an enjoyable experience. Wouldn't we all rather feel fresh than stale? Isn't it obvious that continual quality improvement (CQI) depends upon fresh new ideas about how to operate more effectively and fresh, new energies for actually doing so?

But, if keeping oneself fresh is such an intuitively appealing idea, why is this personal and organizational condition that is at the heart of the Magician/Witch/Clown/ Foundational Community stage of development (see Tables 5.1 and 5.2 in Chapter 5) so rare? Why, if refreshing oneself is such a simple and appealing idea, are the names we give this next stage of development so strange and unfamiliar? Why do we use names like 'alchemist',[1] 'sybil',[2] 'wanderer',[3] and 'community of inquiry'[4]? Why is development to this stage so rare that we find no managers who score at this level in our general samples of managers (see Table 11.1)? Why is it so rare that when we speak about this stage in public, managers ask us whether anyone approaching this stage could even work in an organization? Why is it so rare that, even when we set out to search for innovative leaders who might measure at this stage, we found that fewer than half of the extraordinary persons who took the measure scored at the Magician/Witch/Clown stage?

Let us offer a series of diverse illustrations in an effort to catch brief glimpses of the answers to these questions. We can begin by explaining why it *must* be true that 'brief glimpses' are the very best we can hope to achieve in this regard. Think about it this way: once an answer to these questions becomes a settled intellectual truth—a *mindset*—it is no longer fresh; it is no longer in contact with the colour and shock and feeling of a fresh perception.

Table 11.1   Distribution of managers by developmental position

Position	%
Opportunist	2
Diplomat	8
Technician	45
Achiever	36
Strategist	9
Magician	0
	100

Sources: Results of Loevinger Sentence Completion Tests administered to 497 managers in studies of first-line supervisors ($n=37$), nurses ($n=100$), junior and middle managers ($n=177$), senior managers ($n=66$), executives ($n=104$) and entrepreneurial professionals ($n=13$). For citations, see note 2 to Chapter 5.

For example, in the previous chapter we presented the elaborate senior management structure (Figure 10.1) that the consultant at one point created from the scattered information senior managers gave him in their phone interviews and from the new structures suggested by the manager for employee development and the president. Then, in the very next conversation with the president, the elaborate structure—of which the consultant was so proud, and which he had imagined could be a major long-term contribution—slipped silently under the waves of fresh ideas. The elaborate structure turned out to be useful for jogging the president's awareness to consider a wider range of ideas of structure, but it also turned out *not* to be *the* answer.

When we initially presented this sequence of events, we did not pause to consider how it came to pass. How did the consultant come to treat the elaborate structure, not as *the* answer, but rather as a 'brief glimpse of truth'? The consultant required a peculiar blend of audacious enthusiasm and modest tentativeness to propose and believe in the structure to begin with, yet to 'let go' of the idea soon after. That blend of feelings is *not* a permanent characteristic of the consultant, but rather an alchemical process cooked up on the spot through the stirring of conflicting feelings. First, he wanted to 'fight for' the idea in the face of the president's initial scepticism; secondly, he did not want to appear noncredible to the president; thirdly, he was searching for a perspective that 'fit' the team as a whole and simultaneously challenged it. Such is the clownish tumbling from moment to moment of a person at this stage. Such is the witch's brew of feelings she stirs. Such are the 'wandering' and unpredictable twists and turns and 'magical' outcomes when experience is engaged with reframing mind.

So, at this stage of development, neither the person nor the organization is based on, or finds its identity in, a particular mindset or structure. Instead, the person or organization continually retastes four 'territories of experience'—freshly seeking harmony among them. For the person, the four territories are: intuition, thought, actions and external effects. For the organization, the four territories are: mission, strategy, operations and bottom-line outcomes.

The transformation from the Strategist stage, like all other developmental transformations to later stages, is a movement from *being* something to *having* that kind of thing. This time the transformation is from being *in the right frame of mind* to having a *reframing spirit*. A reframing spirit continually overcomes itself, divesting itself of its own presuppositions. A reframing mind continually reattunes itself to the frames of reference held by other actors in a situation, and to the underlying organizational and historical developmental rhythms, seeking the 'common sense' of the situation and seeking the motivating challenge of the situation.

Discovering the motivating challenge can create a social ju-jitsu effect: just as total disintegration is threatening, the person or organization or nation suddenly fluidifies and acts with unforeseeable vigour and resolve. For this reason, this vulnerable power is often experienced as magician-like, witch-like or clown-like.

In transforming to this managerial style, the person must face and learn how to transform the entire dark side of the human condition as it manifests itself in the person and the person's surroundings. Unlike the Strategist, who may believe that he or she is on the side of good and can beat evil, the Clown* recognizes that the polarization between good and evil—between victory and defeat, between the sacred and the profane, between classes, races, and sexes, between I and Thou—is recreated at each moment by our relatively fixed and one-sided perspectives on the world. Evil emanates from the character of our own fallen, passive attention; it cannot be permanently defeated. Indeed, to fight against it as though it were only outside ourselves is to reinforce it. Action inquiry becomes, for the Magician/Witch/Clown, not

---

* In this chapter, we refer to the person at this stage variously as Magician/Witch/Clown, or as Magician, or as Witch, or as Clown to emphasize that such a person is not anchored in a particular mindset and cannot be categorized in a simplistic fashion.

so much a theory of managing as an ongoing jousting, at one and the same time, with one's own attention and with the outside world.

Such a person requires no official role. His or her power and authority derive from listening to developmental rhythms. By virtue of this four-territory listening, he or she takes the 'executive role', a sense of responsibility for the whole that is open to anyone, regardless of official role. Listening in this way, with a sense of wonder repeatedly reawakening in body, heart and mind, the Witch experiences the rhythms of a particular conversation, of the lives of the individuals conversing, of the particular organizational setting where the conversation is occurring, and of still wider historical circumstances as radiating from the past and the future into the only time when awareness and action are possible: this inclusive present.

A study of six Magicians

Let us explore further whether and how these theoretical speculations are illustrated in the activities of several late-stage executives. Because of the difficulty in finding managers in large samples who measure at the Magician/Witch/Clown and at the still later Ironist stages of development, we have for the past eight years been searching out persons who, on the basis of public reputations for uniqueness and unusual success, or on the basis of personal testimony by close associates, may be measured at later stages of development.

More than half of the persons so discovered have *not* measured at the two latest stages; but we have observed in great detail a half dozen who *have* measured at the Magician or Ironist stages. Of these, some have agreed to tape their predictions and reflections on work days for a week on their drives into and away from work. Some have agreed to let one of us follow their footsteps for entire days. And all have submitted to two or more hours of interviewing. In four of the six cases, one of us has had long-term contacts with the persons in one or more of the following roles: consultant, member of a board of directors, teacher, friend, fellow participant in a spiritual community.

For our present purposes we wish to provide a few glimpses of these people in action, in an effort to convey the sense of moment-to-moment attention, unpredictability, uniqueness and cross-level analogizing that characterizes much of their work and play (or 'work/play', a conjuga-tion that comes closer to describing the actual interweaving of business, art and leisure in the lives of these individuals).

More 'brief glimpses' of Magician-like experiencing

The first thing that struck us forcibly as we became more intimately connected to our subjects' work days was that they were key players, not just in one organization, but in *many*, with their days unpredictably divided into initiatives and responses across the organizations. Perhaps the most extreme example of this was the woman who interacted with between five and seven organizations each day of the week that she documented. Her primary organizational affiliation was as a member of a global consulting firm, and she acknowledged that when she was visiting a particular client, she would occasionally have brief contact by phone with no more than one or two other organizations in the course of a day. But this week she was at her own firm's offices throughout. There, she: (1) trained junior consultants, (2) served on a performance evaluation committee, (3) developed an affidavit for a suit against a board of which she was a member, (4) billed 37 hours to three different direct client firms as well as five other engagements that she more indirectly supervised, and (5) initiated 42 telephone calls and received 19 on behalf of a newly organizing industry trade association (she called this effort 'market development'). In addition, she offered two different, ongoing workshops from 8 to 10 p.m. on two of the evenings. The participants in these workshops included former and current organizational clients who wished to explore their own personal development at a deeper level. Although this illustration is offered from the outside in, giving no direct taste of this woman's experiencing, it suggests to us one way that persons who measure at the late stages of development tend to live at once 'symphonically' and 'chaotically'. In our next illustration, we look at this same phenomenon from the inside-out perspective of another of our Clown executives.

The second thing that struck us when we observed these executives directly was that within a given day their pace varied enormously. There was a sense of leisure and playfulness at times; a sense of urgency and fierce efficiency at others. Indeed, in one case the two types of responses coexisted simultaneously. This CEO intentionally works and lives in a different city from his corporation's headquarters. His office takes up parts of two floors in a large Victorian house, the rest of which is his home. The first floor office consists of an impressive, but more or less normal, outer office for the secretary and visitors, along with his inner office, including an informal seating area, a working table for meetings of up to 8 or 10, and a private bathroom. Within the bathroom is a spiral staircase to the second floor. The second floor room is dominated by a large exercise mat, a wall of books, and comfortable seating. A speaker phone makes it possible for this man to be exercising or lounging in a totally relaxed fashion, yet project his voice over the phone as though he is rushing and distracted. This technique, he explains, encourages callers to come to the point more quickly and seems to increase their cooperativeness when he slows down, momentarily, to give them what they can appreciate as 'quality attention'.

Even in his busiest times in the office downstairs, he escapes upstairs for two or three minutes each hour to do sit-ups, push-ups, aikido, or yoga postures. Challenged about the manipulativeness of his telephone technique, he responds unabashedly,

> I *am* giving them quality attention. In fact, I am giving them a far higher quality attention than most of them can imagine. This way of working increases the quality of my attention, saves their time and money, and apparently serves them well, since many of them are long-term clients of our firm. My closest colleagues are aware of the set-up and joke over the phone about what I'm probably doing as we speak, and that seems to heighten the creativity of our exchanges.

The World Bank executive

A third element in common among all six executives is their apparently equally deep fascination with three different sociological levels: with personal detail at the individual level; with the dynamics of group and organizational issues; and with how the organizations with which they are involved relate to national or international developments. We have already seen this pattern in our first example of the global consultant who attends to personal development, organizational development and interorganizational networks. Another dramatic example of this theme was the World Bank executive from Sweden, with whom we conducted our research during the 1980s when former Congressman Conable (R-NY) was serving as president of the World Bank and launched a major reorganization and downsizing.

Conable's procedure was to redraw the organization chart, with far fewer positions, and invite everyone in the organization to become a candidate for any position (thus effectively 'killing' the former structure [and generating skyrocketing anxiety among its personnel]). Conable himself hired fewer deputies than previously, and they in turn followed suit, hiring a reduced number of subordinates, and so on. Although the espoused theory of this change was to profoundly shake up the perceived complacency of the World Bank while downsizing, the actual outcome was in no way transformational. Because of the intense anxiety and politicking and the lack of any formal performance evaluation procedures, with few exceptions former bosses hired back former subordinates for similar positions as before.

The late-stage Swedish executive whom one of us was observing and interviewing at the time took a different approach, however. She began by telling her current subordinates that the problem of personnel evaluation and organizational transformation were, in her view, the bottlenecks that most frequently inhibited success in third world development programmes. Therefore, she regarded a person's ability to solve the current organizational dilemma in a way that could be applicable to third world projects as a primary (but not the only) criterion for rehiring, and she asked them to propose methods and other persons in the World Bank whom they regarded as most highly qualified to resolve this kind of dilemma in a transformational fashion.

Initially, most of the former subordinates did not recommend any other candidates for the positions, evidently regarding it as contrary to their career interest to do so. Only one of the former subordinates met the executive's request. This person also offered some inventive structural suggestions on how to proceed. The Swedish executive hired this person and let the rest of the group know the basis for her decision, as well as the additional structural features for the remainder of the selection process. One of these features was that, in order to be considered for any of the remaining three positions, each of the remaining five former subordinates absolutely must recommend the most qualified person outside the group for the particular position, documenting the process that she or he had used to reach that determination.

Three of the five subordinates felt trapped, insulted, and/ or betrayed by this procedure. Two of them refused vociferously to participate, while the third masked his alienation (although the Swedish executive was well aware of it). This person 'pretended' to participate, but in a way that was ineffective. The constructive, negative feedback from the Swedish executive persuaded this person to change his strategy for his continued search within the World Bank for a position, and he ultimately succeeded. The two 'vociferous refusers' were not appointed. The Swedish executive invited each of the remaining two persons (who responded positively to the Swedish executive's second 'wake up call') to take the position for which, based on prior experience, they were *least* qualified. She explained her decision to them as a challenge to increase their attention to teamwork and to learning from others, and both accepted. The final position was offered to one of the candidates recommended by the three rehired subordinates. At the end of the following three years, this group had one of the best performing loan portfolios among all the area groups within the bank.

This story not only illustrates a manager's analogical attention to individual, group and international issues, but also illustrates, from a distance, a fourth theme in common among the later stage managers we researched. This theme is the charismatic quality of their personal relationships, but in the service of challenging others rather than generating worshipful subservience. The women and men seemed to use their sensitivity to initial conditions, to the particular language meaningful to their interlocuters, and to new initiatives throughout ongoing encounters, along with their capacity for intelligent analogy and an evident relish for unpredictability, in a way that increased their own and others' alertness, learning and sense of mutuality.

One of us saw a touching example of this as another of the six executives we observed—an artist, entrepreneur and civic leader—fed supper to his three-year-old twin son and daughter. With humour, and largely through the medium of babytalk, he conducted a meandering lesson in arithmetic and lifetime personal development, syncopated by their initiatives as well. The fact that this interaction does not occur at work illustrates the point made earlier, that persons at this stage of development treat their interwoven work and leisure life equally as opportunities for widening awareness. Their interest in such awareness is neither a means to an end nor instrumental in order to achieve something else, but is rather an end in itself.

In a different room of the house immediately following the scene, the researcher tape recorded his memory of this conversation, trying to capture its spirit, tones, timing and exact phraseologies. Once again, the rhythms, paradoxes and spontaneities of this encounter give us an impression of conducting social interaction and personal experiencing as a 'chaotic symphony'.

Child's play

To set the scene:

The artist–entrepreneur had returned the two miles from his office to his Denver home on what I (the researcher) found to be utterly unwieldy, three-wheeled roller skates invented by him and manufactured by his own company.

I drove.

His wife, an educational administrator, left for an accounting class as he entered.

Still sweating, he commandeered their three-year-old twins for a brief 'jog' to the elementary school they would attend in three years, and back again. (The jogging actually involved one kid or the other on his shoulders most of the way.) Once home again and showered, the executive fed the children, and the following conversation unfolded.

'Books,' said Alexander, neglectfully dropping a spoonful of squash on the large stuffed lion's head.

'Library,' said Rebecca gravely.

'Elementary school', added their father.

'Elementary school!!' they both chimed in with relish.

'Eat excellent,' their father reminded them.

'Meatloaf,' enunciated Alexander, through a mouth full of it.

'Elementary school is where you'll go in three years, when you're six years old,' the father said, holding up six fingers.

'Six years old!' they both declared with emphasis.

'How old is mama?' the father asked.

'Thirty-one,' they said promptly, evidently rehearsing a well-known sum.

'How old is dada?'

'Thirty-six.'

'How old is Grandpa Henry?'

'Sixty-eight.'

'Happy birthday, Grandpa Henry!' interpolated Rebecca.

'Grandpa Henry have a brown car. Sedan car,' announced Alexander, as if not to be outdone.

'That's true,' their father acknowledged. 'How old is Old Nonie?'

'Eighty-five,' they said with the willingness of responsive readers at church.

'Go to elementary school, six years old,' reiterated Alexander.

'Yes, and after that, when you grow up more you'll go to another school, junior high school.'

'Junior high school,' repeated Rebecca, concentrating.

'When you're eleven years old, you'll go to junior high school. And then, when you grow up more, you'll go to high school. You'll go to high school when you are fourteen years old.'

'Fourteen years old,' murmured Alexander softly, eyes now glazed from looking into a new dimension.

'And then you'll go to college when you are eighteen years old,' continued his father.

'University of Denver?' queried Rebecca.

'Yes, maybe University of Denver. Where mama is now.'

'Mama go to work on the bus,' incanted Alexander, dissolving his distant reverie.

'Yes, but now mama at University of Denver in a class. In the grey car.'

'In the grey car,' acknowledged Alexander.

'Mama and dada went to elementary school when *they* were six years old,' continued his father, reinforcing the orthodox creed. 'And then they went to junior high school when they were eleven years old. Then mama and dada go to high school and then to college.'

'College eighteen years old,' said Rebecca, displaying her capacity for holding together the different pieces of this game.

'Yes, go to college when eighteen years old and then, after college, go to work twenty-one years old.'

'Go to work twenty-one years old! ' shouts Alexander gleefully.

'Why go school?' ponders Rebecca.

'Go to school to learn new things,' her father parries. And now he really bears down. 'When twins are three years old, learn new things in family, like now, learning "years-old" and "schools". When six years old go to elementary school to learn new things. When eleven, learn new things in junior high school; when fourteen, learn new things in high school; when eighteen, learn new things in college; and then, when twenty-one years old, go to work to learn new things.'

'Mama has brown hair,' says Rebecca, in a self-evident bid to change the subject.

'Twins have blond hair,' says Alexander.

'Dada,' concludes Rebecca, with the mock sly glance of someone who knows she has a sure-fire joke, 'has *some* hair.'

'Rebecca is a muffin-brain,' counterattacks her father in self-defence.

'Insults,' remarks Alexander, thrusting out a waggling finger in preparatory emphasis. 'Dada is a dinosaur foot!'

And so, future lessons instantly forgotten, a fusillade of 'insults' pours forth from all three:

'Elephant toe!'

'Popcorn knee!'

'Zucchini nose!'

'Cauliflower ear!'

'Giraffe neck!'

'Bumble-bee bellybutton!'

'Tickle-massage, dada.'

'Okay, come over here.'

'No!'

'Then I'm-a-goin-to-haf-to-cum-git-you!'

'No, dada. Mercy!' as he starts for them and they pretend to try to get away.

'Justice!' he says as his fingers reach them.

Uncontrollable giggling and gasping for breath until each twin manages to wheeeze 'Massage', whereupon the marauding hands move gently into a massage for the period of two in-breaths. Then they again invite 'Tickling' and the fingers again begin flying.

See how the dialogue between the artist–entrepreneur and his three-year-old twins zigzags back and forth, with initiatives by both the father and the children that either develop or interrupt what emerges as the main theme? Our division of the dialogue into 'verses' roughly shows how it starts over again and again, 'chaotically', while simultaneously reaching a symphonic crescendo. Is not the entrepreneur clearly engaged in an exercise of widening the children's comprehension and imagination, while simultaneously aware that their attention span is short and concrete, and that long, abstract disquisitions (such as his 'long' talk that starts 'Go to school to learn new things') will not necessarily mean anything to them? The father is sensitive, not just to initial conditions, but to the new conditions at each later moment. Thus, when Rebecca changes the subject after his 'speech', the father playfully yields to entirely different kinds of awareness expansion such as the impulsive insults, the physical tickle-massage and the metaphysical play between 'Mercy' and 'Justice'. Such is the wandering, reawakening path of action inquiry between persons at very different stages of development when at least one of them is seeking simultaneous awareness of the educational aim, the strategic relationships, the ongoing actions and the outcomes of the present situation.

Chaos theory as map of late-stage action awareness

Chaos theory has recently become fashionable in the natural and social sciences. Chaos theory highlights processes that are non-repetitive and unpredictable—apparently irrational—when mapped in two dimensions, but which reveal astonishing shape, order and singularity when mapped in three dimensions.[5] Instead of learning the truth by dividing the phenomenon into parts, the chaos theory approach is to look at the phenomenon as a whole from a higher dimension. In this regard, chaos theory is about how apparently formless qualities like smoke and clouds, ocean currents and weather, moods and organizational norms can be seen as moving rhythmically and taking shapes, when viewed mathematically as $(x+1)$-dimensional phenomena rather than as x dimensional.

Chaos theory also introduces the notion of fractals—self-similarities or analogies across micro/meso/macro scales. The idea here is that you cannot measure many shapes precisely (such as the shoreline of England, or the surface area of a mountain, or the play of a person's stream of consciousness) because the more closely you focus on an area of detail the more squiggles or bumps you can see and measure. Therefore, what becomes important is not precise measurement, but an equation for the overall quality of the shape. What is remarkable is that for some phenomena that shape is reproduced at whatever scale of size one examines the phenomenon. Approximate analogies for wholes become more important than precise measures of parts.

Let us say a little more about chaos theory, not only because it relates to inside-out, Witch-like awareness, but also because it will help us to reconsider the nature of developmental theory, which, until this chapter, has been presented as though it is a Strategist-like, right mindset.

Another characteristic of chaos theory is that it focuses on a system's enormous sensitivity to initial conditions in its further development. Small differences in initial conditions can generate great differences in the eventual shapes of two systems. Moreover, activity and inactivity, meaningful communication and noise (as, for example, over a phone line) are not evenly distributed in such systems. Therefore, means are not particularly meaningful, and evenly spaced interventions will not generate calculably cumulative effects. On the contrary, activity and noise occur in spurts. Consequently, no overall equation is sufficient for predicting when to act to effect a certain change. The actor also requires awareness of initial conditions and of the ongoing syncopation in the sytem's development, since the effect of a given action will be determined in part by whether it occurs during a spurt or a pause in the system's activity.

At first glance, all three of these qualities of chaos theory—
(a) shape as discernible from a higher dimension when treated as $x+1$ dimensions;
(b) fractal self-similarities across scales; and
(c) sensitivity to initial and ongoing conditions

—appear disconnected from, or directly contrary to, developmental theory. Does not developmental theory suggest a predictable, orderly development through tightly defined stages, whatever the initial conditions?

But, if we consider further the illustrations of late-stage executives just offered, we shall find that there is not just a strong contrast between developmental theory and chaos theory, but also a close kinship between the two. In fact, the chaos theory propositions presented in the previous paragraphs and the version of developmental theory that corresponds with Magician/Witch/Clown-like awareness are strikingly self-similar—like fractals.

With regard to the notion of shape as discernible from higher dimensions, if we think of each of the four territories of experience as a different dimension, things that appear shapeless and arbitrary at an earlier developmental stage gain shape when viewed from the next higher dimension. For example, behavioural norms don't mean much to a person at the Opportunist stage who is mastering the outside-world territory by means of his or her own actions. They (behavioural norms) become meaningful at the Diplomat stage, when a person is gaining control of the personal action dimension by conforming to the normative patterns that his or her thoughts and feelings infer. However, for this person the world of systemic logic is still only implicit, not yet controllable. He or she is ruled by cultural or peer-group convention, not by an independent application of an explicit and internally consistent logic.

With regard to seeing self-similar fractals at different scales, it is only at late stages, when a person seeks to experience the different territories of experience simultaneously that he or she can see whether there are successful analogies—self-similar fractals—or significant incongruities across the territories. Only at late stages, for example, do executives see, care about and attempt to create fractal-like relationships among mission, strategy, operations and outcomes, as the Swedish World Bank executive does in the earlier illustration. At earlier stages, executives are more likely to care only (or primarily) about outcomes, or only (or primarily) about operations, or only (or primarily) about strategy.

Finally, with regard to the issue of sensitivity to initial and ongoing conditions, developmental theory appears invariant only when considered as an abstract theory. In practice, persons spend longer or shorter periods of their lives at different stages, spend longer or shorter times in the 'chaotic' transitions between stages, and conclude their development at different points along the developmental continuum. Moreover, at later stages a person's attention becomes both more inclusive and more discriminating. An early-stage person may say that 'nothing' happened at an hour-long meeting, implying that it was boring and that he or she takes no responsibility for the overall shape of the event. A late-stage person at the same meeting may have experienced it as an intense drama with much at stake, during which he or she failed to find the moment and the action that could transform an inconclusive process into a more meaningful and creative event. In short, the drama of development, influenced by the tone set at the outset, perhaps even by the arrangement of furniture in the room, and by each wisp of interruption, is occurring at many intersecting scales for the late-stage person on a daily and hourly basis—not just over a lifetime. Thus, the 'inconsequential' suppertime play between the artist–entrepreneur and his daughter and son in the earlier ilustration is permeated by a lively dia-logic, at once coherent and open to surprise.

Why is there such a strong contrast between the initial view of developmental theory as a rigidly sequential, linear theory, and the view of developmental theory offered here as opening towards chaos? One way of embracing both horns of the dilemma is to interpret the 'rigid' version of developmental theory as resulting from taking a reconstructed, outside-in perspective on development—a type of perspective consistent with the overall outside-in, bird's eye approach of the Technician and Achiever stages of development and of contemporary mainstream social science.[6] At the same time, the dynamic/chaotic version of developmental theory presented in this chapter can be interpreted as corresponding with a constructive, late-stage, inside-out perspective on development consistent with the action inquiry paradigm of social science[7] as well as with the actual action awareness of late-stage transformational leaders, as illustrated in the previous section.[8]

From chaos theory to chaotic action awareness

What the chaos theorists' elegant theorizing does not address is how human beings in their day-to-day organizational and family lives can come to appreciate the complexity, indeterminacy and higher-order orderliness that the theory of fractals reveals—and that effectual organizational management in turbulent times demands. Developmental theory, which at first blush contradicts chaos, actually describes how persons and organizations can evolve towards just the complex, analogical appreciation of experience that chaos theorists speculate about.

In a passage on improvisational flute playing, mathematician Michael Rossman brings chaos theory to life in a description of the interplay of four territories of experience (external sound, the hand working the flute, the pattern of the music and the intuitive intervention of each next note):

> Sometimes the music itself leads me forth, embracing even my tremors and contradictions in something whole. Playing free, every so often I realize that the note I have just begun is not the one 'I' had intended and sent out orders to produce, but a different one chosen confidently by my body to extend the music—quite independently of the listening-and-scheming me who flashes with resentment at the *mistake*.

> . . . When I am free to uncover in the instant the dancing logic of those next notes that will weave the slip into consonance, make it have been inevitable, I feel involved in some transcendent mathematics. To reduce it to the simple case of improvising alone, it is as if, on some cosmic abscissa and ordinate, I were living out the construction of a complex curve while simultaneously deriving its equation, unifying induction and deduction in a way inverse to their unity while playing Bach. The curve comes to a point not predictable from the equation known up to that moment; rather than reject the point as anomalous, a discontinuity, I continue the curve through it and beyond in a way which yields a new equation, one containing its previous version as a limiting case valid up to that odd point, and embodying a deeper notion of continuity. And so it goes, when I am moving in the spirit of a world in which chance and accident and will are subsumed in a higher order.[9]

Seen from the inside-out, developmental theory is the story of how consciousness of four territories of experience and of the harmonies (analogies, self-similarities) and disharmonies (incongruities) across them can evolve. We can hear the 'freshness' in Rossman's improvisational flute playing, and it again raises the question we asked at the outset of this chapter. Why is this freshness so difficult to rediscover in the ongoing struggles and tensions, habits and comforts, of our lives?

The optimistic language that we have used about harmonizing the four qualities of experience from intent to effect—hides as much as it reveals. What it hides, when that is made explicit, will go another long step towards making clear why so few persons and organizations move towards this kind of continual-quality-improving experiencing.

What the language of harmonizing the four territories of experience hides is the distances, disharmonies and incongruities among these different qualities of experience that are revealed to a widening awareness. To experience such incongruities is not just an intellectual exercise, but an existential, emotional shock. For example, to experience oneself as lying when one believed oneself honest, or as acting unilaterally when one advocates acting collaboratively, generates suffering. Who wishes voluntarily to take on the continual suffering of witnessing the gaps in oneself, in others, in organizations and in larger social processes between intentions, espoused values, actual practices and outcomes?

One answer, we believe, is a person at the Magician stage who is intuitively trying to create a business or a family setting where inquiry about the most difficult issues is valued and practised. We call such a setting a *Community of Inquiry* and will be giving it fuller description in the next chapter. By way of warning that such a setting will be no comfortable Utopia for anyone and that it is 'bought' through suffering the gaps, we present the following journal excerpt about work and family by one of the Magicians we have studied.

One of the partners of a major executive search firm, this man is also a trusted board member of a company we shall call Blue Corp. Here he describes the whirlpool of issues and difficulties in his life, as he participates in merger meetings between Blue Corp and Red Corp, as he engages his angry teenage son, and as he suffers his separation from his fiancée who is stuck on the other side of the world:

What a witches' brew this merger negotiation is becoming. Today, in fact, I took my small bronze witches' cauldron to the meeting at the Meridienne, along with my three juggler's balls.

I never did bring out the cauldron, but the meeting came to a gentle boil at one point nonetheless. The soft juggler's balls occasioned some good humour, as well as some good squeezing by members of both teams.

It's fun to watch the relationships form, carefully but also enthusiastically. In general the spirit has been good during the first three meetings. Then the concerns of the absent CEOs and Board members drag us back some between meetings. We are gaining respect for one another within the meeting room. Everyone is working very hard to be constructive, flexible, and creative. Still, it's easy to get stuck and start blaming the other team. Amazing how difficult it is to agree on what a 50/50 merger means in specific terms. I keep reminding our team to test their inferences with the others before drawing conclusions. Twice now, when we've publicly tested, they've helped us see what's really at stake for them; and it's *not* what we had imagined.

Today, the problem seemed to us to be that their CEO is stuck in some old thinking. We have agreed from the start that he will be the CEO of 'Newco'. But he says that he has never had good experiences with a COO, so he doesn't want our man, who couldn't be more competent, as his COO, but as one of the division heads along with his current division presidents. We wondered whether he was trying to be loyal to his divisional presidents, one of whom will very likely succeed him within the next couple of years if there is no merger.

Our team leader, the Information Services VP, made a nice statement, concerned but not accusatory, about our sense that their CEO isn't joining us in building a *new* company by thinking 'outside the box'. (Wonderful the benign, integrating influence such clichés can have.)

Their team leader, who likes my ties and my stories so much, made a marvellously diplomatic response, saying that their CEO has already been rethinking several points, that he is generally hard to move initially, but that he is also very firm in his commitment, support, and loyalty once he makes a decision. Although this statement is open to various interpretations, we do repeatedly sense they are sincere because they acknowledge problem areas.

I had urged our team to directly raise the issue of whether the Red Corp representatives in this very room (two of whom are themselves divisional presidents) might be opposed to having our man as COO. No one else seemed about to, so I now did. I talked slowly, saying that those of us in the room might either help or hinder the two CEOs in resolving this issue, giving the Red Corp guys time to weigh the risks of speaking truthfully about their own ambitions, before I actually asked them.

This is when the meeting seemed to me to reach a gentle boil. Two of them quickly made strong statements about their willingness to work for our man. And our team leader got a laugh from everybody by quipping that they had now been exposed to the sort of treatment our senior management had learned to expect from me: being inescapably invited to comment on the most delicate and potentially embarrassing of issues.

Of course, we know that the most likely heir-apparent wasn't in the room, so our concern may yet prove true. But their sincerity was again evident and generated trust. And they certainly heard unmistakably that the deal's off unless they can agree, so that should give them some leverage with their CEO, if that's what's needed.

I wish I could see the same ambiguous progress with Jarred.

What an agony he now is to himself and to his brothers and parents. Neither a single exclamation point, nor a dozen, can evoke his sound and fury, as twice a week now he enters his seventeen year young rage and lashes out at: Milt, who can more or less take care of himself; or at his stalwart and long-suffering little brother, Phil; or, more often, at his mother; or at me. On Sunday night, after a good day, he completely destroyed the cookout that his mother prepared, as only a fabulous cook like her can, for Nana and Grandpa. First, Jarred threw the basketball at Milt; then he 'taught Phil a lesson' which left the latter's left face dramatically scraped; and, for dessert, began frothing and screaming at his mother and even his grandparents. As his *pièce de resistance*, he accused his mother of ruining his supper, because the meat was cold when he finally got to it (the microwave was within two steps of him at the time)! I was ashamed and furious when told.

Yesterday morning at 7:15, as the final arrangements for the day were reviewed, Jarred again suddenly provoked extreme tension over the time of his dentist appointment and the idea that he should ride the 'shame train' (the bus, to you and me) from school to dentist. He proceeded to break the tension he had created all by himself by flying into another rage against getting manipulated by the whole rest of the world.

This artistic movement and self-expression brought Jarred the outcomes for which he, no doubt secretly even to himself, wished—namely: the departure of his immediate family on their separate ways to schools and work; his temporary release from school; and my advent.

Our six hours together were great—the very picture of a boy and his Dad jogging about woodland paths, talking seriously, developing a list of projects that *he* wants to complete (e.g. get driving licence and contact lenses). And I was an exhausted wreck afterwards. Will any of it make any difference tomorrow? Why are my two oldest sons prone to such extremes of rage? Will Jarred come through this in the end as well as Milt did after a briefer period of rages last year? How to conduct myself with Jarred from moment to moment, when any hint of irritation on my part provokes an explosion from him, yet all my efforts to meet him four fifths of the way to him leave me apprehensive that I am colluding in his manipulation of me?

Meanwhile, literally in the background because she is on the other side of the world, but very much in the foreground of my feelings, is Regina (Sui-Lin, in Chinese). She is trapped in Vietnam by her Confucian parents' insistence that she choose between them and me, by her refusal to do so, and by the bureaucratic eternity that arranging a fiancée visa requires. The dry dust of official paperdom threatens to dissolve all memory of love in sheer boredom.

The agony is made infinitely worse, however, by the knowledge that Regina's father is at this very moment envoying her, complete with her MBA and her silent eros that has already hooked the oily man who can offer the price concession, to dine alone with him. Her commission is straightforward and business-like: to extract the price concession for the textile factory her father is planning to build.

'So what?' you say. 'Pretty much business as usual, isn't it? She's an Asian woman, with a Confucian obligation to her father. She's collected her MBA and her individuality in the good old U.S. of A. This is no doubt a very minor trick in the world of Confucian business practice. What's the big deal?'

Well, it's a mystery to me what the big deal is, though I've been learning more and more about it during our past nine months of separation. One thing is clear, however. Regina's low whisper over our $800 per month phone bill tells me that she is truly sick with self-disgust. Self-disgust that she should attract such attention in the first place. Self-disgust that she should feel as irritably alienated from her father as she now feels. Self-disgust that she cannot please her parents by so much as glancing in the direction of the eligible young men they are so diligently assembling for her. Self-disgust that she should find herself complaining to me. She is in agony, and her parents' decree of last November that she choose between them and me has kept her locked there.

In her absence, I am drying out, stiffening, daily. My voice withdraws deeper within me. Without the holy rock and roll of our struggles to understand one another and our embracing silences, the dancing moments are fewer and fewer, the aspirins more and more frequent, my life less and less well lubricated. I feel alternately chilly and feverish. The pains from my lower back operation, and my many childhood tumbles on my head that have so jammed my cracking neck and jaw become more and more prominent features of my daily life, despite my vigorous counterattack. . . .

Walking, jogging, twirling, swinging, balancing, and running near dawn around the sacred woodland circle that Jarred and I rounded earlier today. . . .

Shiatsu massage, with chanting, every week with my gay friend, Coz. . . .

Entering, last night, the three-week bath of glory I have contrived to give myself each summer by teaching masters consulting students at the local university. . . .

All these vigorous countermeasures are intended to assuage the tug and scrape of my lonely heart and the petrifaction of my post-50 body, and they fail in every moment . . . except the truly dancing ones.

What we hear in these amused and pained reflections hardly sounds like what we might envision as a community of any kind. On the contrary, this sounds like the most fragmented of modern lives. The man is getting his professional kicks from a very temporary job (or maybe two very temporary jobs, if you count the part-time teaching he mentions towards the end). He is divorced and does not see his sons during the week (anybody have a clue why his sons are angry?). And he is a world apart from his fiancée.

He certainly sounds as though he is engaged in difficult forms of inquiry:

• how to increase the likelihood of a successful merger (a little-known art!)
• how to raise a teenage son (a still less well-known art, despite our billions of opportunities to practise it!)
• how to consummate an Asian–American marriage in a way that integrates two families and two traditions instead of further dividing father from daughter and sister from brother.

But is he engaged in a Community of Inquiry? Certainly not from our understanding of the situation. If there is a community, where is it? In the hotel suite rented by the hour? In the family rent by divorce? In the lovers on opposite sides of the world? Like Gertrude Stein's Oakland, but even more so, 'there's no there there'.

Can the relationships that the executive search firm partner describes *evolve* towards a Community of Inquiry, whatever that turns out to be when we examine it more closely in the next chapter? Perhaps they can. But, someone may counter, so can all relationships, according to developmental theory. True in theory, we respond, but in practice relationships are more likely to evolve towards a Community of Inquiry the more late-stage participants, like the executive search firm partner, act in truly mutual, vulnerable ways that accept the contingent validity of all participants' perspectives while creating transformational conditions. (Of course, we have too little data from the journal entry to know precisely how this man acts in every moment, but we do get a few hints about his mutuality in making sure the Red Corp members don't feel attacked by his inescapable question and in his uncertainty about how to act with his son. We also sense his vulnerability throughout his stories; and his ability to entertain multiple perspectives simultaneously is illustrated in his belief that the other business team is sincere at the same time as fearing that he may be being tricked.)

Conclusion

We have offered glimpses of evidence from a small sample of late-stage executives. They provide suggestive illustrations of what 'chaotic' action awareness looks like. Since these illustrations all occurred among persons measured at the Magician stage of development, and since ealier studies of managers at earlier stages have generated no such illustrations, the data is consistent with, and therefore not disconfirming of, the hypothesis that development to the later stages generates 'chaotic' action awareness.

Obviously, much more research will be necessary to generate confidence in the general validity of this hypothesis. To determine whether this hypothesis is valid, not just generally but also in your case, will require still further research by you in the action inquiry mode.

Notes

1. M. Yourcenar (1976) *Abyss*, New York: Farrar, Straus & Giroux.
2. P. Lagerkvist (1958) *The Sybil*, New York: Random House.
3. The Wanderer is one of the 64 hexagrams of the Chinese Book of Changes. R. Wilhelm (trans.) (1967). *The I Ching*, Princeton, NJ: Princeton University Press.
4. W. R. Torbert (1976). *Creating a Community of Inquiry*, London: Wiley.
5. Chaos theory is described and illustrated in F. Dubinskas (1992) 'On the edge of chaos: a metaphor for transformative change', Las Vegas, NV: Academy of Management Symposium paper; J. Gleick (1987) *Chaos: Making a New Science*, New York: Penguin; B. Mandelbrot (1977) *The Fractal Geometry of Nature*, New York: Freeman; M. Wheatley (1992) *Leadership and the New Science*. San Francisco, CA: Berrett-Koehler Publishers. See particularly the photos and models in Gleick.
6. R. Evered and M. Louis (1992) discuss the distinction between 'outside-in' and 'inside-out' social science in Evered, R. & Louis, M. 1981. 'Alternative perspectives in the organization sciences: "inquiry from the inside" and "inquiry from the outside"', *Academy of Management Review*, **6** (3), 385-95.
7. Torbert and Reason discuss the action inquiry approach to social science. See W. R. Torbert (1991) *The Power of Balance: Transforming Self, Society, and Scientific Inquiry*, Newbury Park, CA: Sage Publications; P. Reason (1994) 'Three approaches to participative inquiry', in N. Denzin and Y. Lincoln (eds) *Handbook of Qualitative Research*, Thousand Oaks, CA: Sage, 324–40.
8. Our approach builds on the developmental theories of Perry and Kegan. See R. Kegan (1982) *The Evolving Self*, Cambridge, MA: Harvard University Press; R. Kegan (1994) *In Over Our Heads: The Mental Demands of Modern Life*, Cambridge, MA: Harvard University Press; W. Perry (1978) *Forms of Intellectual*

and Ethical Development in the College Years: A Scheme, New York: Holt, Rinehart & Winston. Kegan and Perry have also focused more on the dynamic process of transformation among stages than on the formal logic of each stage. They too see development as a movement in the direction of an increasing openness to context, to relationship, to the limits of formal reasoning, to moment-to-moment primary experience, and to the inescapable process of commitment and responsibility to particulars across time. Interpreted in this way, developmental models appear to be telling a story of movement by living systems from relatively inadequate, overly static and simplistically deterministic logics to perspectives compatible with chaos theories.

9. M. Rossman (1971) 'Music lessons', *American Review* **18**, 21–31.

12   Creating a Community of Inquiry

In this chapter and the next, we address ourselves to the future. In the next chapter, we ask you to join us in exploring what you and we regard as the primary goods that, taken together, constitute the good life. If you and we agree enough in our visions of the good life, then it is likely that you will want to join us at a distance in working towards creating real-time cultures of inquiry at work, in personal relationships, and in spiritual, political and artistic actions.

In this chapter, we offer brief glimpses of what such interorganizational cultures of inquiry may look like, as we discuss the Foundational Community or Community of Inquiry stage of organizing that parallels the Magician/Witch/Clown stage of personal development. We are hampered by the fact that we have only shadowy and fragmentary exemplars to help stimulate your imagination, for we believe that no fully embodied exemplar of this stage of organizing has ever existed historically.

Table 12.1 shows the theoretical characteristics of the Foundational Community or Community of Inquiry stage. These two names for this stage of organizing sound very different—the one suggesting foundational stability, the other suggesting transformational disequilibrium. A first approximation of a current interorganization that can help us imagine what this stage of development means and does not mean is Alcoholics Anonymous, to which we have referred earlier (Chapter 8). Alcoholics Anonymous, in its effectual practice of inviting its members to refound their lives and transform, may represent the closest approximation to Foundational Community to date. Its members have come near to dying, literally in some cases, and have begun to grasp the need to die to their former assumptions about their own power and control. Members of Alcoholics Anonymous in general feel themselves as equal to one another in a profound way, rather than as hierarchically related to one another. They also feel grateful for one another's attention and influence in general, rather than resistant to it. And a very high percentage, compared to members of most organizations, feel that their lives are transforming through their participation in the organization. All these are characteristics of a Foundational Community. Do these Foundational Community features explain why 12-step programmes are at present proliferating in so many countries and in regard to so many different aspects of life?

Table 12.1   Characteristics of a Community of Inquiry

1. Political friction among different paradigms/frames/stages within the organization and between the organization and the wider environment; all fundamentalist, universalistic ideologies challenged by the community's emphasis on peer-like mutuality and on the humble, vulnerable practice of inquiry.

2. Regular, experiential-empirical participatory research on relations among the spiritual/intuitive, theoretical/eternal, own-behavioural, and 'external'/'outside world' qualities of experience; such research generates sense of peerdom, mutuality.

3. Collaborative Inquiry structure fails ('dies') because it does not meet the alchemical challenge of timely collective action; preverbal, shared purpose revealed as sustaining and as generating multiple momentary structurings that invite enactment choices and feedback on the consequences of such choices.

4. Appreciation of continuing interplay of opposites: action/research, sex/politics, past/future, symbolic/diabolic, etc.

5. New experiences of time: his-story becomes my-story; interplay of timebound needs, timeless archetypes and timely creativity.

There are also essential ways, however, in which Alcoholics Anonymous (AA) does *not* qualify as a Foundational Community. It is primarily a community for *reflective* inquiry, not *action* inquiry. Its meetings are basically for talking about the past and the present ('I am an alcoholic', 'One day at a time'), not for acting into the present and the future (although the saying 'Easy does it' does provide a profound and humorously generalizable hint). Consistent with this point, AA is, so to speak, a purely spiritual organization for the transformation of a spiritual condition, rather than one that is also concerned with the political and economic structuring of one's life. For example, AA members do not rely on AA for work or for judicial decisions. A true

Foundational Community will integrate personal/spiritual and political/economic transformation.

Boards of directors of organizations, when the chairman of the board is not the CEO and when the majority of the board is not employed by the organization, are the foundational interorganization of that organization. And boards of directors function, at best, as communities of inquiry for the organization, testing the clarity of, and the congruity among, mission, strategy, operations and outcomes.

The United Nations, if it were supported by a tax rather than by 'contributions', could more straightforwardly explore what it may mean to become a global, foundational inter-organization. It might, for example, create an Intercultural Inquiry and Investment Corps to identify businesses and community projects that deserve micro-development investments and to provide leadership and assessment training that will help those organizations to develop later-stage cultures of inquiry and accountability. The Inquiry Corps might be composed of six-person teams from six different countries assigned to a seventh country. Thus, the Inquiry Corps teams themselves would need to become cross-cultural, cross-paradigmatic micro-organizations, basing their work in the host country on the vulnerable, mutual, transforming power of timely inquiry and action. The degree to which nations contributed to, and invited the presence of such teams would provide an immediate measure of their openness as a polity to inquiry and self-transformation. Veterans of the Inquiry Corps would represent a growing, global leadership cadre with transnational loyalties.

The Society of Friends—commonly known as Quakers—is another peer-like organization that illustrates characteristics of a Community of Inquiry. Its members place themselves in permanent political tension with their own countries by refusing to engage in war, seeking to become conscientious objectors and peace mediators in times of war. They have no official or professional ministry. Their meetings for worship, as well as their business meetings, are characterized by a silent listening for an inner voice or inner light that may correspond to what we are calling in this book intuitive, multi-territory awareness.

The Chinese Communist movement became at least the shadow of a Foundational Community during the long march in the 1920s from the south to the north, harried by Chiang Kaishek and his American warplanes, with only 10 000 of the original 100 000 surviving the march, but attracting allegiance from whole territories and populations along the way because of its relatively just principles and practices, even under such duress. With innumerable particular failures, the Chinese Communist movement continued to operate attractively, and with regular efforts at self-criticism, up through the land redistribution of the late 1940s.[1]

Like Lech Walensa, Adam Michnik, and the Solidarity movement in Poland, however, once Mao and the Chinese Communists gained the preponderance of control and legitimacy over their homeland, their solidarity and justice began to wane. Although their aim is CQI through the correction of gaps between theory and practice (a Collaborative Inquiry stage concept), in actual practice they did not evolve beyond the Systematic Productivity stage of organizing. During the Cultural Revolution of the 1960s, Mao's attempts to revolutionize the educational system and the government bureaucracy so that they generated action inquiry by individuals, and Collaborative Inquiry on a wider scale, became a grizzly parody of the work illustrated in this book.

Another example that suggests at least the shadow of a Community of Inquiry is a para-organization conceived at a picnic one day in the 1500s. Six University of Paris students who did not all know one another were brought together that day by a former Spanish soldier, Ignatius of Loyola. Together, they dedicated themselves to founding the Society of Jesus, the Jesuit Order. Within a decade, Jesuits were beginning to travel, often alone, to the far corners of the world in order to immerse themselves in the cultures of India, China, the Paraguayan natives and others. Rather than seek to impose the European structure of Catholicism, they sought to reconceive how the Christian spirit could be communicated in each distinctive culture. So influential and so controversial did the Jesuit Order become in global exploration, politics, education and science, as well as within the Catholic Church itself, in theology and in spiritual exercises, that it has twice during its history been proscribed and later resurrected.[2] Its womanless, non-procreative aspects obviously restrict the generalizability of this quasi-illustration of Foundational Community.

This same limitation, comically enough, applies to the Beatles, who also represented at least the shadow of Foundational Community during the late 1960s. Exploring the meaning of life, both individually and corporately, the Beatles inspired a more far-reaching—certainly a more artistic—cultural revolution than Mao. Or was that the Rolling Stones who were the shadow? Or is the still-vivid Grateful Dead really the example we are looking for? In any event, all of these are peer organizations with global cultural impact in both economic and cultural terms.

We hope that this book helps more people to recognize and appreciate the challenging 'stews' that Witches and Fools cook up with others. We also hope that, by examples such as the one with which we ended the last chapter (i.e. the search firm executive involved with a merger, an angry son and an absent fiancée), we shall dissuade anyone from imagining that a Community of Inquiry will be a blissful Utopia, or one that emerges full-blown on a global basis.

Conversations, triangles and quartets

So far we have been imagining Communities of Inquiry on a large, highly visible, and even global scale. But the challenge of creating Communities of Inquiry exists simultaneously on the small and personal scale. On the most micro social scale— the scale of single conversations—we have said earlier in this book (Chapters 2–4) that talking can be seen and participated in as an exemplary form of action, where, as in World Cup football, the conversational ball is juggled and passed gracefully from one speaker to the next, or speedily and forcefully taken away momentarily by a subgroup with another agenda. When conversation is treated artfully—with a concern for increasing productivity, friendship, justice and inquiry into assumptions—speech generates an atmosphere of alertness and timely, transforming contributions, as well as appropriate non-verbal action. Less effective speaking, on the other hand, can inhibit collective action or descend into more unilaterally controlling forms of speech and non-verbal action. Untested inferences, undiscussable issues, and constraining group norms then proliferate and choke off significant quality improvement and transformation.[3] The question of whether the speaking at 12-step meetings, or board meetings, or our proposed UN Intercultural Inquiry and Investment Corps meetings, or any other meetings, represents ineffective or effective action or inquiry must be alive in participants' awareness at each meeting if the collective is to function as a Community of Inquiry. Otherwise, the most recent joke we've heard about 12-step programmes becomes truer and truer. The joke goes: 'Did you hear about the new 12-step programme that's started for people addicted to talking?' 'It's called "On-And-On-And-On-And-On . . . ".'

The simplest ongoing form of a Community of Inquiry is a triangle in which each of the three members is consciously and explicitly related to the other two. The distinctive quality of explicit relational triangles is that, by contrast to the single relationship between a couple, there are *four* relationships that can unbalance and rebalance one another (three couple relationships and one three person relationship). It may be that thousands—nay, literally millions and eventually billions—of triangles begin to evolve into mini-Communities of Inquiry. Each unique, experimental version of such dynamic, dialectical, transformational triangles may exist only briefly, like a two- or three-year soap bubble that then collapses again. Eventually, through such experiences, a sufficient proportion of the globe's population may develop a taste for adult development to the later intercultural stages. Eventually, we may become skilled at dancing with paradoxical simultaneity in the social and spiritual worlds—with the near and the far, with hierarchy, heterarchy, and peerdom, with initiative, collaboration and accountability. Thus, may we develop beyond the CQI groups proposed in Chapter 7 to a fuller taste for creating late-stage learning organizations.

Isn't it fascinating that throughout the modern era, with Foucauldian intensifying intensity,[4] our arithmetic of friendship has focused, almost solely, on the simplest possible form of friendship—the couple or best friend, the two-person male, female or intergender relationship? By contrast, the human subconsciousness during the modern era is constantly seduced and obsessed by covertly triangular dynamics—for example, the husband, the wife *and* the lover; the boss, the favoured subordinate and the more competent subordinate; or the parents taking out their problems on one of their children. So common are such implicit triangulations that many therapists take as a prime directive to seek them out in their clients' practice and unmask them, sometimes with the intention of eradicating them.

But what if good friendship is really about cultivating an awareness of one's limits and shifting emotional alchemy? What if good friendship is really about enacting mutuality across different preferences, feelings and intellectual assumptions? What if good friendship is about exposing one another's verbal maladroitnesses and learning more sharp, more caring, more transformative speaking? Would not explicitly triangular relationships, much more easily and continually than the too-easily polarizable couple relationships, test one's ability to maintain a changing balance, to fall gracefully out of balance, and to rebalance? Might not aspiring members of a Community of Inquiry choose to hone their relational abilities and awareness in several experimental triangular friendships prior to making lifelong couple commitments, if indeed such a form remains a treasured ideal?

Mihaly Csikszentmihalyi makes a distantly similar proposal to ours about triangles when he proposes a type of quartet as the embryonic cell structure of society in the future. In a book that towards its end looks to the future as this chapter does, Csikszentmihalyi proposes creating quartets rather than triangles—small, voluntary 'cells' of four persons.[5] Each such cell helps members develop political skills by having each member focus on a functionally different area. Two members concentrate on assembling information about (1) the economic conditions and (2) the political forces of the surrounding community. The third member focuses on the internal management of the group, and the fourth member integrates the internal and external information and suggests timely actions for the group to take. These can include publishing information, offering comprehensive analyses of systemic relationships, supporting particular local political candidates, or confederating with other cells to create 'an evolutionary fellowship that could provide a vision and a conscience for society as a whole'.[6]

In some ways, this vision of small cells is similar to the idea of triangles we have just proposed. In other ways, Csikszentmihalyi's idea sounds much more like a Strategist's proposal for Collaborative Inquiry stage groups. We doubt that large numbers of people will be attracted to groups with such a quasi-academic, quasi-political flavour. What is important, however, is not the 'correctness' of any particular idea, but rather the unleashing of creative imagination to invent various new social groupings that encourage learning and transformation among adults.

An evolving Foundational Community?

Let us look at a more home-grown and not-yet-fully-developed organizational exemplar of Foundational Community to find one that is more fulsome and balanced than the

Jesuit Order, the Chinese Communist Cultural Revolution, or the Beatles, and that happens (if, indeed, it is mere happenstance) to be led by a woman. This organization is a relatively small investment advisory firm called Franklin Research & Development Corporation (FRDC). Founded in the early 1980s as an employee-owned firm, FRDC invited each employee who so wished—whether secretary, computer programmer, or president—to buy (at a nominal price) one share of stock and thereby gain an equal vote with the president at the quarterly shareholder meetings. These meetings, in turn, elect the board of directors, including two employee members, and either confirm, disconfirm, or direct other board actions. Today, the one employee–one vote structure is being modified to recognize the differential ownership stake and contribution that longevity of commitment to the company's mission and practice and the level of decision-making responsibility of different members permits them to make. All members continue to become eligible for shares after one year of employment, but now they can accumulate additional shares at slightly different rates each year thereafter.

But this is not the only unique quality of this for-profit investment company. It is not only unusually peer-like in terms of internal ownership, but also unusually mutual in its customer relationships and in its methods of analysing whether companies represent good investment opportunities. FRDC's investment strategy directly contradicts the conventional financial wisdom that your investment portfolio ought to be determined solely on criteria of financial return, starting from the widest possible universe of companies. On the contrary, the FRDC advises its clients on ways to *limit* the universe of companies in which they consider investing on the basis of non-financial factors, such as the social, political and environmental effects of the companies. Thus, FRDC caters to clients concerned with the ethical impact of their investments and works to identify companies that take responsibility for their ethical impact on their employees and the environment while operating profitably. Thus, FRDC seeks a peer-like mutuality both with its clients (inquiring into their investment criteria) and in companies' relationships to their employees, communities and environments. FRDC's corporate vision is expressed in its motto: *Investing for a Better World*.

A decade ago it was self-evident to virtually all financial experts and professionals that FRDC's investment strategy guaranteed lower than average financial returns (not to mention that its one employee–one vote structure seemed the knell of doom for managerial discipline). The conventional wisdom 'on the street' was that only a small market segment of quirky idealists would choose to lose money like that. However, it turns out empirically that, for some reason that is incomprehensible to market economic theory as currently formulated,[7] a lot of potential clients (a rapidly growing number of whom are now becoming actual clients of FRDC and the other social investing advisers that have been springing up) are interested in integrating their spiritual, political and economic commitments. Moreover, it turns out that if you choose the best financially performing companies from among the narrower universe of companies that show signs not only of a healthy short-term interest in profits but also of a longer-range interest in integrating their mission with their internal structure and their community and environmental effects, you get more reliably positive long-term financial outcomes.

Joan Bavaria, the founder and president of FRDC, is also one of the founders of the national interorganization—called the Social Investment Forum—that has helped to define and redefine this new sub-industry over the past decade. She is also on numerous boards and is one of the writers of the environmental principles (originally called the Valdez Principles, now the CERES principles) that such companies as Sun Oil and General Motors are currently signing.

Today, FRDC competes on even terms with the traditional investment houses. It has spawned a whole sub-industry of social investing, and more and more mainstream financial houses are developing social screens for investing groups. Moreover, FRDC has accomplished all this while shadowed by a law suit that has threatened the survival of the company for several years and has only recently been settled to the satisfaction of all parties'. Thus, FRDC has survived a prolonged 'near-death' experience, as well as significant political and economic friction with the dominant paradigm of the financial industry.

The future holds almost unfathomable demands and rewards for FRDC and all its fellow pioneers (for example, Sun Health Care, the company we examined so closely in Chapters 9 and 10). These social pioneers are leading us to a new, multi-cultural global society that can only become more civilized as the new kind of interorganization outlined here evolves. This new kind of interorganization will integrate for-profit concerns with a not-for-profit dedication to mission. (Indeed, such interorganizations will often be legally structured as a not-for-profit parent with for-profit subsidiaries, or as a parent holding company with both for-profit and not-for-profit subsidiaries.) This new interorganization will develop and continually amend an explicit and justifiable governance structure,[7] and its members will cultivate CQI through the daily exercise of something similar to what we describe as action inquiry in this book.

No one has yet developed a theoretically coherent measure for distinguishing companies, churches, schools, industry associations and other interorganizations that systematically and reliably seek to act in a socially and environmentally, as well as financially, responsible manner. Until the present, indeed, there has been no theory from which such a measure could be constructed. Perhaps the developmental theory presented in this book can become the basis for such a measure. For this theory explicitly traces the CQI path that an organization can follow beyond a Systematic Productivity stage preoccupation with short-term effects, such as increasing market share, increasing profits and reducing costs. Developmental theory suggests measuring the degree to which an organization has evolved to the Collaborative Inquiry stage concerns and processes, such as continually reducing product development time from conception to strategic planning to effective implementation, and concerning itself with its members' life-long development. This developmental theory also suggests that a good measure will explore and integrate multiple insider and outsider stakeholder perspectives on the organization's success. A good measure will also tap into the degree that the company enacts the Magician/Witch/Clown/Foundational Community concern with integrating spiritual awareness, political structure, economic operations and social/ environmental effects.

The Dutch consulting firm

Here is another short story about a small organization developing towards an interorganizational Community of Inquiry.

Once upon a time, 15 years ago, there were two strangers—Netherlanders—each of whom was a capable, professional help-giver. One—a male—was a therapist; the other—a female—was a social worker. One was more sensitive and steady; the other was more mercurial and hyperactive. Each yearned for more and for something different. Eventually, these two Dutch strangers met (Conception). They were attracted to one another and became a couple. Soon, they began to work together on occasion as business consultants doing training and team building (Investments). Within a year, they created their own consulting organization (Incorporation).

Over a period of five years, the organization became very successful financially and reputationally. Instead of increasing the size of the firm, however, this couple experimented with many dimensions of growth. They experimented with integrating their business and their home, creating a unique blend of countryside farm and fully equipped office of the future with two administrative assistants on the ground floor, elegant dinners, frequent developmental retreats and adventurous vacations to all continents (Experiments).

Through their developmental retreats, the couple met several potential colleagues, and either partner worked with each of these on occasion. One other man joined the business as a junior partner, and two relatively senior women began to discuss possible partnership roles in the business. All five of these persons found that the developmental theory and the action inquiry process presented in this book significantly illuminated the developmental challenge for senior managers as persons, as teams, and as re-inventors of their organizations (beginning of evolution to Systematic Productivity).

The founding partners took the initiative to contact three academically based scholar-consultants who had long studied and worked with these developmental ideas. These three were invited to participate in a two-day, twice-yearly meeting of eight persons in order to create a learning organization among themselves. All eight filled out, and later discussed the results of, the Loevinger developmental stage measure, which showed four of the members scoring at the Strategist stage, two at the Magician stage and two at the Ironist stage.

The consultants also arranged for the senior management teams of two client companies to take the developmental measure, with the academics participating in feedback and further consulting to those teams. In both of the cases, the company presidents were scored at the Achiever stage. Both presidents gave their vice-presidents considerable autonomy and support, but in both cases the presidents were passive about restructuring in the face of environmental demands to do so, while several vice-presidents who scored at post-Achiever stages were in fact leading restructuring initiatives and feeling the 'drag' of the presidents.

Working together in both the consulting–action mode with clients and in the research–inquiry mode among themselves led the group of eight to the gradual design of new executive development and organizational change programmes (the final step in a Collaborative Inquiry process outlined over the past three paragraphs).

At this time, the original couple took the lead in designing new financial partnering arrangements that permitted other members to gain increasing ownership stakes in the business. Also, issues of commitment, of lifestyle, of intimacy and of different competences and limits all arose, sharply etching each member's boundaries and making them discussable— even, sometimes, transformable! With the inspiration and model of this evolving community, a similar group has begun to form in the United States (beginning of evolution towards Community of Inquiry?).

Our final illustration will exemplify how we can begin to attend to our ongoing, daily conversations and organizing experiences as processes that challenge us to participate with others in repeated ongoing transformations towards a Community of Inquiry. As we have already suggested, we shall discover in greater detail what organizing looks like at that late stage, not by reading any particular book or by legislating any particular policy in a general way, but by practising in the direction of such a community in our family, religious and working lives.

Envisioning and enacting the future: social science fiction

Let us examine another small-scale organizing experience-evolving towards Foundational Community. We say that this is a small-scale organizing experience because there are only two principal players and the action occurs over a very short period of time. But their experience influences other members of the organization and raises profound interorganization and cultural questions about the relationships between superiors and subordinates, men and women, and working and loving. As these two players come closer to establishing a Community of Inquiry between themselves, they generate political friction between themselves and other members of the organization.

The organization of which they are members has arguably been the most widely and closely observed organization in the world during the early 1990s. Like Alcoholics Anonymous, the Jesuits, the Beatles, and the Franklin Research & Development Corporation, this organization does not coerce the wide range of people it influences; rather, they seek its influence and can cease attending whenever they wish. To be more specific, we are speaking of the senior management team of the crew of the Starship Enterprise in the *Star Trek: The Next Generation* television series.

We describe here a particular episode in which the principal players are the captain of the Enterprise, Jean Luc Picard, and a new Lieutenant Commander of Stellar Cartography, Nella Daren. Captain Picard is a classic hero— reserved, inventive, trustworthy, stern. Commander Daren is a strong, intelligent, determined officer, as we quickly infer upon first meeting her during the initial sequence of the episode.

But before launching into this story, before highlighting its distinctive developmental stages, and before focusing in particular on what it tells us about evolving towards Foundational Community, let us take a moment to justify why we are presenting this analysis of a fictional story instead of another contemporary business case. One reason is to emphasize that in acting towards the future, each of us is guided by a vision which, however conventional it may be, is also, in all its concrete aspects and in its point of view, fictional.

Points of view are constructions of our imagination, hence fictional (*fiction* comes from the Latin *fictio*, to shape, *fictus*, moulded). We shape our own points of view in interaction with the communities to which we belong, though we only begin to become aware *that* we do so and *how* we do so as we evolve beyond the Achiever/Systematic Productivity stage. The more we become aware of the fictional aspect of our vision or faith, the more we can distinguish its 'essential' features (i.e. its theoretical/archetypal/eternal features) from its 'accidental' features and from its 'intended' (by us) features. The more we can suffer these differences between the intentional, the archetypal and the accidental features of our vision, the more we can be flexible enough to allow such accidental features to drop away and alert enough to move among eternal patterns according to our own intention rather than passively and imitatively.

A second reason for ending this book with a fictional story is to emphasize how fiction communicates truths, for it does so in a much more lifelike way than does social science writing as it is currently usually practised. Fictional writing or film-making, at its best, asks us to enjoy and be enchanted by the specifics of the artfulness of the story . . . while simultaneously remembering that it *is* 'just' a story. Remembering that it is just a story helps us to detach ourselves from it and see through it and ourselves to its hidden lessons for us and our lives. These lessons can be so cunningly subtle that we may not be sure that the authors intended them. Therefore, we must take responsibility for the fictional lessons we are constructing for ourselves, as well as for the brew of faith and courage that we are concocting in order to walk our revisioned path.

Let us see, now, how developmental theory helps us reconstruct the following *Star Trek* episode.

Conception

The *Star Trek* episode begins at 3 a.m. with Captain Picard repeatedly being frustrated in his attempts to get both information and tea from the ship's systems. The ship's computer repeatedly tells him, 'Stellar Cartography is using all auxiliary power at the present time.' He decides to find out what is going on in Stellar Cartography, and walks in on a darkened room where an experiment is in progress.

'In or out! Just close the door!' brusquely hisses the woman we shall learn is Commander Daren. But the experiment has already been unbalanced by the interruption and fails. The lights go up, and Commander Daren turns on the intruder, only to be brought up short as she recognizes that it is the captain. She apologizes for her brusqueness and says she hadn't expected anyone at this time of night. Captain Picard advises her to learn to 'expect the unexpected' on board the Enterprise—Magician-like advice indeed. When he says that he was prevented from getting his Earl Grey tea, she responds in a rather motherly way, 'No wonder you can't sleep if you're drinking caffeine. Try some of *my* special blend.' His restrained facial expression as he tastes the tea tells us that he does *not* like this blend; but he asks what experiment she has been doing. She begins talking in some detail about her attempt to model the birth of a star system. Commercial break.

In these opening scenes, we are shown several versions of the *Conception* stage of organizing (see descriptions of each organizational stage in Table 8.2):

(a) a new officer learning a new (to her) organization's culture
(b) the not-particularly-propitious beginning of a relationship between Captain and Commander
(c) the beginning of a study of the beginning of star systems
(d) the vision of the interplay of opposites captured in the phrase, 'expect the unexpected'.

In showing this episode to several audiences, we have found that a number of viewers believe that Commander Daren has made a very bad start in her relationship to her boss, in snapping at him to begin with, in 'matron'-izing him next, and, third, in boring him with her intellectual excitement about her research. Others, however, suggest that her overall 'enterprise' may seem admirable to the captain. Either outcome seems plausible. Our allegiance to developmental theory suggests to us that the captain's developmental perspective will determine the actual outcome. Will he react negatively to the 'insubordinate' aspects of her behaviour, or positively to the independent, motivated, peer-like aspects of her behaviour?

Investments

After the commercial break, we first see the second in command, Will Reiker, refusing Commander Daren's request for use of auxiliary power the next day. She attempts to continue the discussion, but he ends it with a 'No! That is all, Commander Daren.'

Next, we see Captain Picard at dinner in his quarters with his old friend, the ship's doctor, Beverly Crusher. He asks whether she has met the new crew members, then mentions that he has met Commander Daren. Beverly signals her approval of the new lieutenant commander, whom she has also met briefly, by calling her 'forthright', accompanied by clenching her fist and lower arm in a small and amusingly androgynous gesture of strength. This is all the support Picard needs to become more voluble than usual and to begin to bore her with a mathematical description of the birth of star systems.

But they are late for a concert which features Data, the 'android', playing the violin, and Nella Daren at the piano. A music lover himself, Captain Picard is clearly bewitched by her playing, to the approving smile of the 'witch' sitting behind him—ship's counsellor (and empath), Deeana Troy.

During the after-party, the captain and Commander Daren talk, the captain complimenting her on her playing by commenting on a particular choice of notes and emphases, in a way that shows he is a *connoisseur*, and by saying he hadn't known she could play the piano. 'On the Enterprise,' she replies, mimicking his earlier comment, 'you'll come to expect the unexpected!'

With the second commercial break, we recognize that we have witnessed the Investments stage of this story. Commander Daren shows her investment in her research project by championing it to Commander Reiker. Other women senior managers—Dr Crusher and Counsellor Troy—show their investment in Commander Daren as a competent, creative, forthright addition to the leadership group. Captain Picard shows his budding investment in Commander Daren by his vulnerability to her sophisticated 'charms'—her mathematical theory and her musical practice. And she in effect invites him, in a somewhat competitive way, towards a vision of a peer relationship when she one-ups him for having one-upped her earlier.

The audiences who have viewed this segment with us have added two further impressions. First, some viewers see Commander Daren's gesture of one-upping the captain as dangerous for her, or as hostile and inflammatory. They themselves seem to be becoming increasingly invested, as they watch the show with these discussion breaks, in a negative interpretation of her actions and her attitude towards an authority figure. This is their fiction about the fiction. Similarly, but conversely, we have found ourselves becoming increasingly committed to a positive interpretation of her interesting brew of gumption, competence and artistry, which is our fiction about this fiction.

A number of women viewers of this segment have expressed delight at:

(a) the images of feminine solidarity (the generosity and lack of competitiveness in Dr Crusher's and Counsellor Troy's responses to Commander Daren);
(b) the feminine practice of artistic power (the aforementioned gestures, along with Daren's piano playing)
(c) the artistic subtlety with which the show conveys these artistic subtleties (Dr Crusher's small but highly evocative arm gesture; Counsellor Troy's faint background smile [which it turns out many of the men in the audience did not see because they were concentrating exclusively on Picard in the foreground (no soft, action inquiry focus there!)]).

Incorporation

The third segment begins with Commander Reiker again refusing a request by Commander Daren. He clearly feels she is being too officious, just as a proportion of the show's audience does.

This interpretation seems about to be confirmed when Captain Picard hears the door buzzer to his private quarters, and Commander Daren enters. Perhaps, we imagine, she is about to 'go over Reiker's head'. Picard puts down the small

'Ressican' flute which he taught himself to play during a 25-minute lifetime on that planet (which regular viewers know from another episode).

She asks him to play it for her, but he is shy and refuses. Undaunted, she asks if she may try it, and he politely agrees. As she (coyly?) begins attempting the fingering, he fumblingly tries to explain to her and then takes back the flute to show her . . . and is soon playing.

Now, she becomes a proud-teacher-acting-like-peer, congratulating him on his playing. Her praise draws from him an innocently joyful grin such as his regular viewers have never before seen or imagined possible. It is as if he were looking into the sun, having a 'close encounter of the third kind'.

Then, producing a futuristic, roll-up piano from her purse, she proceeds to lead them in improvising on the French children's song, 'Frère Jacques, frère Jacques; dormez vous? dormez vous?' Picard whistles, glowing and gleaming, until the picture fades for the next commercial break.

The segment we are now discussing can be interpreted as an Incorporation stage segment in the simple sense that it is the first time that Captain Picard and Commander Daren actually *do* something *together*—they play music.

A second sense in which this third stage of the story represents its *Incorporation* is that, just as the third point defines the plane of a portrait, so this third point or stage in the story defines its overall archetypal character for us. Here we have a promising subordinate, a woman of genius, who is 'outside the box' for her immediate, bureaucratic organizational superior (Commander Reiker), but is simultaneously attracting the attention of his superior (Captain Picard). Put simply, we have here a budding, subconscious work/love triangle. In more complex terms, this triangle can be interpreted as an archetypal triangular tension in spiritual development between following the rules (i.e. obeying Reiker) and engaging directly, through one's own initiative, with the source of power (represented by the musical interplay between herself and Picard). Such, ever, is the story of spiritual development, especially as retold in the Gnostic, Sufi and Vajrayana Buddhist traditions.[8] In the Gnostic version, for example, humans host and nurture an embryonic spark of light (the feminine subordinate) which grows through contact, not with the religions dedicated to the Yahweh-type 'enforcer' gods of this sector of the universe who are believed to be keeping us enslaved in relative darkness (the Commander Reikers!), but rather with their superiors (the Captain Picards of the celestial hierarchy).

In terms of the developmental archetypes, Commander Reiker can be seen as a typical Achiever-stage COO, trying to get the job done and not play favourites. Captain Picard represents an Ironist CEO, accustomed to wearing an objective, impartial and impenetrable mask of command, but able to doff it when he comes face to face with, and is properly challenged in a playful manner by a true peer, such as a Strategist-and-at-least-aspiring-Magician/Witch like Commander Daren apparently feels herself to be with anyone, whether Reiker-like or Picard-like.

Again, part of the audience responds to Commander Daren's leaderly and supportive comments about Captain Picard's flute playing as 'matron'-izing. They are more than ever irritated by her and speak of her as competitive and scheming. The fact that she has not actually asked Picard to override Reiker strikes these viewers as evidence of the subtlety of her manipulativeness.

Experiments

In the next episode we find Commander Daren leading the way up ladders, with Captain Picard following, to an obscure intersection of tubes in the bowels of the ship. When they reach her chosen spot, she asks him if he knows where they are. He answers with the technical coordinates of the intersection, but she says, 'No, we are at the most acoustically perfect spot on this ship.' They then take turns playing some extremely resonant and passionate music, his coming from his Ressican lifetime. She is truly moved. Her husky, passionate voice emerges and breaks as she tells him, 'That's beautiful. I've never heard you play with such feeling.'

Meanwhile, other crew members hear ghostly sounds of unusual music faintly reaching their ears; but when they begin to investigate, they can no longer hear anything. When the camera returns to Picard and Daren, they are engaged in a long embrace and kiss. This is definitely most irregular for the entire series. Captain Picard in love? What can this portend? Time for another commercial break.

This scene has many Experiments stage qualities. The twosome is experimenting with music making and love making. In 'getting involved' with one another, they are exploring beyond the conventional wisdom about how superiors and subordinates ought to relate in professional settings. And she, not he, is clearly taking the lead.

Some viewers immediately conclude that this experimenting is unwise in principle, for all the conventional reasons. Others are delighted by the 'cracks' in Captain Picard's loner façade and take the relativistic perspective that 'anything goes' in love and war. But the developmentally oriented viewer sees the *timing* of these moves as critical and as propitious, given the developmental 'moment' of the relationship. Such a viewer also realizes that the couple is moving at a rapid developmental pace and is 'asking for trouble'—that is, asking for the even more difficult balancing acts that each successive stage mandates.

Systematic Productivity or Collaborative Inquiry?

Let us not forget, in the midst of the magic of this love making, who the *real* leader is! As the next scene opens, Picard and Daren are taking the ship's elevator along with other crew members. She says in an informal and friendly voice 'I'll be finished with my survey at 11 hundred hours.' To which he responds in his flattest, most formal voice, 'Very good, Commander' and steps off the lift without looking her way as the door opens. Is this appropriate *etiquette* in public, so as not to show favouritism, or is it a betrayal of their budding friendship?

Are we back in the Systematic Productivity mode, with its impersonal, hierarchical ranks, the mode that almost always appears dominant in any large organization when observed over short interactions? Or is there a way to evolve beyond this mode without altogether destroying its code and its discipline?

We next see Captain Picard himself struggling with these questions, with the help of Counsellor Troy. 'Relations with co-workers can be fraught with consequences,' Picard pontificates, having difficulty even naming the situation for which he is seeking her counsel.

'So can cutting yourself off from your own feelings,' she counters pointedly.

'I'm afraid of compromising my objectivity,' says he.

'Are you asking my permission to conduct a friendship with Nella Daren?' asks she, in an amused but unthreatening tone.

Now he lightens a little for the first time: 'And if I were asking your permission, would you grant it?'

She pauses and smiles, 'Yes.'

This is, of course, not the end, but at best the beginning, of a Collaborative Inquiry that must engage not only the couple itself but the other significant stakeholders in this couple's destiny if it is to be negotiated successfully. At minimum, these stakeholders include the senior management team that operates—in bureaucratic, military, Systematic Productivity terms—*between* the captain and the lieutenant commander. Counsellor Troy has signed up for Collaborative Inquiry. Will anyone else? Will Will Reiker? As this segment continues, we see Picard re-entering the Stellar Cartography laboratory (recapitulating the beginning of their relationship) to apologize to Commander Daren. 'Nella?'

'Can I help you, sir?' she answers flatly, again mimicking an earlier gesture of his.

But he continues, and we soon find them back in his cabin and him with tears in his eyes as he tells her how much his Ressican life and music mean to him and how precious it is for him to find someone with whom to so actively share it. So, now they are launched into their own private Collaborative Inquiry.

But what of their relations to the rest of the senior management team—Commander Reiker, in particular—not to mention that large part of their audience that may feel extraordinarily uncomfortable with, and even censorious of, their conduct? After all, they appear to be collapsing the distinction between work and love, between the rational and the emotional, between the professional and the personal, that orders modern life.

The following scene addresses this question. Commander Reiker has asked for a few moments of the captain's time. He is uncomfortable with Commander Daren's assertive conduct on behalf of her department's interests. Picard sees his worst fears already coming true—fears about personality conflicts growing out of the perception of illegitimately interwoven personal and professional relationships. But he does not simply defend himself, nor does he conclude that he ought to discontinue the relationship.

'Do you feel that her requests are inconsistent with the proper performance of her duty as chief of Stellar Cartography?' he asks. Reiker pauses, and to his immense credit, fairly computes his answer: 'No, sir.'

'Then let her do her job, and you do yours,' replies Picard. 'I've always had the greatest confidence in your judgement.' With this response, he catches both the highest Systematic Productivity wisdom relevant to the situation, and then, with his fulsome compliment, includes Reiker in the Collaborative Inquiry now underway.

But Daren herself is assailed by doubts when she rehears the story about Reiker, along with the moral that Picard draws from it that they must conduct themselves with great care in public. 'I don't like to have to second-guess others,' she says, in an Achiever-like, none-of-that-process-stuff mode. 'It can take my mind off what I am trying to do.' 'No, don't let it do that,' responds Picard, 'just add in the possible effects that you may have as you think and act.' Thus does Picard recommend Witch-like simultaneous awareness of intentions, thoughts, actions and effects to Daren.

So goes Collaborative Inquiry—two steps forward, one step back; slide to the side and twirl about. Are we acting more deliberatively or more spontaneously? What logic are we enacting? Where is the source of our spontaneity?

Foundational
Community

After the next commercial interruption, we near the climax of the episode. On the planet below them, a firestorm is approaching the outpost they are trying to evacuate. Commander Daren is now sitting with the senior team, brainstorming a solution. She makes a tentative suggestion on how to create a firewall that Geordie, the chief engineer, is quickly able to technologize. Picard accepts the strategy and turns to Reiker for the implementation plan. Reiker assigns everyone, with Daren assigned to the on-planet away-team.

Now it is Picard's turn to strain against the Systematic Productivity logic of the situation, fearing for Daren's safety. He asks Commander Daren to remain after the meeting, but she quickly asserts that the assignment is justified and parts.

In fact, as we were beginning to expect, based on our use of the developmental lens, the transition from the Strategist/ Collaborative Inquiry logic to the Magician/Foundational Community logic dictates that the relationship must die and be reborn, in both actual and mythical terms. The firestorm rages out of control, despite the firewall. Most of the persons on the planet surface are successfully evacuated, but when Reiker beams back up, he is forced to report to the captain that the last two groups of crew members, including Commander Daren, appear lost to the fire.

We see a stunned and infinitely heavy Captain Picard in his quarters, walking with meditative dignity and sitting, having shut, with finality, the box that contains his Ressican flute. We can feel the irretrievable loss that this fine man feels—this man who had never hoped for such a love, but had then seemed to find it, only to lose it.

The intercom sounds, announcing that a few more survivors are beaming on board. Picard rises, knowing that he must not hope, yet, unable not to, already preparing himself for further disappointment.

The crew members who arrive do not include Commander Daren. Again crushed, he turns away with unbearable dignity. Then, as he turns, a final twosome arrives: Daren holding a more seriously injured subordinate.

We next see her speaking to him in his 'ready room', grieving for the crew members lost. They share how they felt during the crisis, and Picard says that he can never again give a command that risks her life. A wonderful sentiment, but one that, in its conventional dichotomization of work and love, misses an essential element of the Community of Inquiry they have just been enacting. Put differently, instead of describing how vulnerable he feels about her and what a dilemma that creates for him as her superior officer, Picard tells her how he will act to reduce his vulnerability, without inquiring into her view. Thus, he is espousing making her safe and he is enacting making himself safe.

But in creating a Community of Inquiry there is no safe haven. A Community of Inquiry is a cross-gendered, cross-generational, cross-cultural community through which we wager our lives on behalf of integrating work, love and frame-challenging inquiry. Nor is creating a Community of Inquiry a one-time wager, such as the wager that Captain Picard, Commander Reiker and Commander Daren have just survived. It is an ongoing wager, inspired by an increasing appreciation of the ongoing interplay between light and shadow, foreground and background, life and death. In transforming to the Magician/Witch/Foundational Community stage, we cease clutching fearfully at life and security and give our lives freely instead.

In any event, the entire relationship between Picard and Daren immediately deflates after he makes his heartfelt, but conventionally protective statement. Without realizing what he is doing, because explicit triangling is not yet a known art, Picard is attempting unilaterally to withdraw their relationship from the triangle with Commander Reiker. As we can see, the triangular tension, though difficult to manage, is central to both Picard's and Daren's commitments. The captain and the commander bicker politely and painfully about whose career will defer to whose (he suggesting hers, she suggesting his). Then she says that she will seek reassignment, and he concludes lamely that that doesn't mean they can't see each other again, does it?

Thus, as this episode of *Star Trek* ends, it appears once again that their relationship has died. Through the evolution of their relationship, we have glimpsed the fictional Foundational Community to which we and they can aspire. But the fuller realization of such a community lies, still, in our future. Will they be reunited in the future? Not on a *Star Trek* television episode, for the series as a whole has now come to an end.

Is the limp ending of this episode dictated by the predefined Systematic Productivity boundary of creating a one-hour show? To answer 'Yes' gives too little credit to the creativity of the show's writers who usually offer more satisfying endings and have more than once offered us two-hour sequences. If that is not the answer, is the limp ending dictated by the developmental limits of the show's writers? To this way of asking the question, the answer is more plausibly 'Yes.' As creative and as Strategist-like as the plots, the character development, and even the varied frames or genres (comic, action, mystery, horror, etc.) of the *Star Trek* series have been, it does seem as though they ultimately fall short, again and again—as this particular episode does—of fully evoking the 'indomitable vulnerability' of the Magician/Witch/Foundational Community stage. For example, no episode that we have ever seen (or heard of from other *afficionados*) either reveals or confronts the political realities of the Federation itself. Occasional hints are offered that not all is well in the upper echelons of the military/scientific/governmental complex of the Federation, but this potential story-line is never pursued.

How will all this affect *your* life? How will the *Star Trek* episode just retold and this chapter about a form of organizing that may never yet have been generated affect *your* life? How will this book as a whole, about the multiple personal and organizational transformations that we invite if we commit ourselves to the path of CQI, affect *your* life? That is, of course, for you to determine. Your decision will, in turn, depend on the degree to which you share or do not share the underlying values that guide one towards a Community of Inquiry.

Our next and final chapter engages you in questioning your version of the good life, and the path you wish to follow towards your fictional vision.

Notes

1. W. Hinton (1966) *Fanshen: Documentary of Revolution in a Chinese Village* , New York: Monthly Review Press; E. Snow (1973) *Red Star Over China*, New York: Grove Press; Postscript to W. R. Torbert (1987) *Managing the Corporate Dream: Restructuring for Long-Term Success*, Homewood, IL: Dow Jones-Irwin.
2. R. Fulop-Miller (1930) *The Power and the Secret of the Jesuits,* New York: Viking; Ignatius of Loyola (1900) *The Spiritual Exercises*, London: Burns & Oates.

3. In the field of political theory, Seyla Benhabib (1986) *Critique, Norm, and Utopia* (New York: Columbia University Press) comes closest to outlining our sense of what good conversation and Foundational Community entails, Donald Moon's (1991) critique notwithstanding ('Constrained discourse and public life', *Political Theory* **19**(2), 202–29).
4. M. Foucault (1993) *The History of Sexuality*, Vol. 1, New York: Random House; J. Miller (1993) *The Passion of Michel Foucault*, New York: Simon & Schuster.
5. M. Csikszentmihalyi (1993) *The Evolving Self*, New York: Harper Collins, pp. 285ff.
6. Note 5, p. 289.
7. W. R. Torbert (1993) *Sources of Excellence: An Unorthodox Inquiry into Quality in Recent U.S. Presidencies, in Business Leadership, in Management Education, in Adam Smith's Ethics, and in Pythagorean Mathematics*, Cambridge, MA: Edge\Work Press.
8. H. Jonas (1963) *The Gnostic Religion: The Message of the Alien God and the Beginnings of Christianity*, Boston, MA: Beacon Press; H. Corbin (1969) *Creative Imagination in the Sufism of Ib'n 'Arabi*, Princeton, NJ: Princeton University Press; C. Trungpa (1991) *Crazy Wisdom*, Boston and London: Shambhala Press; D. Finnigan (1993) *The Zen of Juggling*, Edmunds, WA: Jugglebug.

13 Seeking the good life: the CQI Path

Now, as we near the end of this book we wish to ask you, our readers, one of the most profound questions it is possible to ask: 'What is the good life and what is the path towards it?'

It is time to ask this question for two reasons. First, we have seen in the previous two chapters, especially in the dialogue between the father and his twin son and daughter in Chapter 11 and the *Star Trek* episode in Chapter 12, that the understanding of CQI that emerges at later stages of development is one that concerns not merely work, but rather our lives altogether—the quality of our moment-to-moment awareness, the quality of our love, and the quality of our incidental family games and jokes. The inspiration for such an all-encompassing commitment to quality improvement clearly will not come from a merely instrumental concern for improving the efficiency of work processes in order to cut costs. It can only come from a wholehearted and increasingly well-aimed search for the good life.

The second reason why it is timely to ask explicitly what are our, perhaps quite different, versions of the good life is that we have been witnessing, at least since the introduction of developmental theory in Chapter 5, that the path of CQI described in this book is one that includes repeated radical transformations of our own ability to experience. One question that naturally arises is, 'Where are these changes ultimately taking me?' Another question that arises is, 'Are there any ultimate values that remain constant throughout this journey and are they values that I can ascribe to?'

Or, the question may arise in a more sceptical form for you, such as, 'Is not the question of the good life more like a religious question—a question that is one's own private business, rather than one to be addressed in the context of management, organizations and economics?'

Still other readers may suggest, 'Doesn't the market system

and market theory presume that each consumer has his or her own utility function, which is not the business of economic theory *per se*?' The simple answer to this question is, 'Yes.' Market economics has assumed that it need not concern itself with people's utility functions. Market economics 'works' (according to the theory) no matter what you like or value. But this book argues that companies can make significant long-term progress towards improving the quality of their products and services and of their market and financial positions, *only* if senior executives engage in a CQI process in regard to their own leadership and to the organization as a whole, and this requires that they value one particular dynamic—self-questioning-in-action—as perhaps no one has since Socrates and the philosopher kings whom he imagined as the best possible executives.

We have suggested in earlier chapters that 90 per cent of all executives (all those at the Achiever stage or earlier) require at least *two* developmental transformations before they become capable of reliably and effectively supporting CQI throughout the organization and in their own moment-to-moment actions. In other words, executives must somehow, paradoxically, be open to a level of questioning that more than once leads them through upending developmental transformations that recast their assumptions about the aims of life and work BEFORE *they become fully open to moment-to-moment questioning that can improve performance.* During such developmental transformations, the very meaning of questioning itself, the very sense of how time works, and the feel for what kind of exercises of power generate CQI all change in ways that the person rarely if ever imagined before the change.

Put still differently, our argument is that, unless the senior managers and boards of organizations fundamentally reconsider the value of self-questioning-in-action in attaining the good life for themselves, the globe's economic, political and spiritual problems and polarizations will not abate. Our grotesque inequalities of wealth and power will continue to become more extreme, so too will the more subtle but even more significant inequalities among people of the world in their sense of the meaningfulness of their lives.

Yet virtually all persons tend to resist the disorientation and suffering of periods of upending questioning (with the exception of those evolving to the Magician/Witch stage). Few leap at the opportunity to repeat the upending sense of their teenage years, especially when they hold major corporate responsibilities. Perhaps the only way to become as enamoured of questioning-in-action, as executives must become who wish to lead a successful CQI process, is to make questioning-in-action the primary commitment and practice in one's personal search towards the good life—as this chapter will suggest.

You will have the opportunity to wrestle with the question of how much to value what type of questioning as the chapter continues. By way of preview, we propose that a good way to approach the good life is to see it as composed of four primary goods—namely, good money, good work, good friends and good questions.[1] As you can by now imagine, these four goods relate closely to the 'four territories of experience' we have been discussing throughout the book—the realms of outcomes (money), actions (work), thoughts and feelings (friends), and intuitive vision (inquiry). But before turning to the discussion of good money, good work, good friends and good questions, and of why they may be good candidates as criteria on which to focus in the search for the good life, let us examine some other areas of life that need to be addressed anew today by a constructive definition of the good life.

Communism's claim to have a workable answer to the 'good life' question has lost much of its credibility. At the same time, in America, fewer feel wealthy, or even comfortably middle class, and the gap between the richest fifth of the population and the poorest fifth has been widening for the past decade.[2] We are no longer certain that the individualistic capitalism of the economics texts works so well, especially when we compare it to the productivity of East Asia's clan capitalism.[3] Nevertheless, few of us wish to imitate the Japanese approach of this past generation, which too often virtually indentures persons to their work, leaving wives estranged from husbands and husbands in their forties dying of heart attacks in lonely hotel rooms. Nonetheless, we are not content with our Western forms of life. Cynicism, discontent and disillusion with regard to virtually all professions permeate broad layers of our population.[4]

From another angle, we are increasingly realizing that the entire modern way of life, with its predominant emphasis on the values of production and consumption and its spiritual relativism, is endangering the planet—from the Himalayan forests, to Madagascar's waters, to Brazil's plant and animal life, to Mexico City's air, to the thinning ozone layer over the North and South poles—and intrudes into the foreground more and more frequently. From the point of view of the market model of economics, these are mere 'external diseconomies' in our quest for the good life. But since the effects of our choices and actions may threaten our very survival, surely an appropriate definition of the good life and of the path towards the good life will properly subordinate both production and consumption to higher values, as does the Franklin Research & Development Corporation's motto, 'Investing for a Better World', that we reviewed in the previous chapter.

On the cusp of the third millennium, the global nature of the political economy and of its environmental effects dictates that our answers to the perennial question about the good life will this time have global—not just local or national—consequences. Therefore, this additional question arises: 'Is there a way of defining the good life that can have global validity—leading, for example, to a more just global monetary system—without obliterating justifiable differences in values?'

Another question, yet more ambitious: 'Is there a way of answering all these questions that leaves the market system intact as a method of determining prices *and* leaves broad leeway for different individuals and societies to evolve *distinctly*, while simultaneously posing a challenge to all individuals and societies to evolve *constructively*?' This would be the most conservative possible path towards the good life from our present condition.

We believe that there *is* an answer to these questions that is at once immediately practical within the *mélange* of market-like systems that now exist, is broad enough to allow for infinite variety among personal and societal value systems, is deep enough to embrace many transformations of under-standing, and is mysterious enough to allow a lifetime of continuing questioning. The most succinct way of stating this answer is that the good life consists of an appropriate blending of *good money, good work, good friends* and *good questions*. Towards the end of this chapter, we will ask you whether any of these four goods are among your primary goods and what *other* goods strike you as primary. Now, let us examine more closely what we mean, and what each of you may mean, by each of these four criteria that *we* claim constitute the good life when appropriately blended together.

Good money

We shall be surprised if very many of you who have ever tried to make ends meet don't agree that making good money represents positive net personal and social value.

But some of you are probably aware of the ambiguity in

the cliché 'good money'. When we say that someone makes good money, we typically mean simply that he or she makes quite a lot of money. There is an implication that the person makes more than an average amount of money, an ample amount of money, comfortably enough money, maybe more money than we can imagine we would really 'need'.

In the context of talking about the good life, however, the phrase 'good money' also carries an ethical overtone of some initially unclear sort. Can we imagine making 'bad money'? Perhaps such a phrase applies to illegal profits, such as those of Michael Milken based on insider information in the Wall Street junk bond market of the 1980s. Not all of us, however, would agree that all illegal profits are 'bad money'. In the Soviet Union of the 1970s, the only free markets were illegal black markets, yet some would argue that such illegal profits contributed more to personal and social net value than the money made by legal means under that system.

No. According to the four criteria of the good life that we are here proposing, what is ethically good about making good money is that one makes money in a way that blends best with the other three criteria of the good life. One can see plenty of examples of persons who accept jobs they don't regard as good work in order to make more money. One can also see examples of persons whose dedication to making more money leads them to sacrifice more and more of the leisure time during which one can cultivate good friends and good questions. Although there may be extenuating considerations in particular cases and for short periods of time, in general making more money in these ways reduces rather than increases the overall goodness of one's life. Hence, no matter how great the amount of money made in such cases, they are not examples of 'making good money', according to this definition of the good life. (Of course, these arguments only have weight if you agree on the importance of the other three criteria which we have yet to discuss. Therefore, you are quite right to feel tentative about accepting our claims at this point, before the discussion of the meaning of the other three criteria.)

Another way of putting this is that, of the four criteria of the good life, three of them—good work, good friends and good questions—are intrinsically valuable (we value the time actually spent engaged with them). By contrast, good money is only extrinsically valuable (valuable as a means to obtain other values, not as an end in itself). Therefore, any time we spend making, managing or spending money—when we are not simultaneously doing good work, meeting good friends or raising good questions—is not intrinsically valuable time. Indeed, every moment we spend in this way reduces the amount of intrinsically valuable time in our life.

At one extreme, according to this definition of the good life, if the richest person in the world spent all his or her time making money in the way just described—thereby leaving no time for good work, good friends and good questions—that person would have the 'poorest' life of anyone, would be making absolutely 'bad money' and would be living an ideal case of 'the bad life'. The reclusive, addicted, suicidal millionaire Howard Hughes seems to have exemplified this case.

At the other extreme, making no money at all could be an ideal case of 'making good money', if one's entire life were spent doing good work and engaging with good friends and good questions. (This extreme may initially strike readers as even more unlikely than the other. In fact, however, it is much *more* likely, since whole cultures have functioned altogether without the symbolic token of exchange value that we call money.)

Turning away from these extremes to the vast middle range of situations that virtually any adult reading this book inhabits, *one can be said to be* **making good money** *insofar as one spends the* **least** *amount of attention to making, managing, and spending money consistent with spending the greatest amount of attention to doing good work and engaging with good friends and good questions.* Note that this way of defining 'making good money' says absolutely nothing about how much money one makes. Note also that this way of defining 'making good money' is perfectly consistent with spending as much time as one wishes making money, so long as one constructs such money-making activity in such a way that it simultaneously involves doing good work, engaging good friends and asking good questions.

In any event, this gives you a sense of what we mean by 'making good money'.[5] Does it sound more—or less—like what you mean by 'making good money'?

Good work

Of course, we would all rather make good money by doing good work than by doing bad work. But what do 'good work' and 'bad work' mean, and how important is good work?

To us, good work means work that invites the development of craft-like skills and aesthetic judgement (whether in the realm of materials or of language). Such work calls for a kind of mastery that is never fully achieved, in the sense that it can thereafter be exercised in a rote, repetitive or mechanical fashion. Instead, good masterwork requires and reflects an active attention by the masterworker at each moment to the interplay between one's own body-in-action and the material. This active attention integrates knowledge and application, prior experience and future ideal, disciplined sobriety and spontaneous responsiveness. In the case of soccer, the World Cup competition exhibits the ideal of grace and social artistry that masterworks can achieve. In the case of executive level work, the principally influential artistry is exhibited, for better or worse, each time the executive speaks. (Hence the importance of crafting effective, artistic speech, as we began to study in the early chapters of this book.) In short, good work raises the consciousness of the worker. It generates mind–body integration and good health.

But our description of good work is still radically incomplete. Left as it is, this definition can give the impression that good work is good just for the worker—is nothing more than a form of narcissistic self-stimulation. Such an implication does violence to our most primitive intuitions about what work is—namely, that it produces something of value to some person(s) other than the worker. And indeed, this *is* another essential element of the definition of good work advanced here: good work produces something of value to some person(s) other than the worker. Everything in the prior paragraph about good work actually implies this without making it explicit.

Another way of seeing the social nature of all craft mastery is to remember that such mastery is defined in relation to a tradition (even when it redefines the tradition in creative ways). All craft traditions represent at once sacred and social trusts: they are dedicated to the creation of *genuine*, rather than false, *social* value. (Of course, how to differentiate genuine from false value in particular cases—whether in food, in works of art, in legal arguments, in accounting audits, in political candidates, or in spiritual teachers, to mention only a few—is among the best and most difficult of good questions . . . a matter to which we shall return below.)

Furthermore, the masterworker can only properly appreciate all of his or her own prior experience and future intention in their embeddedness within social relations—relations to mentors, peers, and apprentices within the craft tradition, relations to specific clients and the general public who receive the work (be it product or service), and relations to past and future generations.

'Delighting the customer'—the current cliché about how to

succeed in business—is certainly one of the alchemical outcomes of good work, according to this definition, and one of the ends towards which the masterworker aims. But it is just as certainly not the only end. 'Delighting the customer' is a great phrase in that it evokes the spontaneous enthusiasm of response—the raising of consciousness and the arousing of appreciation—that the very best products and services generate in their recipients. On the other hand, 'delighting the customer' can become a murderously narrow and inadequate criterion of good work when it becomes the only or the overriding criterion.

All of human history in any field of endeavour instructs us that there is no simple public measure of good work. In the short term and even in the middle term, good work may or may not be rewarded by good money, by promotions, by awards or by positions of communal esteem and trust (e.g. board memberships). Nevertheless, there are two reasons that doing good work is a more significant criterion of the good life than making good money. First, as already stated, it is intrinsically valuable, not just extrinsically valuable. Second, good work *can* generate good money, whereas good money can only support, not generate, good work.

The public judgement of good work is so problematic because the very best work does not generate a passive result, but rather acts on the public, raising consciousness and questions about the very boundaries of the product, service or medium. This is most evident in the realm of the creative fine arts, but it also occurs in the most down-to-earth products such as shoes, which recently have been filled with air and advertised as vehicles for flight by Air Jordan and other colleagues of his (former) craft tradition. In addition, we have traced the consciousness-raising aspects of good organizational leadership throughout the later chapters of this book, and very much hope that these chapters raise many questions for you.

We know best the cases when such boundary-questioning-and-crossing experiments succeed in commercial terms. But such success hardly proves that those experiments provide much genuine value (as the rapid succession of fads suggest), and many more such experiments fail than succeed. Many of the failures deserve their fate. Others have simply asked questions for which the public is not yet ready.

Recognized geniuses like Shirley MacLaine of Hollywood and various astral dimensions, or Edwin Land of Polaroid, or Pablo Picasso, or Marguerite Yourcenar, the first woman elected to the French Academy, integrate an enormous span from indigestible questions to delighting the customer (and they often exhibit extraordinary endurance throughout their lifetimes in their experimenting towards such a span of consciousness).

As the foregoing paragraphs suggest, good work unveils questions that evoke wonder in the worker, in co-workers and in the audience. But *wonder* is a gentle word, and questions sometimes act more roughly. The commitment to do good work can badger and bedevil the worker with such questions. A final criterion of good work is that, through such questions, the work remains lively for the worker and keeps the worker lively 'til death doth them part (at least insofar as those of us still living can see).

A brief postscript: if an increasing proportion of the members of a society seeks to live a life that includes good questions, good friends and good work, then good work that raises good questions is increasingly likely to generate good money and esteem for the masterworker.

Such, then, is the definition of good work offered here. This definition emphasizes the challenge of CQI inherent in good work and shows that this is not just measured by an increase in the external quality of the product, but also by the vivification of the awareness of the worker. This more vivid awareness is what we have been describing in the previous few chapters when we speak of the freshness of simultaneous insider/outsider awareness.

How do these ideas accord or not accord with your own sense of good work? To what degree do you experience yourself as currently doing good work and preparing yourself to further improve the quality of your work, either by this definition or by your own?

As a fringe benefit, we predict you will enjoy working more and more the closer your work comes to embodying the characteristics we are ascribing to good work.

Good friends

A common way of describing good friends is to speak of 'mates' who have a lot in common (like to shop together, or play basketball together, or get along at work). They can trust one another's reliability. They support one another—perhaps casually, but nevertheless reassuringly. And they don't get into fights . . . (too often).

What do you mean by good friends?

This common way of describing good friends is emphatically *not* what we mean by good friends. No. We mean more nearly the reverse.

Good friends, as we understand the relationship, are persons who wish to meet and celebrate their differences, in part because these differences clarify who each is and what each values. Good friends often act unpredictably because they are growing and seeking to promote one another's growth. Good friends actively develop trust by disclosing their own efforts to grow, by supporting the other's efforts, and by getting into fights of a certain kind—by struggling together over what each means by the good life and by confronting one another when possible contradictions appear between a person's espoused principles and actual practices.

'Mates' share norms and values which remain implicit. They thus tend to become more alike, or at least *appear* to become more alike, until some rift separates them. By contrast, good friends, as here understood, *explicitly* test their differences and become *more different* from one another—stranger and stranger—even as they also develop shared aims, respect, and love at the deepest level. e. e. cummings' lines about friends and lovers bespeak this kind of love:

love's function is to fabricate unknownness . . .

how lucky lovers are (whose selves abide
under whatever shall discovered be) . . .[6]

This kind of friendship is highly challenging and dynamic. It is essential for discovering and defining for oneself what the good life is and what one's own particular good work is. Persons who begin to taste and value this kind of friendship tend to be attracted to, rather than repelled by, strangers who come from different cultures, generations, sexes, religions or races. And because such friendships are rooted in concern for one another's development, they tend to become *lifetime* friendships that can span great distances and long periods of absence, rather than temporary friendships founded around some specific age-related activity. Developmental transformations tend to occur within the friendship rather than ending the relationship.

No matter what the beginning circumstances or formal roles of the participants in such a friendship—even when they are hierarchically related as mother–daughter, boss–subordinate, or teacher–student—the friendship evolves towards a peer relationship in its maturity.

By this definition, family relationships are a subcategory within friendship. Marriages and parent–child relationships at their very best cultivate mutual development and, over 25 year time periods, peer relationships can evolve. According to this definition of the good life, the proper aim of marriage and family life is to generate the kind of friendship described here.

Many persons in today's world have no friendships of this kind. Others have one or two friends with whom they border on the kind of experience described here on rare occasions. Because the kind of friendship we are talking about does not treat either person's current equilibrium as sacred, it can feel threatening. Persons frequently shy away from this type of friendship without fully realizing it—for example, laughing away the beginnings of what for the other would have been a significant disclosure. The degree of male violence against wives and of parental abuse of children is one raw indication of how far many families are from creating the conditions for true friendship.

Who do you count as good friends? Do the names differ if you use your own prior definition and if you use the definition presented here?

The definitions of good work and good money offered earlier are probably fairly easy to understand and probably contain some attractive elements, whether or not you fully agree with them. By contrast, the definition of good friends offered now is more likely to seem strange and problematic. Although this definition contains echoes that go back at least as far as Plato's dialogue *Lysis* on friendship, this kind of friendship has never flourished widely in any society. It has often been regarded as dangerous to family, church and state because it generates a deeper loyalty to 'whatever shall discovered be' than to any taken-for-granted, prestructured institutional authority.[7] It is a late-stage Magician/Witch/Clown experience of friendship—an experience that only a minuscule proportion of the human race has initiated before now. Both the CQI groups we suggested in Chapter 7 and the even more provocative suggestion of 'triangular friendships' that we offered in Chapter 12 can be steps in the direction of such friendships.

Whereas it is at least conceivable that global consensus could be achieved about the positive value of good work and good money, as we are defining them, it seems much more likely today that global consensus would form *against* our definition of good friends than for it. Neither American individualism, nor European postmodernism, nor Middle Eastern fundamentalism, nor Japanese clannishness predisposes persons towards such friendship.

But this is just the (paradoxical) point. *No* taken-for-granted culture can generate such friendship. The aspiring intercultural friends must generate such friendship for themselves by offering their allegiance to good questions. This kind of friendship is not personality-bound and culture-bound, but personality-transforming and culture-transforming.

Because this kind of friendship welcomes strangeness (weirdness, queerness) and transformation (as long as these present themselves in a mutual and vulnerable manner) rather than protecting against strangeness, such friendship is consistent with a global society which allows for local and personal differences.

This kind of friendship is also just what you'd want in a board of directors, or a senior management team (or a team at any other organizational level). For a work team's ultimate constructive purpose is surely to question whether its members, both collectively and individually, lead/act in ways consistent with the organization's mission.

Good questions   Most people treat questions as leading towards answers—the point being to discover the correct answer. In such cases, questions serve at best as a means to an end. From this point of view, it will no doubt seem peculiar at first to hear our claim: that good questions are intrinsically valuable—indeed, more valuable than good work or good friends (though truly good questions often insinuate themselves *through* good work and good friends).

Of course, what we mean by good questions are not mere questions of fact, e.g. 'Where's the bathroom in this place?' To such a question, we wish an immediate answer. Nor are good questions mere questions of theory that deserve and repay eternal rumination. Good questions are intrinsically valuable because they heighten our awareness of external facts, of our own acts, of theories, and of our own attending in the moment—make us more alive and more related to the rest of our own lives and everything else.

Good questions, insofar as we can attend to them, connect us to a wider, living universe. Every time that the scene before our eyes comes to life and we really see the colour, the movement and the relationships—every time looking becomes seeing—we are looking with a question. Every time we truly listen to the sounds reaching our ears, we are hearing with a question. Every time we actually taste the food we are eating, we are . . . actually tasting.

To taste is to test. To test is to question. To question is to taste. The subtlest taste of all, and the trickiest to develop, is the taste for continuing questioning. Initially, we can't help hoping that we'll find an answer that ends our agonizing questions. We'd rather not be *that* alive! We're anything but sure that we want to learn how to see answers as leading to better questions. . . .

Questioning may or may not be translated into words. In poetry, at its best, every word is tasted as it is written (and as it is read). In prose, too.

An organization's mission or purpose is, properly, an undying question—sometimes prodding, sometimes alerting, sometimes guiding its members. But how many members of an organization treat it this way? How to focus, how to formulate, how to wake up to an organization's mission is itself a good question. How to wake up others to this questioning is another good question. Is *anyone* in the organization awake to these questions?

What are the questions guiding your life? What are the questions you are trying to evade? What is the single question that integrates those different questions? Are you asking every day? Every moment? Are you fully alive—let alone living the good life—when you are not tasting your experience? Are you embalmed within your thoughts right now, or are you tasting your thinking along with your embodiment, outcomes and your changing quality of attending?

Inquiry and faith

Perhaps you are a committed believer, with a deep, embracing and comforting faith. Whether your faith is in the Koran, or in the miracle of Jesus' birth, death and resurrection, or in an 'a-theistic' scientific method, or in constitutional democracy, you may feel that you have passed beyond this 'adolescent theology of questions' to a wonderful, well-founded answer.

Yes. But if your answer is truly wonderful and you are truly alive to its wonder now, then you are 'wonder-ing' and 'wonder-ful': alive to its mystery—questioning. To advocate scientific method without question, or Christ's resurrection without appreciation for the mystery, are grand self-contradictions indeed!

Good questions never die. It is only our attention to them that dies. Good questions enliven parties (even political parties!), organizations and each of us individually (even those of us who avowedly and emotionally hate to be put into question). Good questions grow relationships ('What thoughts, feelings, and actions are truly loving now?'). Good questions grow vocations ('How can I excel my current attention in the service of excellent work'). And good questions grow wealth ('Who are my customers and what will tickle them pink?'). Whereas 'right answers' have a way of forming armies and generating destruction, good questions generate conversation and good spirits.

Good questions rise outwards towards the very nature of nature, towards the very nature of the universe. Good questions deepen inwards towards the very mystery of one's own and others' human being, attending finally to one's own and others' attending, bestowing the gift of developmentally meaningful glances, silences, words. Good questions expand flirtatiously along the boundaries and surfaces of the present. We can only work, love and question in the present. Can we remain present to the present, even as our hearts remember the past, our minds roam the future, and our bodies fall towards sleep?

As we grow older and begin to stiffen physically, are our questions becoming increasingly lively? Do they guide us towards increasingly fluidifying exercise?

Not all questions become increasingly lively. Not all questions awaken us to the present. Not all questions meet any of the criteria for good questions advanced in the foregoing paragraphs. Indeed, the experience of good questions is likely to be relatively rare, and may be felt as somewhat illicit or dumb in a society such as ours, conditioned for the past five hundred years by the quest for scientific certainty.

If you immediately and fully agree with our sense of what good questions are and with our sense of their centrality to the good life, we shall be astonished. For we have never seen the matter presented so.[8] Moreover, we have heard many initial reservations and objections to these ideas when we share them verbally—objections which are by no means fully dealt with in this brief introduction to the notion of good questions. So . . . what are your initial responses to this notion?

Prioritizing and blending the four goods

In beginning to draw together the thoughts you had as you read the foregoing pages, you may wish to consider the following questions:

1. What additional criteria for the good life—besides good money, good work, good friends, and good questions—have occurred to you?[9]

2. How do you prefer to reformulate the four goods we have tried to describe?
3. How do you prioritize the four goods presented here and/or the goods that seem primary to you?
4. On which of your 'primary' goods have you mainly concentrated in your life?
5. How successful do you feel you have been so far at generating each good that seems primary to you?
6. When you share such reflections with your friends, or the members of your CQI group (*which you have no doubt started by now*), what do you and they together suggest as the most significant blocks that you must overcome or dissolve or accept now and in the near future if you are to make your way towards your version of the good life?

We have been quite explicit about *our* rank ordering of the four goods that we believe are conducive to the good life. Good questions, we have asserted, grow relationships, vocations and value/wealth. Good questions are therefore, in our understanding and experience, the primary aim of anyone seeking the good life. As strange as it may sound from the modern point of view, a practitioner of this path towards the good life might say—even cheerily:

'Good questions bedevil me;
therefore, my life is good'.

Good friends are the second highest priority in our version of the good life, and friendships are good to the degree that they are based on good questions. The more you take the risk to bring the questions that bedevil, bewilder, and bemuse you to your friends; and the more you take the risk to listen to their questions; the better your friendships will become, even when the questions are addressed to the friendship itself. (Along the way, you are likely to lose some 'friends' who don't want to face such questions, at least not just now or not in just such a way.)

Good work is the third priority among our four primary goods. Work is good to the degree that it revivifies good questions (raising the worker's awareness); to the degree that it spins off good friends and the leisure to enjoy them (indeed, the best work, and all truly artistic work, is itself leisurely in this respect); and to the degree that it embodies itself in ways that others, including Mother Earth herself, value.

Money, we have asserted, (including bankable credit,

which it is far more useful to have, in most cases, than mere literal cash), ranks lowest of the four goods, having no intrinsic value. Money, therefore, functions as a good only insofar as it supports the other three goods.

The very best way for money to support the other three goals is to make it (enough of it so that one is not distracted by its absence) *by doing good work with good friends addressing good questions.* To create such conditions is a high challenge indeed! If one succeeds, the issue of how to divide one's time among the different priorities obviously fades, since one is attending to all four goods at once. This represents the ultimate blending of the four goods—the good life.

At least, this is our current belief. We are in the midst of testing it—each in our own different ways—in the daily living of our own lives.

Conclusion

These pages have attempted to raise questions with you about what you regard as the good life and as the path towards the good life. We have attempted to provoke you in two different ways:

(a) by asking you what approach to the good life is compatible at one and the same time with a market economy, with cultural and personal diversity, and with the developmental transformations that adulthood can entail; and

(b) by offering you a set of four, rank-ordered criteria for the good life and the path towards the good life for you to compare to your own evolving criteria.

We have not attempted to make a strong, closely knit argument in favour of our particular criteria. Instead, we have attempted to say just enough to display the outlines of each criterion, the outlines of their overall coherence with one another, and the outlines of their consistency with a globally universalizable definition of the good life which does justice to local differences.

Of course, you may not agree that we have succeeded in displaying either the beneficence, or the coherence, or the universal applicability of our four criteria for the good life. We shall welcome your comments to that effect, since it is altogether in our own self-interests to improve our approach. Please tell us also how your favoured criteria fare in response to the demand for beneficence, coherence and universalizability.

Good wishes on your path. If you believe you are choosing something like a path of CQI, we hope you are beginning to find of use the action inquiry approach that we have introduced in this book. If you practise this action inquiry 'gait' very far along the CQI path, we hope this book will serve as a kind of companion through one or more significant transformations in your relationship to the rest of the world.

Notes

1. John Rawls (1971) in *A Theory of Justice*, Cambridge MA: Harvard University Press offers another, related theory of what anyone can be presumed, minimally, to mean by the good life. While his theory is not synonymous with the one offered here, it is not fundamentally inconsistent with it either (see W. R. Torbert (1974) 'Doing Rawls justice', *Harvard Educational Review* **44** (4), 459–69). Rawls' candidates for the four primary goods are: (1) self-esteem; (2) a rational plan of life; (3) the opportunity for good work; and (4) wealth. The last two obviously bear some relation to the ideas of good work and of good money.

2. The well-known conservative Kevin Phillips has written two books on this topic: (1990) *The Politics of Rich and Poor: Wealth and the American Electorate in the Reagan Aftermath*, New York: Random House; and (1993) *Boiling Point: Republicans, Democrats and the Decline of Middle Class Prosperity*, New York: Random House.

3. The distinction between individualistic capitalism and clan capitalism is based on William Ouchi (1980) *Theory Y*, Reading, MA: Addison-Wesley; William Lazonick (1991) *Business Organization and the Myth of the Market Economy*, Cambridge, UK: Cambridge University Press; and Lester Thurow (1992) *Head to Head: The Coming Economic Battle Among Japan, Europe, and America*, New York: Morrow.

4. Best known among the recent cultural critiques is Robert Bellah *et al.* (1985) *Habits of the Heart: Individualism and Commitment in American Life,* Berkeley, CA: University of California Press. More recently, there is Donald Kanter and Philip Mirvis (1989) *The Cynical Americans: Living and Working in an Age of Discontent and Disillusion*, San Francisco, CA: Jossey-Bass.

5. The most provocative extended treatise on the relation of money to the good life that we have encountered is Jacob Needleman (1991) *Money and the Meaning of Life*, New York: Doubleday. Although the flavour and style of that book are very different from our brief comments here, we do not sense any fundamental inconsistency in the underlying argument.

6. The lines from 'Love's function is to fabricate unknownness' are reprinted from *Complete Poems, 1904–1962*, by e. e. cummings, edited by George J. Firmage, by permission of Liveright Publishing Corporation and W. W. Norton and Company.

Copyright © 1935, 1963, 1991 by the Trustees for e. e. Cummings Trust.

7. Carey McWilliams (1973) *The Idea of Fraternity in America*, Berkeley, CA: University of California Press.

8. A fuller and different discussion of questioning occurs in Chapter 15, 'Living Inquiry', of W. R. Torbert (1991) *The Power of Balance: Transforming Self, Society, and Scientific Inquiry*, Newbury Park, CA: Sage Publications.

9. Actually, we are currently arguing together about whether 'good sleep' should be considered the fourth primary good, thereby reordering 'good money' to the fifth rank among primary goods. Arguments in favour of 'good sleep' over 'good money' include: (1) good sleep is an intrinsic good; (2) good sleep implies a 'free' conscience; (3) good sleep requires good exercise; (4) good sleep implies learning from altered state experiences not bounded by one's habitual, waking assumptions; (5) good sleep implies being on relatively good terms with developmental transformations, such as the transformation from life to death can be. The conversation continues.

Appendix A Action inquiry exercises

We found that our students, the managers with whom we work, and prior readers of this book all asked for additional exercises to support their action inquiry efforts. For this reason we offer additional exercises in this appendix, which is divided into five sections:

1. Analysing framing, advocating, illustrating and inquiring
2. Enacting framing, advocating, illustrating and inquiring
3. Experiences in trying out the Chapter 4 exercises
4. Analysing developmental frames
5. Experiences with continual quality improvement groups

You are, of course, welcome to peruse them in any order you wish, if you wish to peruse them at all.

Analysing framing, advocating, illustrating and inquiring

Let us start again with the importance of close attention to on-the-job conversation, as we did in Chapter 3. We find that, even when you make the commitment to write such a conversation in your journal, it is often difficult to break through the next barrier and to analyse, slowly and thoroughly, your own relative ineffectiveness using the categories of *framing, advocacy, illustration* and *inquiry*.

Frequently, when you record in your journal a dialogue that is significantly troublesome, you may be so focused on the anger or the helplessness that the other person's unhelpful actions generate in you that you fail to attend to the ways in which you are, in effect (though of course not *in intent*), colluding with that person by your way of acting.

Below, we offer a sample conversation that you can analyse. As usual, we suggest that you *do* analyse it and that you record your analysis *before* you read on into our analysis of the conversation. You can also mentally role-play various different responses that Grace could make to John, or John to Grace.

Before reading the dialogue, it will help you to know that Grace experiences herself as having been harassed by John since his recent appointment as her supervisor, and she dislikes interacting with him.

The day before this dialogue takes place, she is helping a colleague from another team with a problem at a point when (in her version of the story) John interrupts, raises his voice, and demands to know why she was working on another team's problem. She stands up and walks out of the office, passing her former manager who sees how upset she is.

The next morning, the former manager takes her aside, apologizes for having made John her supervisor and promises she will soon be removed from John's group. A few minutes later, as she is speaking to another co-worker, John announces they should both come to a 10 a.m. meeting and that his third subordinate will also be present. Grace asks if any preparation is necessary, and he says 'No'.

John opens the 10 a.m. meeting by turning to Grace. Here is her reconstruction of the dialogue that follows:

John: What happened yesterday?
Grace: I got upset. I didn't know I wasn't supposed to work on that problem. I was trying to help Scott out.
John: You don't have to help them out. They don't help us out.
Grace: Scott is always helpful to me.
John: You created a real problem yesterday.
Grace: How did I create a problem?
John: There were other people around. You created a problem for me and for all those people. You are *never* to *not* answer me again. Sometimes people ask me questions that I don't want to answer, but I *have* to.
Grace: I was obviously upset. Where's your sensitivity? Maybe my dog died and I was having a bad day.
John: Well, I'm the boss, and if you don't like it you can leave. You have to respect me.
Grace: You have to earn respect.
John: I let you do whatever you want.
Grace: I am achieving the goals that Harry and I put together. If you want to put together new goals, I would be happy to. Besides, I want to be evaluated by my goals.
John: That's not the way it works in real life.
Grace: Well, you're right. I'll try harder. (At this point I had realized that the best thing to do was end the confrontation because no solution could be found.)

Perhaps the first thing to point out is that different readers will have very different reactions to different aspects of this exchange. Because your own particular reactions may be quite strong, you may find it difficult to believe that anyone else could seriously hold another view. But, we assure you, some will (partly based on their own particular developmental frame for interpreting events). Some will feel that John is basically right about several different things: that it was inappropriate for Grace to leave the room without speaking the previous day; that life isn't fair; that as boss he legitimately has superior power.

Some may feel that Grace is quite courageous in standing up to John: not just accepting that she created a problem; telling him he had to earn respect; highlighting the achievement of her goals.

Others may interpret this as a typical example of sexist domination of a woman by a man.

Still others may feel frustrated at the ways Grace 'unnecessarily' surrenders, from her initial description of 'What happened yesterday?' to her apparent validation of John's entire position at the end ('Well, you're right. I'll try harder.').

And yet another subgroup will be focusing on the fact that Grace does not seek the views of the two other participants in the meeting, and that they do not volunteer to intervene.

Let's put these various inferences and interpretations aside for a moment and try to analyse whether and how each speaker frames, advocates, illustrates and inquires. As we have before, we encourage you to write your own line-by-line analysis of which of the four types of speech are used, how explicitly they are crafted, and how influential they are in generating more valid information and better judgement. Before looking at our analysis, go back and try to score each comment, using as many of the four categories as seem appropriate, and noting when it seems to you ambiguous how a comment should be scored.

Analysis and commentary

John begins with *inquiry*: 'What happened yesterday?' In opening with an inquiry, John does not reveal what he is thinking or feeling, thus making himself relatively invulnerable, while at the same time asking the other to make a commitment—to become vulnerable—by offering a description of a controversial event. An inquiry is an archetypal opening gambit for a person at the Opportunist stage of development.

Almost anything one says at the outset of a conversation

implicitly frames what follows, but we only score it as *framing* when the frame is *explicitly* stated. Thus, John's opener is *not* scored as *framing*. This is not merely a technical point about the scoring. Being able to make these four types of speech explicit when one wishes to, and in the combinations one wishes, is a critical point that distinguishes between effective and ineffective speech in our actual practice. (We invite you to confirm or disconfirm our advocacy here by actual observation of your own practice *as you practise*.) For, as long as the frame within which you are speaking is primarily implicit:

(a) others may not understand the speaker's intention;
(b) it is unlikely that the speaker will test publicly whether others share his or her frame; and
(c) it is more difficult for others to inquire about or challenge the frame.

Our experience is that, if we remember the four overall territories to which these categories refer at the time of an interaction, we can respond to an opening inquiry such as John's by seeking a clarification of his frame or by proposing our own frame.

Thus, Grace could reflect John's manner back to him by asking: 'What's your point in bringing this up now?' This would then force John to make an explicit commitment to a frame for the conversation. Or, she could say, 'I'm glad you are bringing up yesterday's incident in a meeting with others at which they can help each of us see how we could have dealt with the situation more effectively. As you probably gathered from my reaction of walking out of the room, I considered your action incredibly rude, unprofessional, and destructive of trust in several directions.'

Let us look next at Grace's *actual* response to John's initial question. She begins by *advocating* what her feeling was (leaving unmentioned John's action that generated her feeling). Then she *illustrates* why she felt that way, but does so by accepting John's interpretation (that she was not supposed to work on that problem) and speaking only about her internal dynamics ('I didn't know . . . I was trying . . . '). So, by looking at Grace's response in terms of the four categories, we see that she accepted an implicit and unclear *frame*, offered a remarkably one-sided *advocacy* and *illustration*, and did not use inquiry to give any of her own direction to subsequent comments.

John's next comment is pure *advocacy* without illustration.

Neither we nor you can form a picture in our minds based on his universalistic abstractions. (In addition, we may note that, if the universalistic statement that 'They [members of the other department] don't help us out' is true, then the organization to which the two departments belong is apparently forfeiting that part of its effectiveness as an organization.)

Grace responds with something more like an *illustration*. The 'always' is a universalistic element that puffs up the statement a little beyond itself. Had she offered a single instance in some detail—let's say, the last bit of help Scott gave Grace prior to her effort to help him—her illustration would gain more ballast than her 'always' gives it. But her statement *is* an illustration by comparison to the prior advocacy for at least three reasons:

* it is more specific about the persons involved,
* it is less propositional, and
* in being less explicit about how future action ought to be influenced if it is true, it becomes less likely to influence future action at all.

This relative non-influentialness of a 'naked' illustration, such as this last one by Grace, is immediately illustrated by what occurs next in the dialogue. Despite the fact that Grace's illustration directly contradicts John's advocacy, she gains no ground, for he simply ignores her comment entirely and moves from his prior paternalistic advocacy to a well-crafted, attacking advocacy: 'You created a real problem yesterday.'

This attacking advocacy is well-crafted as an *initial* attack in a *professional* conversation because it is non-emotional in content, confronting about performance (as so many more managers need to learn how to be), and implicitly concerned with problem solving. That it is also conclusive rather than inquiring; that it offers no supporting illustration; that it is a *non sequitur*; that it is blaming; that it deflects attention from his behaviour—all these elements that are not conducive to mutual learning and quality improvement can go unnoticed by those not practised in observing the action effects of speaking as they engage together in conversation.

Breaking away from the analysis of the conversation, we wonder to what degree our analysis agrees with yours? To what degree is our analysis helpful in beginning to give more sinuousness and significance to your sense of *framing*, *advocating*, *illustrating* and *inquiring*?

Let us now move on from after-the-act analysis to before-the-act rehearsals of scenarios that can more directly influence our ability to act effectively.

Enacting framing, advocacy, illustration and inquiry

In a new situation, Greg has shown Jane up in a meeting with clients in a way that hurts client confidence in their company, according to Jane's version of our next story. Jane uses her journal to rehearse how she can frame, advocate, illustrate and inquire when she next takes up the issue with Greg. Here is her plan:

Framing
I am going to walk into his office and ask if he has a minute because there is something on my mind. He will invite me in and ask me to sit down. I will take a deep breath and begin.

Jane: Last week at the Goldman Sachs meeting, I felt as if you embarrassed me in front of the traders and several other of the portfolio managers. I am not sure that you are fully aware of how the conversation appeared to others in the room. I felt as if I was under direct attack from you because I had not shown you bonds that I did not think our guidelines permitted and did not offer any real premium. The bonds I am referring to are the 144As. I understand that each of the portfolio managers has a different style and each runs money in a very different manner. I have spoken to Jan on prior occasions to ask her if we can use 144As. Her response was and remains 'NO'.

Greg: 'Mmmm . . . ' (He is extremely forgetful and at this point is probably desperately trying to remember what he said or did.)

Advocating
Jane: In the meeting you mentioned two issues which you had participated in that were 144As. Both of those issues had regulation rights which means that if the company does not register the bonds within a certain number of days, they must pay a penalty. As soon as the company registers the bond, the issue will be publicly traded. Do your guidelines permit 144As? If so, we had a lack of communication and I will be happy to show you the issues which I find offer value. The ones which Goldman Sachs was talking about were very expensive.

Greg: (Fumbling through his account guidelines in an effort to demonstrate that he can indeed use 144As.) Yes, I would like that.

Illustrating

Jane: Do you understand why I was upset during the meeting? I realize that you did not mean to embarrass me, but I felt as if you did. You as much as anyone understand the need to act as a cohesive group in front of the Street. It is very important for our image. If I do not look tough to the Street, our overall trading performance will suffer. When a portfolio manager publicly humiliates a trader, the image is shattered. In the future, if a similar situation arises, I think it would benefit both you and me if you spoke to me after the meeting rather than during the meeting.

Greg: Yes, DEAR (he is a bit of a sexist). I did not realize I embarrassed you. Jeez, I certainly did not mean it to come across like that.

Inquiring

Jane: I must admit I was not happy. I hope this does not happen again. And please tell me whether your accounts can use 144A without regulation rights.

Greg: Yes, I will do that.

Now, you are welcome to critique Jane's sense of what these four categories are about. In her framing, for example, she *does* frame the content of what she wants to talk about, but she does *not* frame the action outcome she is looking for in this conversation. What she labels as illustrating, to take another example, is more a combination of inquiring and advocating, as much or more than it is illustrating.

But our main point here is not about perfect rehearsal. Our main point is about the importance of rehearsing, however imperfectly. This is what the rehearsal led to:

I cannot believe that I carried it through as planned. I am sure I fumbled through what I had to say, but the fact that I confronted the situation was most important. . . . I walked towards his office and caught him just as he was coming out. You say in your book that action inquiry will feel awkward at first, as if everyone is staring at you, and that is exactly how I felt as I walked up to him. The conversation went as follows:

Jane: Greg, do you have a minute? There is something I would like to talk to you about.

Greg: Sure, come into my office.

Jane: I would like to talk to you about what happened at the Goldman Sachs' meeting last week. The situation with the 144As.

Greg: Yes, yes, the 144As.

Jane: The issues they were mentioning did not have any value in them. Sarah (our bank analyst) wrote up a memo on them last week. Do you have a copy? I felt embarrassed by the way you asked if the salesperson had shown them to the desk.

Greg: Oh no . . . you see, I was just so surprised. I can use 144As (he fumbles through his papers to show me).

Jane: (Some of his accounts DO allow 144As.) I will be happy to show you the 144As which I think have value. These did not. You understand as well as anyone that we are trying to build a relationship with Goldman and how important it is to appear as a cohesive unit in front of the Street. In the future, if there is something you would like to discuss, please do it with me after the meeting. The Street does not need to see internal differences. I was very embarrassed.

Greg: I am sorry. It will not happen again.

Jane: Thank you. I will get you a copy of Sarah's memo.

And that was that. I walked out of the office very proud of myself. The hardest part was getting the guts to walk into his office.

Feb 24

I was working this morning when Greg came into the trading room. He tapped me on the shoulder and said he called Goldman Sachs, but that our salesperson was on vacation. He said he would try again next week. I am shocked. I am sure that he is calling to apologize. I never thought he would call Goldman. Am I glad he is calling? Yes, absolutely. I am not sure whether he has more respect for me, but I certainly have more respect for myself.

I feel more confident about my dealings with managers. This was only one situation, but I feel as though it now leaves the door open for me to speak up more readily. This was really the first time I have stood up to a manager and said I was unhappy with his behaviour.

Feb 28

Greg did indeed call Goldman Sachs and apologize for his behaviour at the meeting. My coverage called me first thing this morning wondering what on earth I had said to him for him to have called. At the end, the salesperson said, 'That is not the Greg I have heard about'. Furthermore, Greg went in to speak to Mary, the head of the trading desk, and informed her of my action and praised me for it. Who would have thought! Mary said I handled him beautifully by not going into his office and screaming at him.

We cannot all hope to have quite such a positive and rewarding outcome—both internally in terms of enhanced sense of self-respect and externally in terms of recognition—to our first major experiment with action inquiry. But the magnitude of the effect that Jane's action had suggests how rare such behaviour is in business and what a competitive advantage it can be to display such action inquiry. Her careful prior rehearsal also seems to have been critical in giving her a kind of Pole star to steer by during the actual encounter.

We urge you to rehearse in writing (or orally in a CQI group if you are participating in one) a significant on-the-job action you feel you are challenged to take, but are uncertain about how to take.

Experiences in trying the Chapter 4 exercises

The exercises proposed in Chapter 4 strike many readers as inviting actions which, because they are unusual, also feel risky and even foolish. It may be of use, therefore, to share two brief accounts by prior readers of Chapter 4 about their initial experiences in approaching the exercises:

March 8
After reading Chapter 4, I realized (that) . . . I had become 'lazy' with my awareness. It has become a habit for me to 'just do it' because there never seems to be enough time.

I am going to test this assumption by experimenting with taking a short vacation at work, twice a day at 10 a.m. and 2 p.m. (typically these are very hectic times). I am going to stop for five minutes and just *think* about what I am doing.

Frankly, I am actually looking forward to this time. Lately, between work and school and planning this wedding, I have truly felt caught in the rat race. I have felt like I can't stop for a second, when in fact this may be just what I need. At the same time, I know this will be a struggle: even as I write, I can feel the tug to move on to the next item on my list.

March 9
So, I held my bargain. I took my breaks at 10 a.m. and 3.15 p.m. (I didn't quite make the 2 p.m. deadline). My 3.15 was actually much better than my 10 because, honestly, I felt absolutely stupid doing 'nothing' at 10. I just sort of announced I was going for a Coke and went downstairs, outside to a bench, and sat. I was fidgeting almost instantly. I must admit, however, that by the end of five minutes I did seem 'calmer'. I don't know why. Maybe because I had reflected about my priorities for the morning, or maybe because it seemed just plain ridiculous to be spending five minutes on myself when I know there is no way we will finish the job as it is. I guess the key is the time was just for *me*.

> Anyway, I did seem more productive after the break. This may be because during my five minutes I had a revelation—I could only get done what was physically possible to do. So I refocused on *finishing* one piece of the project. All five of us have been running to the next piece because the schedule called for us to move on. We have been trying to finish the documenting after work and on weekends. This approach just isn't working. We are spending hours reacquainting ourselves with the product.
>
> When I forced myself to take the later break, I just sat in my office and stared at a memo—others thought I was reading. This time I spent most of the period reflecting on what I am now putting down on paper.

This reader's experience, as commonplace and even trivial as it may appear at first reading, strikes us as an illustration of immense significance. Note that this person tried the experiment even though it seemed 'stupid' and 'just plain ridiculous' from the point of view of her Technician-like logic of getting many things done fast and treating herself as less significant than the job. Even after she did it, she claims not to know why she felt calmer. But then, as she continues, with the benefit of having taken a second break later during the day to think about what occurred, she realizes that: (1) the very fact of treating herself as more important than the job may be key; and (2) the decision to finish what she could rather than interrupt herself may be key. Both of these reversals of priorities represent double-loop changes from a Technician frame to an Achiever frame. These unexpected reframings were the 'fruits' of her non-habitual action inquiry exercise.

Here is another prior reader practising the 'unfocusing the eyes in meetings' exercise from Chapter 4.

> I am practising unfocusing my eyes at our daily meetings. Every morning at 9.30 a.m. the head of the department will come into our open area and will run through the activities that affect us, from the tone of the mortgage market to the latest events in Mexico and Indonesia. In unfocusing my eyes, I have discovered that many people do not pay attention to what is being said until he addresses their area.
>
> Is the meeting well framed at the outset? No. Are inquiries used as weapons, or as genuine ways of generating clarity or including more colleagues' perspectives? I think that the inquiries are usually used as ways of generating clarity, though some people think they are used as weapons.

Although this short excerpt, like the previous one, does not seem earth-shaking in terms of its external significance, it marks a profound change in the writer's position within the meeting. The writer is now actively engaged in 'following' the action 'dance' of the meeting from moment to moment. As a result, this participant is now in a position to act with an awareness of the ongoing pattern of action and with an awareness of how his action either conforms to that pattern or 'leads' the dance into a different pattern. This participant is now actively managing both the content of what he says and the process of how he says it. He is in principle more likely to be effective because he is managing more of the variance in how his actions influence others.

Analysing developmental frames

Whereas the dialogue analysis we have just been practising examines managerial events on a more 'microscopic' play-by-play level, the analysis of developmental frames invites us to look at ourselves and our colleagues in a more 'macroscopic' way—to see the kinds of persons we are and are becoming.

Here is one manager's journal entries during his early days of attempting to diagnose his colleagues' developmental frames.

Today I was part of a meeting to discuss a new product line, where I was able to watch and become increasingly aware of the developmental styles of members of my management team. I will list the three individuals and their themes:

QT (Technician):   Critical of others' methodologies
                      Wants product to be better than it has to be
                      Tries to solve problems by formulations
SJ (Strategist):   Process oriented towards flow of product
                      Thinking ahead to exploitation of this
                        technology for another product line
                      Smooths over differences between opinions
MD (Achiever):   Focuses on bottom line in $
                      How to get to market as soon as possible
                      Cut out cost

SJ is the company's quality manager and is newer to the organization than the others, but I see him subtly exercising more influence. One way he does this is by being a good sounding board for me and others. He listens well and can play the devil's advocate role well. He also can switch roles rapidly, as I saw when we visited a customer the other day.

The customer has been experiencing recurring layflat problems with our casting film. We have been in a 2-year co-development effort with our raw material supplier, duPont. The 'blame' tends to fall on them. However, during this meeting, SJ put himself and our company squarely in the middle by opening up our process conditions and the latent issues of thermal history to the customer. He reaffirmed our vendors' support and engaged the customer to take some ownership of their handling of the casting sheet by changing machine infeed equipment. He walked the delicate line of supporter and instigator. I watched how he effortlessly changed his role in the interplay—at one minute being the dutiful QC manager, then a Process Engineer, then part of the marketing strategy team on how to exploit this newfound expertise in the ceramic casting market. Actually, he carries two business cards to play out his different roles.

I saw his Strategist qualities again at the company Christmas party. Of all the speakers, including the president, SJ's talk was the longest, the most thought out, and the most engaging of the night. He drew the audience of 100+ people into an interdependent 'contract' to be more conscious of how their individual actions impacted the success of the company and their own self-worth. His words and gestures bespoke a spirituality of knowing one's role and being comfortable with it. He was the only speaker to ask for participation, and he got it.

Watching my superiors act out these developmental roles makes me better able to predict their attitudes and responses and better prepared to act in ways that accomplish my objectives without getting stalled or having them feel strong-armed. I have noticed that the perception of my abilities has gone up since I have been able to control these interactions better.

What developmental role, we might ask ourselves, do we infer that this writer is enacting as he writes? It seems to us that he evinces considerable Technician-like pleasure at mastering the category system he is applying, as is perfectly appropriate in an early stage of one's learning process. Then, towards the end of his comments, we see increasing evidence of an Achiever-like concern 'bottom-line' benefits of this kind of work. At the same time, he demonstrates throughout a strong sense of SJ's Strategist-like actions as a kind of 'ideal type' for himself. Thus, we tend to infer that the writer is at the Achiever stage of development overall, opening towards the possibility of experimenting with Strategist-like actions. However, up through this excerpt in his journal, he has not yet explicitly applied the theory to himself. Thus, we have no evidence that he is as yet involved in the Strategist-like practice of reframing his own assumptions. Of course, it is critical in offering all of these inferences to be aware of how narrow is our base of evidence. At best, such inferences are to be held as tentative hypotheses which our future actions can seek to test.

Experiences with continual quality improvement groups

Probably the most significant 'trick' one can learn in creating or participating in a continual quality improvement group is that any time one is experiencing a block in effectiveness it is possible to frame, advocate, illustrate and inquire about that block in a non-blaming way, rather than to take the block for granted as a boundary on one's activity. This applies not just to whatever blocks one has experienced elsewhere, but to the moment-to-moment activity of the CQI group itself. The following short description shows how one CQI group dealt with blocks at the very outset of its first meeting.

The group work seemed awkward at first. Who should start? What should we do? The four of us agreed we didn't know how to proceed. Paradoxically, that seemed to relieve some anxiety right away. We agreed to explain our current positions, say a little about our companies, and try to formulate what we experienced as our most important and difficult challenges.

We then role played our difficult situations and found them to be similar in that we are all 'stuck' in a framework of confrontation with our peers/supervisors/subordinates. By role playing, with each of us playing our 'antagonist' while another member played us, we found ourselves appreciating more why our antagonists are themselves antagonized by our behaviour, whereas before we could only see how antagonistic *their* behaviour was. I think that having that new perspective, as well as hearing the other member play us in a new way, helped us to see how we could reframe a situation and start advocating, illustrating, and inquiring as needed. I found myself able to lift myself out of the 'stuckness' into an analytical position of inquiry into why there was 'stuckness'.

My difficult situation was a classical case of 'Who's in charge?' I believed that my success quotient was the highest of all involved even though my power quotient was lowest. Now I see that even if that analysis is correct, it legitimizes my relative powerlessness and keeps me from adopting different tactics that will in fact give me more influence (make me more powerful) irrespective of my formal power.

So, I have now reframed my overall approach in two ways: first, I will argue why the new slitter will benefit the company rather than why it will benefit me; and second, I have succeeded in getting a champion who has the necessary authority to take the project on. I am also advocating in a new way by publishing information on the costs we are incurring by not having the slitter. The group also suggested that I illustrate by submitting information on relative prices and values of three alternative slitters rather than waiting for approval before taking that step. Amazing how the specifics seem to interest people and invite buy-in. With regard to inquiry, I've put the project on our monthly business review meeting agenda to keep actions/status visible to all.

To us, this is a fascinating excerpt, not only because it shows towards the end how many different ways a group can invent to advocate, illustrate and inquire, but even more because the simple and counterintuitive act of vulnerability—admitting at the beginning that the group itself was 'stuck'—was what caused it to be unstuck. This way of acting immediately transformed this CQI group from one that was anxiously attempting to conform to whatever we, the authors of this book, have in mind by such groups, to a group that was inventing itself (which, as it happens, is just what we hope for in such groups even as we offer these supports for such group self-construction).

Appendix B Liberating Disciplines

This appendix offers a definition and illustration of the latest stage of organizational development, according to the theory espoused in this book. Because few organizations in history can be said to have approached this stage, and because the theory tells us that we shall ourselves have a difficult time apprehending both the definition and the illustration, we have elected to offer these comments in this appendix rather than in the body of the book. On the other hand, it is important to say *something* about this stage, for it represents the most complete realization of a learning organization that we can imagine. We call this stage *Liberating Disciplines*.

Liberating Disciplines cultivate a spirit of inquiry among organizational members, turning the organization's overall mission into a question that alerts and guides its members at each moment. Such an organizational structure does not just enhance members' alertness and liveliness in implementing particular strategies and projects; it also provides opportunities for members to question whether given strategies, actions and outcomes truly further the mission.[1] The leadership of an organization at the most advanced Liberating Disciplines stage of development can only sustain this subtle structure if the leaders are at the parallel Ironist stage of development. Only then will the organization cultivate, *not* members' obedient conformity, nor merely competent performance by members, but rather their continuing transformation from stage to stage of adult development as they increase their capacities to join in the inquiry.

The societal role of transforming inquiry

For a society to be truly and fully self-transforming and self-renewing, institutions at the Liberating Disciplines stage of development that cultivate transforming inquiry must exist at the centre. For example, is it mere coincidence that during that most creative and enduring of social transformations—

253

the American Revolution—most of the signers of the Declaration of Independence belonged to the world's largest organization for adult inquiry at that time—the Freemasons? Today, if we know of this organization at all, we imagine it as a kind of glorified fraternity based on silly mumbo-jumbo. But at the time of the American Revolution it was a genuine esoteric society wherein one built one's own independence by developing an inner, self-transforming conscience (Adam Smith's 'spectator within the breast',[2] symbolized on US dollar bills as the eye atop the pyramid [itself a Masonic symbol]).

Likewise, at the centre of India's transforming inquiry that restructured it from a British colony to an independent nation stood ... Gandhi's ashram. Gandhi's unique fusion of political and spiritual action inquiry between 1918 and 1948 not only generated a process of adult moral development for thousands and thousands of practitioners of 'Satyagraha' ('Truth Force'), and not only led to India's independence, but also produced the leaders of every single major political party in India during the 1950s.[3]

An analogous process would occur in a truly self-renewing organization. In such an organization, the senior management and board of directors properly engage not just in strategic planning and macro-management, but also in a transforming inquiry that gradually aligns the organization's structure, performance, and outcomes with its mission.[2] The board, in particular, properly plays a role that can be described as 'a community of inquiry within a community of social practice'.[4]

Likewise again, an analogous process would occur in a fully self-transforming institution, such as the ballet or finance or social science. For example, a social science committed to self-transforming inquiry would engage not just in empirical and theoretical inquiry but in inquiry that challenges its own paradigm and assumptions. Indeed, each study in such a science would not only offer new empirical and theoretical results, and would not only challenge the received paradigm of social science, but would illustrate how the author/scientist challenges his or her own paradigm of thought and action. It would serve not only as a Liberating Discipline for others, but also as a Liberating Discipline for the creator of the scientific project. (As we shall see, this is one aspect of the general character of Liberating Disciplines— that they can transform the 'boss' as well as the 'employees'.)

How radical such a science is by contrast to social science today is suggested by the comments of Donald Schön, Ford

Professor of Urban Studies and Education at MIT, and a renowned leading edge practitioner of social science today,[5] in reviewing an example of a work where the scientist presents not only empirical and theoretical results, but also critiques science itself *and* the author's own assumptions and practice.[6] Schön describes this 'new paradigm' work as 'a document of shocking grandiosity' that nevertheless 'deserves to be read'. Schön describes the autobiographical aspects of this work as 'profoundly disconcerting, frequently disappointing, and occasionally terrifying' especially in its 'refusal to respect conventional boundaries between personal and professional life'.

A quite different appreciation of the same material emanates from a scholar more closely allied with the effort to explore a social science that is explicitly paradigm-challenging and seeks to reconcile the subjective with the objective. In an *Academy of Management Review* article on the same work, Judi Marshall, Professor of Management at the University of Bath, writes,

> (the author) demands high standards of attention, inquiring action, and truth-speaking from himself, and he exhorts such attention in others. We meet him as an educator devising liberating structures, working to co-create peer communities of inquiry, struggling with the politics of hostile superior power cultures, and as a person managing his commitment to work roles, and involved in divorce and loving relationships. The inclusion of such material challenges preconceptions about appropriate boundaries, and it reunites, as (the author) claims we must, productivity and inquiry, reason and feelings, the professional and the personal. This is a purpose to which I have great commitment.

Just such a vast difference in feeling about a work is what we ought to expect whenever a paradigm-challenging art is displayed (think of the early responses to Gloria Steinem, Jane Fonda or Shirley MacLaine in their various incarnations, or to Tchaikovsky, Freud, Picasso or Ballanchine).

Picturing a self-critical, self-renewing society

Figure B.1 shows how the institutions of an ideal, self-critical, self-renewing society can be conceived as interrelated (the cone is intended to represent a section of a circle, with periphery and centre). At the periphery, the military guards against threats from without—against intrusion by destructive forces. Just inside the periphery, prisons, asylums, police and the court system maintain the internal boundary against threats from within. At the other extreme—the centre—operate the creative, flexibility-enhancing institutions that foster the spiritual exercise of transforming inquiry. Such is the function not only of the Freemasons and of Gandhi's ashram, but also of Quaker meetings, of Native American medicine lodges, of Yoruba trance dances, and of Hindu sexual yoga, among the many attempts to institutionalize transforming inquiry.

Between the stability-maintaining institutions near the periphery and the flexibility-enhancing, transforming institutions near the centre lie the self-reproducing institutions of the commercial, industrial and entertainment sectors. (Again, each distinct institution and organization can be characterized along this periphery–centre model as well.)

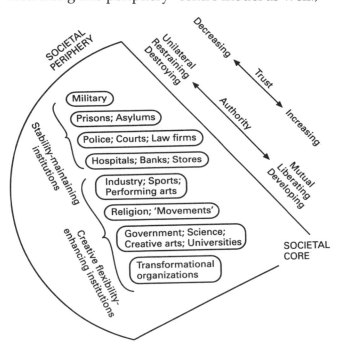

Figure B.1   Creative and maintaining institutions in a self-renewing society guided by the spirit of inquiry

Despite the examples already offered, most readers will no doubt feel unfamiliar with and sceptical about the very existence of Liberating Disciplines. There are three reasons why institutions that cultivate transforming inquiry are relatively unknown and usually invisible. First, such institutions may simply not exist in a given society. Second, even though such institutions may exist in a given society, they may cloak themselves or be suppressed because they question central values. For example, Alcoholics Anonymous is a partially cloaked society. Third, even if such an institution is not cloaked, it may in effect be invisible from the developmental point of view of most members of the society. Most people may interpret the conflict associated with any paradigm-challenging institution as simply distasteful to them, make a negative judgement about the institution, and thereafter simply look the other way.

With regard to the first reason, can the reader point to many schools that cultivate transforming inquiry? Illich suggests that schools today function more like prisons or places of incarceration.[7] Freire suggests they function more like banks, helping the already well-endowed to get ahead.[8] Gintis and Bowles suggest they function more like factories, reproducing the existing social norms rather than challenging and transforming them.[9] Thus, even though schools and universities might be presumed to be intended to cultivate developmentally transforming inquiry among their students, in practice few contemporary schools seem to do so.

Interestingly, the only university that has been able to show empirically that it *does* cultivate developmental transformation is Maharishi International University in Fairfield, Iowa (the university associated with Transcendental Meditation).[10] There can be little question that this university is outside the received paradigm for American universities.

The second reason why institutions that cultivate transforming inquiry are relatively unknown and rarely visible is that, because they cultivate inquiry into the most sacred and taken-for-granted of social values, they are frequently regarded as dangerous and subversive by most persons and institutions. They therefore frequently cloak themselves from public view. Thus, for example, the typical architecture of Zen monasteries was of courts within courts, the inner courts often unknown to novices and the public, accessible only to senior adepts. Gaining entry even to the outermost court was not automatic, but rather required commitment and persistence. Similarly, many of the Sufi schools in the Islamic world remain hidden to this day, so unorthodox does their teaching–learning process appear from the point of view of the literal, hierarchical monotheism of official Islam. Both Zen and Sufi practices are precisely assumption-testing and assumption-transforming practices.

When institutions that cultivate transforming inquiry among their members have been publicly visible for a time, they have frequently been suppressed. Examples include Socrates' teaching, the (Whirling) Dervishes in Turkey, and the Jesuit Order within the Catholic Church, which has twice been suppressed.

The third reason why institutions that cultivate transforming inquiry may be invisible is that their role and purpose are not seen or understood by the majority of individuals. They re-present—and cultivate development towards—the later stages of personal development. Each later developmental perspective introduces a person to a new way of tasting and organizing experience, a way relatively inaccessible and invisible to persons at earlier stages, as illustrated throughout the earlier chapters of this book. According to developmental theory, with guidance we can each understand—though not initially reproduce in our own, real-time action—the perspective one stage beyond our current position; but we shall not even glimpse, just distort and reinterpret, perspectives two or more stages later than our own.[11]

The organizational design of transforming inquiry

The foregoing discussion will suggest that it must be difficult, if not in principle impossible, to describe the internal structure of an organization that truly enacts the mission of cultivating transforming inquiry. Certainly, it must be the opposite of a constraining, inflexible, bureaucratic structure. An organizational structure that cultivates transforming inquiry must be liberating, flexible, paradoxical and self-transforming. Such a structure falls altogether outside the boundaries of what is commonly defined as an organization (i.e. as we ought by now to begin to expect, the idea of liberating structure challenges our very paradigmatic assumptions about organization). Listen to Katz and Kahn's definition of organization on p. 277 of *The Social Psychology of Organizations*:[12]

> The organizational context is by definition a set of restrictions for focusing attention upon certain content areas and for narrowing the cognitive style to certain types of procedures. This is the inherent constraint. To call a social structure organized means that the degrees of freedom in the situation have been limited. Hence organizations often suffer from the failure to recognize the dilemma character of a situation and from blind persistence in sticking to terms of reference on the basis of which the problem is insoluble.

Let us attempt to create the mirror image opposite of this definition of organizational structure, in order to define an organizing process that truly cultivates transforming inquiry through Liberating Disciplines. For the notion of 'constraining organizational structure', with its connotation of an objective, external, social boundary being superimposed upon undisciplined, subjective persons, we can substitute the phrase 'liberating social psychological discipline'. The word 'liberating' mirrors the word 'constraining', and the words 'social psychological discipline' mirror the words 'organizational structure', though less obviously so. Persons voluntarily 'take on' (become disciples of) a discipline based on internal commitment, rather than 'submitting and externally conforming to' a structure. The words 'social psychological' indicate that the social and the psychological interpenetrate one another, whereas the word 'organization' suggests discontinuity between the person (psyche) and the social (organization).

But the phrase 'liberating social psychological discipline' is really too awkward to use. Let us shorten it, therefore, to 'liberating discipline'—a felicitous paradox that may open us to the mystery of effective organizing. Now we have some of the intellectual reasoning that leads to the choice of name for the Liberating Disciplines stage of organizing.

Continuing in this fashion to create a mirror image of the Katz and Kahn definition, with some poetic licence, we produce the following initial definition of a 'liberating discipline' on the left-hand side of the page, with the Katz and Kahn language on the right:

A liberating discipline	*(not) An organizational context*
is by experience	*(not) is by definition*
a set of challenges	*(not) a set of restrictions*
for questioning (the quality of one's) attention	*(not) for focusing attention*
and widening it and	*(not) narrowing*
one's cognitive-emotional tracking	*(not) the cognitive style*
to include the enacted task, process and mission.	*(not) to certain types of procedures.*
This is the enacted dynamism.	*(not) This is the inherent constraint.*
To call	
a social psychological process	*(not) a social structure*
liberating means that	*(not) organized means that*

the degrees of freedom and discipline	*(not) the degrees of freedom*
in the situation are expanding.	*(not) in the situation have been limited.*

Hence organizations that cultivate transforming inquiry rarely suffer from the failure to recognize the dilemma character of a situation and from blind persistence in sticking to terms of reference on the basis of which the problem is insoluble.	*(not) often suffer from the failure*

What can this strange arrangement of words mean? The reader may wish to try translating this somewhat mechanical aping of the Katz and Kahn definition into more congenial language. For example, our colleague Peter Reason of the University of Bath suggests beginning like this:

> We can only fully comprehend a liberating community or organization as we experience it. However, we can say that such communities encourage their members through a discipline of practice to question. . . .

Jay Conger of McGill University suggests that it sounds as though an organization that cultivates transforming inquiry is like a spiritual practice of individual growth within a supportive community. (But, as the illustration in the next section of this appendix suggests, the word 'supportive' is a bit cosier than the atmosphere generated in a community of inquiry.)

Once we domesticate the definition of Liberating Disciplines sufficiently to mean *something* to us (and we suspect such an effort will include a good three readings of this appendix as a whole and some experience in an organization that at least aspires in this direction), the more important question becomes: What will a pattern of organizing based on this definition look like?

First, the definition means that a leadership intent upon generating Liberating Disciplines will regard every organizational dilemma, directive, task or encounter as an opportunity to challenge the attention of self and others. The aim of each action is never merely to accomplish a predetermined end, but equally and simultaneously to widen the attention of participants to question and see whether mission, strategy, present action and outcome are congruent with one another or not. At its most challenging, such leadership action generates tasks that are incomprehensible and cannot be performed without ongoing awareness of the accompanying social psychological processes and purposes.

Second, Liberating Disciplines are inherently dynamic. Whatever structure is created at a given time is meant to evolve over time as the membership's overall awareness and initiative increases. Indeed, the leadership may initiate radical changes in structure as much to heighten inquiry as to accomplish predetermined ends more effectively (thus, for example, a given piece of writing may include multiple genres, as this book does). Both leaders and members properly challenge the passive tendency to treat a given organizational structure as ultimate and encourage instead a continuing search for a thread of meaning from sense of mission or source of purpose, through cognitive structuring and restructuring, as well as through passionate and dispassionate embodied action, into visible events and products.

Two more corollaries about Liberating Disciplines follow directly from the foregoing comments. First, the appropriateness, legitimacy or efficacy of the given organizational structure is open, in principle, to challenge by any organizational member at any time. Such challenges can function both to heighten vigilance of the members and to better align organizational purposes, processes, practices and profits. Incongruities among mission, strategies, operations and outcomes are inevitable. The leadership gains legitimacy and the organization as a whole gains confidence and efficacy by seeking out such incongruities and correcting them.

The second corollary points to the obverse condition: the leadership becomes vulnerable, in practice, to public discrediting if it acts inauthentically. That is, the leadership rapidly loses legitimacy if its tasks, processes and purposes become incongruent with one another *and* it *refuses* to acknowledge and correct such incongruities. Thus, there is a very real sense in which the leadership of an organization that cultivates transforming inquiry puts itself in a very vulnerable position. It is no doubt the dim intuition that such is the case that keeps most organizational leaders from adopting this whole approach to organizing. On the other hand, we may predict that organizational leaders who have participated in Liberating Disciplines for a generation or more of their adulthood will actively seek out such conditions in order to keep themselves vigilant—in order to support their own ongoing efforts to interweave moment-to-moment action and inquiry. Moreover, they will understand that their social authenticity and mutuality with persons at all levels of conventional hierarchies, as well as their organizational transforming power, derive from their vulnerability.

At the same time, there is another side to this leadership vulnerability. Especially when organizational members are young in their commitment to Liberating Disciplines and their attention is therefore still predominantly restricted to what William Blake called 'single-vision(ed) . . . sleep' (seeing the outside world as the only objective territory of experience, and not witnessing their own acting, thinking and attending as equally real), their charges of leaderly or organizational incongruities may well be invalid and untrust-worthy. Such charges may reflect their inability to apply Blake's 'fourfold vision' (simultaneous awareness of purpose, process, action and outcome) to themselves and the organiza-tion. A fourfoldedly attentive leadership will turn such conflicts into educational opportunities, challenging the 'charging' members to 'retreat' and to taste and digest unexpected feedback. Indeed, the more adept the leadership is in interweaving action and inquiry, the more it will risk using all available forms of power to create a rich context for transforming inquiry, recognizing as it does so that no genuine personal or organizational transformation can be forced.[13]

An organizational leadership serving the spirit of inquiry

Let us examine, though no more than briefly and incomple-tely, an organization that we judge offers the best example we have ever found of a multi-generational set of male and female leaders and leadership groups dedicated to cultivating the spirit of inquiry. The organization spans some 80 years at present and consists of more than 100 000 members on all continents. It includes many persons of international repute in the fine arts and the performing arts, in the gamut of scholarly disciplines, and in the professions, as well as members of every race and social class and many ethnic groups.

The mission of this not-for-profit, global, educational organization is to re-present and cultivate a kind of playful awareness and action in its members' lives—a kind of spiritual and mundane inquiry on a moment-to-moment basis—that makes them more awake, more conscious, more true to themselves (selves whom they increasingly realize they have yet fully to meet).

Anthony, Ecker and Wilber compare this organization to others that are explicitly concerned with members' spiritual transformation, and they offer a comparative critique of these organizations' different practices.[14] In addition, a wide range of books by and about several of the organizational leaders provide different views of the organization's history and purpose.[15] One of us has also participated in the organization for over a quarter of a century, but stopped doing so five years ago in order to pursue his spiritual inquiry in a more singular fashion for a time.

This organization—or, better, this set of Liberating Disciplines—is commonly named the Gurdjieff Work, after George Gurdjieff, the Greek-Armenian who first gathered students about him in Moscow in 1913, after having explored esoteric schools from Egypt to Tibet during the previous 20 years. Gurdjieff continued to create unusual conditions for learning until his death in Paris in 1949.

Gurdjieff mounted various public presentations with students on different continents (music, dance, lectures, etc.), among the many vehicles he generated for challenging students towards a more active awareness. One unusual sociological characteristic that members of this organization uniformly report is that the leadership provides consistent, though surprising, direction in the inquiry domain, but *not* in the task-oriented domain. Occasionally, as when preparing for one performance or another, there is a strong, task-oriented demand. But at other times the quality of performance is left very much up to the individual members. This inconsistency of task-orientation is highlighted by the fact that there are continual, highly consistent inquiry activities.

Gurdjieff, like Plato, held that we are ritual creatures who wander dreamily or blinkered through our days—that our ordinary waking state is as far short of full, inquiring consciousness as our night-time sleep is from daytime awareness.[16] The inquiry activities within the Gurdjieff Work include meetings at which members have the opportunity to review their internal efforts at observing the quality of their own awareness and performance throughout the preceding week, while simultaneously engaging in such self-observation at the meeting itself. Another inquiry activity is for all members to take on a particular internal inquiry task ('Listen to how you listen') while performing an external task of some kind (e.g. building a stage and arranging the lighting). For example, one such inquiry activity, which sounds absurd outside the context of studying the quality of one's own awareness, is to brush one's teeth with the unaccustomed hand holding the brush. Setting this small task for oneself can show how difficult it is even to remember what we intend to do, can highlight how habitual most of our actions are, and can show how difficult it is to continue for long with a true spirit of inquiry.

A second striking sociological characteristic of this organization is that the leader, Gurdjieff, intentionally generated conflict with some of his leading students, who in turn set up their own distinctive versions of these Liberating Disciplines. Then, after Gurdjieff's death, many of these erstwhile apparently divergent 'sects' reunited into a single enterprise. In this way, conditions were created both during and after the founder's lifetime that raised questions about the legitimacy of each leader's approach.[17]

At first hearing, this situation of divided leadership no doubt sounds counterproductive. It directly violates the military/bureaucratic dictum about unity of command. But when we remember that one of the oldest and most stable polities in the world—namely the USA—is organized to institutionalize conflict among its three branches and its two parties, with the result that the legitimacy of each president's actions is constantly being questioned and tested, one begins to wonder whether international corporations should consider institutionalizing a more public struggle within their leadership groups. Apparent unity of command may be a necessary feature of an organization at society's periphery whose primary concerns are efficiency and unity against outside competitive threat (e.g. the military). But a core social organization whose primary concerns are continuing dialogue among multiple cultures and continuing inquiry about how to improve quality—an organization closer to the other end of the sociological spectrum shown in Figure B.1 above—may require a more contentious internal environment.

A third surprising and paradoxical sociological characteristic of the Gurdjieff Work is that it has never advertised itself in any way or sought to attract and convert new members. Instead, it remains cloaked, thus posing the potentially empowering challenge to all who come into contact with the rumour of the organization's existence to find their way into it, if they so wish. So begins the study of what one truly wishes. To find the organization, one must truly wish to do so.

When one begins to ponder this anomalous characteristic, one realizes that a slightly less extreme version of this phenomenon of intentionally difficult entry is characteristic of many of the highest quality organizations—consider Alcoholics Anonymous (you have to get there by yourself), the New York City Ballet or the US Marines, the Boston Consulting Group or Yale's secret society Skull and Bones, to which both former President Bush and his nemesis and national court jester, Doonesbury cartoonist Gary Trudeau, belong.

A fourth surprising characteristic of the Gurdjieff Work's web of Liberating Disciplines is that—unlike more commercial self-help organizations or evangelical sects—the new members do not in effect financially support the leaders. On the contrary, as one takes more leadership responsibility within this organization, one is expected to make a more significant financial contribution as well. No one earns his or her living from the organization, and leaders show their fitness to lead in small part by their enhanced ability and commitment to balance high achievement in the everyday commercial world with a deepening commitment to this liberating discipline.

Taken together, these unusual approaches to organizing generate a frequent 'dilemmic' sense for members—that is, the members frequently experience themselves as facing a relatively unstructured dilemma rather than a well-defined problem, and a dilemma that demands a higher awareness than their wavering efforts at self-observation show them they are generating. Such a repeated sense of dilemma can be defeating to anyone accustomed to external success, or accustomed to avoiding responsibility for one's own performance. On the other hand, how else can one cultivate a moment-to-moment taste for improving the quality of one's own awareness and action—for continual quality improvement?

The film
Groundhog Day

If the example of the Gurdjieff Work seems too distant to teach us much, let us consider the story of the popular film *Groundhog Day* as another example of Liberating Disciplines.

In *Groundhog Day*, comedian Bill Murray plays an insufferable, egocentric TV weatherman who reports on the annual appearance of the groundhog in a small western Pennsylvania town, but gets caught in a peculiar time warp whereby he begins that same day over and over again. At first, he is terminally depressed; then he gradually, gleefully and sophomorically realizes he has licence to do whatever he wishes; still later, he begins to take the eternally repeating day as a liberating discipline (see the film for details).

If this interpretation of the story appears a bit like reaching, consider the story behind this story: consider the similarity between the *Groundhog Day* story and the novel *The Strange Life of Ivan Osokin* by Gurdjieff's prime student, Peter Ouspensky, a Russian mathematician and philosopher.[18] In that story, a magician gives Osokin a chance to relive 12 years of his life and correct his mistakes. But can the man correct his mistakes, and can he escape the coil of eternal recurrence? Read the book for details.

If this connection between the Gurdjieff Work and the film *Groundhog Day* appears even more like reaching for a connection, consider a story behind that: that Bill Murray is a member of the Gurdjieff Work.

Now, what *is* the story here? Where does truth end and fiction begin? And how can stories themselves serve as liberating disciplines?

That in itself is a long story. We can start by examining the traditions of Hasidic and Sufi stories. The Disney cartoon *Aladdin* is a Sufi story. . . .

Conclusion

Overall, this brief overview of the Gurdjieff Work, along with the even briefer references to other historical examples and contemporary films, can offer an impression of organizing and leadership that generate Liberating Disciplines—that invite each participant to join in an inquiry that can transform one's present awareness.

As international organizations such as the United Nations and the World Bank struggle with the questions of how to generate a new world order both politically and economically, is there a spirit more likely to increase peace, productivity, tolerance of diversity, creative tension, transformation and harmony than the spirit of inquiry?

As organizations attempt to operate in a manner that fosters continual quality improvement, is any approach less centrally dedicated to inquiry in the moment of action likely to draw us towards that grail?

As persons seek understanding, mutuality and intimacy across boundaries of race, culture, age and sexual orientation, can we conceive of an authentic, mutually empowering and dignifying, covenantal relationship that does *not* invite and welcome an ever-deepening, ever-lighter and more illuminating inquiry in the midst of our relational actions?

These very questions (not the answers to the questions) can guide us towards a wider awareness. Can we see through our impatience to have answers and gradually acquire the taste for incompletion—the taste for being *present* at the very leading edge of our personal development and the very leading edge of an organizational quality improvement process? Will our leadership in our managing, our parenting, our teaching, our consulting or our writing generate Liberating Disciplines and a spirit of inquiry?

Notes

1. W. R. Torbert (1991) *The Power of Balance: Transforming Self, Society and Scientific Inquiry*, Newbury Park, CA: Sage Publications.
2. A. Smith (1759/1969) *The Theory of Moral Sentiments*, Indianapolis, IN: Liberty Classics; W. R. Torbert (1993) *Sources of Excellence: An Unorthodox Inquiry into Quality in Recent U.S. Presidencies, in Business Leadership, in Management Education, in Adam Smith's Ethics, and in Pythagorean Mathematics*, Cambridge, MA: Edge\Work Press.
3. E. Erikson (1969) *Gandhi's Truth: On the Origins of Militant Non-Violence*, New York: Norton; W. R. Torbert (1991) *The Power of Balance: Transforming Self, Society and Scientific Inquiry*, Newbury Park, CA: Sage Publications.
4. C. Argyris, and D. Schön (1974) *Theory in Practice: Increasing Professional Effectiveness*, San Francisco, CA: Jossey-Bass.
5. C. Argyris and D. Schön (1974) *Theory in Practice: Increasing Professional Effectiveness*, San Francisco, CA: Jossey-Bass; D. Schön (1987) *Educating the Reflective Practitioner: Toward a New Design for Teaching and Learning in the Professions*, San Francisco, CA: Jossey-Bass.
6. D. Schön, forward in W. R. Torbert (1991), *The Power of Balance: Transforming Self, Society and Scientific Inquiry*, Newbury Park, CA: Sage Publications.
7. I. Illich (1970) *Deschooling Society*, New York: Harper & Row.
8. P. Freire (1970) *The Pedagogy of the Oppressed*, New York: Herder & Herder.
9. H. Gintis, & S. Bowles (1975) *Nightmares and Visions: Capitalism and Education in the U.S.*, New York: Harper & Row.
10. C. Alexander, S. Cook and M. Miller (1994) *Transcendence and Mature Thought in Adulthood: The Further Reaches of Human Development*, Trenton, NJ: Rowman & Littlefield.
11. R. Kegan (1982) *The Evolving Self*, Cambridge, MA: Harvard University Press. R. Kegan (1994) *In Over Our Heads: The Mental Demands of Modern Life*, Cambridge, MA: Harvard University Press.
12. J. Katz and R. Kahn (1978) *The Social Psychology of Organizations*, New York: Wiley.
13. For greater detail see W. R. Torbert (1991) *The Power of Balance: Transforming Self, Society and Scientific Inquiry*, Newbury Park, CA: Sage Publications.
14. D. Anthony, B. Ecker and K. Wilber (1987) *Spiritual Choices: The*

Problems of Recognizing Authentic Paths to Inner Transformation,
New York: Paragon House.

15. J. Bennett (1973) *Gurdjieff: Making a New World,* New York:
Harper & Row; T. de Hartmann (1964) *Our Life with Mr.
Gurdjieff,* New York: Cooper Square Publishers; G. Gurdjieff,
(1963) *Meetings with Remarkable Men,* New York: Dutton;
P. Mairet (1936) *A. R. Orage: A Memoir,* London: Dent & Sons;
J. Moore, (1992) *Gurdjieff—The Anatomy of a Myth,* Rockport,
MA: Element; P. Ouspensky, (1971) *The Strange Life of Ivan
Osokin: A Novel,* Baltimore, MD: Penguin; F. Peters (1964)
Boyhood with Gurdjieff, New York: Dutton; L. Welch (1982) *Orage
with Gurdjieff in America,* London: Routlege & Kegan Paul.

16. P. Ouspensky (1949) *In Search of the Miraculous: Fragments of an
Unknown Teaching,* New York: Harcourt, Brace & World.

17. R. Collin (1954) *The Theory of Celestial Influence,* New York:
Samuel Weiser. Collin specifically suggests this choreography
of conflict, as does Gurdjieff's own detailed account in another
case (G. Gurdjieff (1975). *Life Is Real Only Then When 'I Am',*
New York: Triangle Publications).

18. P. Ouspensky (1971) *The Strange Life of Ivan Osokin: A Novel,*
Baltimore, MD: Penguin.

Index